THE COMPLETE ENCYCLOPEDIA OF

BIRDS

THE COMPLETE ENCYCLOPEDIA OF
BIRDS

VLADIMÍR BEJČEK
KAREL ŠŤASTNÝ

REBO
PUBLISHERS

© 1999 Rebo International b.v., Lisse, The Netherlands

This 3rd edition reprinted in 2006.

Text: Vladimír Bejček, Karel Šťastný
Photographs: Josef Hlásek 223, Lubomír Hlásek 179, Vladimír Bejček
and Karel Šťastný 69, Jan Ševčík 68, Martin Smrček 52, Jaroslav Klápště 42,
Zdeněk Veselovský 29, Jiří Formánek 1
Production and layout: Studio Granit, Prague, The Czech Republic
Cover design: Minkowsky Graphics, Enkhuizen, The Netherlands
Typesetting: Artedit, Prague, The Czech Republic

ISBN-13: 978-90-366-1594-5
ISBN-10: 90-366-1594-1

All rights reserved. No part of this publication may be reproduced,
stored in a retrieval system or transmitted in any form or by
any means without the prior written permission of the publisher
and copyright holder nor be otherwise circulated in any form
of binding or cover other than that in which it is published and without
a similar condition being imposed on the subsequent purchaser.

Contents

Introduction

Birds constitute a remarkably unified group of highly specialized vertebrates. All have a bill and a body covered with feathers. The great majority of them use active flight as the way of moving. Birds evolved from their reptile ancestors about 140 million years ago. The very first known representative, not bigger than a pigeon, is *Archaeopteryx* whose skeleton remains were discovered in Jurassic sediments in Bavaria. What followed was a comparatively rapid evolution illustrated by a fact that 60 million years ago, the majority of present orders and families already existed. Today, more than 9,000 species of birds with surprising sizes, shapes, colors and acoustic varieties live all around the world.

The goal of this publication is to inform the reader, with the help of a brief description, and a picture about at least a part of the rich spectrum of the world avifauna. When selecting species, we focused mainly on the Northern Hemisphere, and Eurasia in particular. Almost 700 presented species are classified with 16 chapters depending on the relation of bird orders, similarity of their characters, way of living, looks, etc.

Following the species, you would find zoogeographical territory to which its nesting area belongs. **PA**: Palaearctic Region includes Europe, North Asia as far as the Himalayas, North Africa including the Sahara Desert, and the Middle East. **AF**: Afrotropical Region includes Africa south of the Sahara including vicinity of the Red Sea, and Madagascar with neighboring islands. **OR**: Oriental Region includes south Asia including the Himalayas, the Philippines, and the Sunda Islands as far as the Wallace Line going between Bali and Lombok islands. **AU**: Australasian Region includes Australia, and Tasmania, the Sunda Islands beyond the Wallace Line, New Guinea, Pacific islands, and New Zealand. **NA**: Nearctic Region includes North America down to the Rio Grande. **NT**: Neotropical Region includes North America south of the Rio Grande plus Central and South America. **AN**: Antarctic Region includes Antarctica. The map shows the territory boundaries.

Left: *Dendroica petechia*
Map of zoogeographical regions

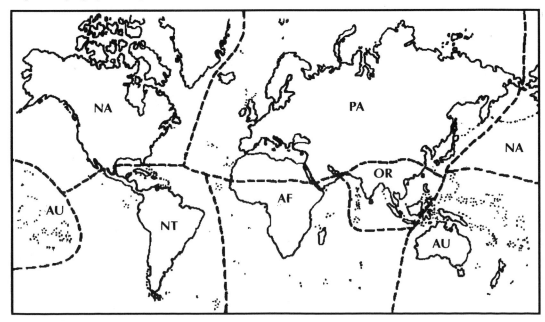

1. Ostriches and Allies

Several families of Struthioniformes *belong to a group of birds often referred to as ratites which include big to huge body types, mostly with vestigial wings and powerful legs with two to four toes. There are common features on their skull, similar build of pelvis, and free tail verterbrae. Also, through evolution the keel on their sternum has disappeared. A number of other characteristics typical for ratites can, however, occasionally be found in the second superorder of flyers, too. Those are namely an evolved penis, simplified featherbed, and a breeding strategy based on the habit of the male bird taking care of the egg incubation and hatched non-breeding*

Left: *Rhea americana*
Struthio camelus

chicks. Palaentological findings prove that ostriches have existed since the early Tertiary period. Only recently have the Moas of New Zealand become extinct. The Moas stood 6.6–13.2ft/2–4m tall, and the largest one, Dinornis maximus, *still lived there when the first Europeans arrived. On Madagascar,* Epyornithidus, *or an elephant bird, 10ft/3m high and 1,000lb/450kg of weight, had a similar fate. One of their enormous eggs, 14in/35cm long and 9in/22cm wide, would hold the contents of about 180 chicken eggs. The last of these giant birds became extinct in the 19th century. Today we find this family of birds living in Africa (Ostrich), Central and South America (rheas), New Guinea and Australia (cassowaries and Emu), and New Zealand (kiwis).*

Struthio camelus

OSTRICH   AF

It is clearly the largest and heaviest living bird. Males grow up to 9ft/2.75m in height and weigh up to 330lb/150kg. Females are smaller. The whole body of the ostrich is fully adapted to running. The strong and very long legs have two prominent toes only, the remaining two appendages are dwarfed. Their body and the lower part of the neck are covered with feathers that are black on males, and grayish brown on females. Beautiful, clear white feathers grow on the male's wings and tail. These come into use during courting when males display them like a fan. The legs are unfeathered, and the birds hide them under their wings when it is cold. The bird's head and neck are sparsely feathered, and the skin is visible. The ostrich feels at home in South African savannahs and semi-deserts that have vegetation not exceeding 3.3ft/1m in height allowing the large bird a good view of the surrounding area. Nowadays, practically all of the free ostrich populations live in national parks. Besides the strength and speed–they can run up to 44mph/70kph–brilliant eyesight helps them to survive in a habitat shared with large predators. During courting, male ostriches go through tough battles featuring dangerous kicks. A successful male may win two to five females. He himself prepares

a nesting depression using his bill and chest. One female can lay as many as 11 eggs during a 2- or 3-day period and up to 4 hens will lay eggs in the same nest. Conceivably, the clutch is then crowded with eggs weighing up to 3.5lb/1.6kg. It is only natural that not all of the eggs are succesfully hatched. The chicks hatch after six weeks. The male ostrich takes a major role during the incubation period and in tending to the chicks after hatching. The family stays together for an entire year. The core of the ostrich's diet consists of fruits, seeds, succulent plants as well as insects and small vertebrates.

Rhea americana

GREATER RHEA   NT

The rheas live in the tall grass steppe of the South American pampas and also inhabit areas of dense grassland and sparse scrub. They are excellent runners, able to reach a speed of 37mph/60kph. Unlike the ostrich, their legs have three toes, and there is feathering on their head, neck and thighs. The most common is the Greater rhea which can grow up to 5ft/1.5m and weighs up to 55lb/25kg. Its body is mostly gray and brown except for white calves and trunk, and black crown and neck sides. Big wings cover all of the body and are used for manoeuvring and making sharp turns while the bird is running fast. A rhea's diet consists of the green parts of

Rhea americana

Pterocnemia pennata

plants, various fruits, seeds and small animals. The males fight tenaciously over the nesting territories in breeding season. Afterwards, each one digs out a nest in the ground and borders it with vegetation. Usually, several females lay yellowish eggs in the nest which are about 1.4lb/600 grams of weight. A full nest usually contains between 15–30 eggs. It is completely the male's responsibility to incubate as well as rear the fast growing chicks. Six months after hatching young rheas are almost the size of adult birds but they do not reach sexual maturity until two years of age.

Pterocnemia pennata

LESSER RHEA   **NT**

This smaller relative of the Greater rhea can be easily distinguished by varying amounts of white spots on its back. It lives in semi-arid uplands south of Peru, at 11,500–14,800ft/3,500–4,500m and also in the areas of steppe woodland and grassland of southern South America. The Lesser rhea picks food off the ground while walking slowly with its head held low. Quite often it mixes with grazing llamas. Breeding takes place between September and January.

Casuarius casuarius

Casuarius casuarius

SOUTHERN CASSOWARY   **AU**

Cassowaries are instinctively shy birds. They live hidden and unnoticed in deep rain forests, coming out as quietly as ghosts to search for food in the evening and early morning. They choose mostly fruit fallen from trees, and insects. When disturbed, they will quickly flee. They are able to run as fast as 31mph/50kph, jump vertically over barriers up to 5ft/1.5m high, and cross rivers by swimming. Such performances are enabled thanks to outstandingly strong three-toed legs. A helmet-like protuberance, known as a casque, filled with a spongy substance, and five long hard quills growing out of the wings in place of primaries help the bird to make its way through dense vegetation. If necessary, they defend themselves by kicking. The 4in/10cm long, sharp claws found on the inner toes can cause the intruders serious wounds.

The most common species is the Southern cassowary which lives in New Guinea, on some of the other nearby islands, and in Australia. It can measure up to 5.6ft/1.7m and weigh almost 132lb/60kg. Conspicuous glossy black plumage gives a hair-like appearance.

The head and the upper neck are unfeathered and brightly colored. Long red skin wattles hang from the neck. Females are larger and also more colorful. The male bird takes care of the nest of 3 to 6 green, rough-covered eggs as well as of the chicks.

Dromaius novaehollandiae

EMU   **AU**

This species lives exclusively in mainland Australia and is the second largest bird after the ostrich, growing up to 6.5ft/2m. With the exception of its legs, it is all feathered, with only blue facial skin showing through on the bird's head. Its short wings are completely dysfunctional and hang down the sides of the body. Emus live mostly in pairs. They are nomadic and always search for places with plenty of water and food which includes flowers, fruits, seeds, and invertebrate animals. The male alone sits on a shallow nest in grass where the female has laid up to 15 dark green eggs. Thanks to built up fat reserves, he then does not eat or drink, nor even defecate for an 8-week period. He continues to look after the black and white striped chicks for at least 7 or 8 more weeks after they hatch from the eggs.

Apteryx australis

BROWN KIWI   **AU**

Apteryx australis

The kiwi genus comprises three species, all of which live in New Zealand. Their wings are stunted to the extent that they remain invisible in long, simple plumage (feathers without beards). The tail feathers are missing. Stout legs end in four toes. Their eyes are small. Quite unusually, nostrils are placed at the far end of the long bill, which also features long tactile feathers at its base. Unlike most of the birds, the senses of smell and hearing are main senses for kiwis. They live in forests, foraging at night for small animals and fruit on the ground. In a similar way to woodcocks, they sink their bill up to its base in fresh soil and carefully pull out annelidans. They nest and also spend days in burrows dug out by a mating pair. The female, which is larger and has a considerably longer beak, usually lays one large egg, which is then incubated by the male for 11 weeks. He goes without food for most of that time.

The best-known kiwi is the uniformly brown and gray

Brown kiwi. It inhabits both islands of New Zealand, and it appears that thanks to consistent protection, its numbers have stabilized. Besides rain forests which are its preferred habitat, it is also found in shrubland and planted pine forests.

Dromaius novaehollandiae

2. Penguins

Oddly enough, flightless penguins (Sphenisciformes) introduce the second superorder of flyers. For it is not a good flying ability which is the main feature of flyers, but a characteristic form of skull or build of pelvis. Owing to this approach, penguins belong to this group, too. Penguins were formerly classified in the superorder of swimmers (Impennes). This classification is not recognized any longer since it seems to have been solely based on observable actions of the bird and not on the penguin's physical characteristics. The order Sphenisciformes *includes flightless seabirds that are excellently adapted to the marine habitat. Six genera with 17 species are known. Their sizes range 15–45in/40–115cm, and weights from 1 to 46 kg. They live only in the Southern Hemisphere and successfully inhabit parts of Antarctica that are entirely unfit for habitation by most other animals. Their thickset, cylindrical bodies are invariably covered with small coverts that notably resemble scales. When moulting, birds discard all of the outer coat of waterproof feathers and then have to remain on land or ice without feeding until their plumage returns to its original condition again. This costs them as much as a third of their body weight. A thick layer of subcutaneous fat protects them effectively against cold. Bones are solid. Small wings without primaries are used as flippers. They provide an effective propulsion for underwater movement. That is also why penguins, like flying birds, have strongly developed keel on their sternum to which enormous breast muscles are attached. The webbed feet are situated far back on the body and perform the function of a rudder. When in the water, penguins can often reach a speed of 3–6mph/5–10 kph, sometimes even higher. When searching for food, they are able to dive as deep as 60ft/200m and stay under water for nearly 30 minutes without taking a breath. All penguins are generally alike when it comes to their shape and color, with upperparts dark or black and underparts white. This combination, observed among other water animals, too, is beneficial for the animal's safety. A white belly is not likely to be seen against the light sky when viewed from underneath, and similarly the dark back blends with the darkness of deep waters when viewed from above. Penguins usually nest in colonies that can be comprised of tens of thousands of pairs. Both parents take turns in incubation and feeding the young. They regurgitate pre-digested portions of the primary adult diet of fish and crustaceans into their bill to feed the young penguins.*

Left: *Pygoscelis adeliae*

Eudyptes chrysocome

ROCKHOPPER PENGUIN   **AF AU NT**

The Rockhopper penguin is one of the smaller penguins that has a thick bill and characteristic crest of bright yellow feathers on either side of its head. It lives in cold, subantarctic waters and nests in large colonies on slopes of scree or rocky shores. It beds its nest with stones, bones and grass. Like five other species of this genus, the female lays two eggs of various size. Even if both chicks hatch successfully, the one from the smaller egg is considerably weaker and usually dies.

Eudyptes chrysocome

Eudyptes chrysolophus

Aptenodytes forsteri

Eudyptes chrysolophus

MACARONI PENGUIN   **NT**

Its habitat includes the subantarctic region from the Southern Shetlands to the Kerguelen Islands. It feeds mainly on crustaceans while diving at depths of 65–265ft/20–80m to prey on them. The population is estimated at more than 11 million pairs and is increasing.

Aptenodytes forsteri

EMPEROR PENGUIN   **AN**

This largest penguin grows up to 45in/115cm tall and weighs as much as 100 lb/46kg. Its upperparts are blue-gray, and the underparts white. The head and neck are black except for pale orange auricular patches. There is a pale base on the black bill. It lives in Antarctic waters. Breeding takes place during the harshest winter in May and June when the temperature falls below -50 °C/-58 °F and winds blow 125mph/200kph. A female lays a single egg on an ice barrier of the Antrarctic shore which the male puts it in a special "pocket" between his feet and folds of skin on his abdomen. The female bird then departs for a long journey to feed in the open sea. This means she may have to walk as much as 125 miles/200km to reach the water. Males gather in tight

Eudyptula minor

Eudyptula minor

LITTLE PENGUIN   **AU**

Being 15.5–17.5in/40–45cm tall and weighing about 2.2lb/1kg makes the Little penguin the smallest living penguin. The male is a bit larger and has a thicker bill. The upperparts and head are dark gray, while the underparts are white. The Little penguin is nocturnal, and fishes alone in shoals of pelagic fish ranging 04–5in/1–13cm in size. It lives on the southern shores of Australia, Tasmania and New Zealand. It breeds colonially from July till December in burrows dug in sand. Parents take turns in egg incubation and look after one or two chicks for two months. Little penguins mainly feed on small fish and crustaceans.

Spheniscus humboldti

HUMBOLDT PENGUIN   **NT**

The Humboldt penguin is grouped among penguins of temperate and tropical zones. All of the upperparts, nape, forehead, throat and face are black. A narrow, black, horseshoe-shaped band is easily visible on its white breast, and the white belly is dotted with black spots. The birds set up small nesting colonies on rocky shores of Chile and Peru. Individual nests are usually placed in rock holes or cracks. The population of Humboldt penguins has been declining since the end of the 19th century. In the last decades, the "El Niño" climatic condition has altered the ocean's stream systems in the east Pacific near the equator. These changes have also contributed to large losses in the Humboldt penguin population.

groups to keep warm with as many as 16 birds per square mile. Even the smallest colonies consist of hundreds of birds. The male warms the egg patiently for two months. The chick hatches, usually at the time of the mother's return. She takes over and feeds it, while the male leaves for a lengthy trip at sea to feed in order to recuperate from the long period of fasting. When they are about six weeks old, the chicks get together to form creches of a sort. This allows both parents to forage for food. In addition, their journey to the sea is gradually getting shorter due to the ice thawing.

Spheniscus humboldti

3. Divers and grebes

Divers and grebes used to be classified in the same order of divers because they shared a number of similar qualities. These similarities result from living in the same environment rather than from a common origin. They spend basically all of their lives on the surface of still, fresh waters. Their legs are located towards the rear of their body, making movement on land almost impossible. They are not able to take off from land. They use their legs for propulsion while diving and their tail as a rudder. Their thick plumage, fattened by secretion of a huge coccyx gland, is waterproof and functions as perfect thermal insulation. The plumage of their underparts which is in constant touch with water is very dense and resembles fur. Their wings are generally short and narrow and tucked under prolonged feathers on their flanks while swimming. They do not usually fly during the nesting season, but cover great distances when migrating to their winter nesting grounds.

Gaviiformes

DIVERS

Divers are relatively large birds weighing 2.2–14lb/1–6.4kg. Both sexes have the same coloring. Their feet feature webbed toes to aid in swimming. Because of their legs being set far back, they are forced to keep their bodies standing upright on land. Even so, they are not able to keep their balance long in this position and soon will fall on their belly. The bird's skeleton, like the penguin's, is not pneumatized and is massive and heavy. When diving, they do not spring upwards such as diving ducks but submerge quickly and effortlessly. They are able to dive as deep as 250ft/75m, and remain underwater for as long as 8 minutes. The narrow, slit-like nostrils on their long, sharp-pointed, and flat–sided bill close under the water. Four species of one genus belong to divers. They can be found only in the Northern Hemisphere, primarily in the tundra and taiga regions of Europe, Asia and North America. They nest near still fresh waters and are very vocal and noisy during breeding activity. Their nests are built of plant matter on land close to the water's edge. The female usually lays two dark spotted eggs there. Both parents take part in incubation. Fish constitute the main part of the divers' diet, which also includes smaller portions of crustaceans and mollusks. Chicks are semi-nidifugous and their parents feed them despite of their relative independence. Divers migrate south for the winter months to inland waters and seas.

Left: *Podiceps nigricollis*
Gavia stellata

Gavia stellata

RED-THROATED DIVER   **PA NA**

This smallest diver is only a little bit bigger than the Great Crested grebe. In nesting season, its head and upper neck are slate gray in color, the back of the neck is striped black and white, and there is a brownish red patch on the foreneck. Its back is brownish gray, while the underparts are mostly white with dark spotted flanks. In winter, the whole underparts turn snow white, while upperparts are brownish gray with oval white spots. The rusty-red patch on the throat disappears completely. Unlike other divers, its bill is slightly uptilted. It breeds close by small bodies of water on the tundras of Europe, Asia and North America. It is the only diver capable of taking off from land.

Gavia arctica

BLACK-THROATED DIVER   **PA**

The Black-throated diver is only slightly larger than the Red-throated variety. Its breeding plumage is distinctively elegant. During this time, the bird's head and the back of its neck are gray, while its throat is pitch-black. Its dark back is chequered black and snow white. There are white vertical stripes on the sides of the neck, and the underparts are white. Compared to the breeding colors, the winter plumage is fairly uniform: the upperparts are solid grayish brown, while the underparts are white. The bird's nesting region reaches further south than the one of the Red-throated diver: it ranges as far as southern Scandinavia and the regions around the Baltic. The bird prefers to breed near large and deep lakes with islets where it builds its nests. The newly hatched chicks stay in the nest for just a day or two and then get on the back of the adult in order to be carried around. They are able to fly at the age of 6–7 weeks. The

Tachybaptus ruficollis

prime wintering habitats are the Baltic, Black and Mediterranean Seas.

Podicipediformes

GREBES

Grebes live on all of the continents except Antarctica. They do prefer standing fresh waters. 22 species of one family are known. Their body weight varies from 0.3lb/120g to 3.3lb/1.5kg. Instead of having webbed toes to aid in swimming, each toe on the foot of their strong legs has an independent flap along it. Bones are partially pneumatized. Their tail is short or missing. When diving, grebes use their legs turned sideways as oars. An unique habit is to swallow feathers they pluck out of their underparts. This may help to protect the stomach wall against sharp fish bones. Digested remnants of food wrapped in this felt-like matter are then regurgitated. Breeding and regular plumage differ tremendously. Grebes build their nests sheltered in a reedbed near the water's edge or in open water. Basically, the nest is a mound of aquatic vegetation with a pit on the top. Its base often does not reach the bottom in deeper waters, and the nest then floats on the surface. The clutch usually contains 2 to 8 white eggs, and both parents take turns warming them. When the parents leave the nest-site, they carefully cover it with rotten vegetation in order to hide it from the sight of potential intruders. The

Podiceps grisegena

chicks have a coat of down with a typical pattern of lon-gitudinal dark bands. Semi-nidifugous chicks spend most of their time resting on parents' backs.

Tachybaptus ruficollis

LITTLE GREBE   **PA AF OR AU**

Besides Eurasia, it lives in large areas of Africa, Indonesia and New Guinea. It is the smallest grebe in Europe, about as big as a blackbird. It is for the most part dark brown with a paler underbelly. In the nesting season it has chestnut cheeks and throat, with a distinctive yellowish-green spot at the base of its bill. This infrequently observed bird lives on small lakes with plenty of vegetation. It feeds mainly on water insects. Its presence is often revealed only by a long piercing trill.

Podiceps grisegena

RED-NECKED GREBE   **PA NA**

Its breeding plumage is distinguished by a black back of the neck and a crown with small ear-tufts, chestnut neck

and whitish throat and cheeks. The bird chooses over-grown pools and lakes for nesting. It is relatively shy and often hides in reeds and vegetation by the shore. Sometimes several couples nest in close proximity. It is rare in Central Europe, more abundant and commoner further east and northeast.

Podiceps cristatus

GREAT CRESTED GREBE   **PA AF AU**

In breeding season, both male and female have black frills on the sides of their heads which can become erect, and rusty-red dark brown neck collars. Regular plumage lacks all of the head decorations. In Central Europe, these grebes fly in to breed from mid-March until April. They choose ponds or lakes with vegetation near the water's edge and large open water surfaces. Soon after arrival at the breeding grounds, elaborate display ceremonies begin. Partners swim towards each other from a distance, their necks held straight ahead. After getting close, they rise up facing each other and spread out the neck collars. Rituals then proceed with various posi-

Podiceps cristatus

tions and are completed by diving together. The nest constructed from dead water plants is usually built in rushes providing protection from waves. It is 24in/60cm in diameter and 32in/80cm high. Most of it is under the water; only a small part is seen above the surface. The female lays 3–4 eggs that first are green-white but eventually turn brown due to the rotting vegetation in the nest. The chicks hatch after a month and instinctively know from the moment of hatching how to swim well. The chicks also like to be carried about on their parent's backs. Parents even dive with the chicks, hiding them under their wings. The winter habitat of European grebes is Western Europe and the Mediterranean regions.

Podiceps nigricollis

BLACK-NECKED GREBE   **PA AF NA**

Universally distinguished from other grebes by its black, slightly up-tilted bill, it is about the size of a partridge. In the breeding season, its head, neck and upperparts are black, with a tuft of fan-shaped feathers on either side of its head. The bird's sides are reddish gold, while the belly is white. It also has remarkable ruby colored eyes. It breeds usually in scattered groups in overgrown quiet or slow moving waters, often together with gulls and terns that help to defend it against predators. A colony of Black-necked grebes can have more than 100 nests. A full clutch generally numbers four eggs. They stay at European nesting grounds from April till October.

4. Tubinares and Pelicans

The common features among species of both groups include marine habitat, superb flying abilities, nesting colonies, and feeding of the young by regurgitation of partly digested food from the gullet.

Procellariiformes

TUBINARES (ALBATROSSES, PETRELS, SHEARWATERS)

All of the 108 species spend most of their life on the open ocean. Their body length ranges from 5.5–53.14 in/14–135 cm. Larger species glide on their long, narrow wings just above the water using updrafts on the windward side of high waves. Smaller species use sustained flapping flight. A common characteristic of all the "tubenoses" is a special structure of their bill with distinguished tubular nostrils lying on its upper part. Birds approach shores and islands at the breeding season only. When threatened, they attempt to drive the invader off by spitting out a foul smelling stomach oil which turns solid in the open air. Petrels, which are as big as swallows, are among the smallest members of this group. The largest ones are albatrosses whose body size is similar to that of a goose. The greatest abundance of these species can be found in the Southern Hemisphere.

Diomedea melanophris

BLACK-BROWED ALBATROSS   AF AU NT

Albatrosses are indeed huge birds with a short, stout neck. The long, mighty bill ends in a big hook. Their

Left: *Phalacrocorax carbo*
Diomedea melanophris

wings are remarkably long and narrow. The birds are capable of gliding above the endless ocean waters without a single wingbeat for thousands of kilometers. Calm weather doesn't produce the updrafts they need for soaring and they must land on the water surface. The Black-browed albatross breeds on oceanic islands of the Southern Hemisphere. With 2.2–2.4 million birds, it is among the most abundant and widespread of albatrosses. Its weight of 6.6–11lb/3–5 kg and the wingspan of 7.8ft/240cm place it with the smaller to medium-sized species. Nesting in colonies begins at the end of September and the beginning of October. A female lays one egg which is then incubated for 10 weeks in a large

Diomedea cauta

ground nest built of mud and grass. The fledging of a chick takes an additional 17 weeks. The birds reach sexual maturity at 7 to 9 years and often live for 34 years.

Diomedea cauta

SHY ALBATROSS   AU AF NT

It breeds on islands between South Africa, South Australia and the western shore of South America. The species is less tied to the high seas and frequently can be found close to land masses. The black edging of the white underwings stands out in gliding. The bird feeds mainly on fish and cephalopods, capturing them by surface-seizing or diving. It often follows fishing boats and cetaceans.

Macronectes giganteus

Puffinus tenuirostris

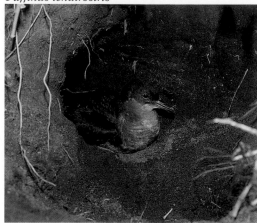

Macronectes giganteus

SOUTHERN GIANT PETREL　　　　**AF AU NT AN**

Petrels are also very well adapted to living at sea. Their plumage is mostly dark gray. Weak legs are set far back on the body. Most of them are gregarious birds living in groups or large flocks, with the highest concentration in places with sufficient sources of food. Huge colonies are formed in breeding season, sometimes consisting of several million nests. Diurnal species nest in the open places, while nocturnal ones nest in burrows. The Southern Giant petrel is the largest representative of the Procellariidae family which includes nearly 70 species. Its body reaches the length of almost 3.3ft/1m, with a weight of 4 to 5kg, and a wingspan approaching 6.6ft/200cm. Two color morphs exist, a more common dark one and the less frequently seen white one. It inhabits oceans of the Southern Hemisphere from a subtropical zone to Antarctica. It breeds in loose colonies up to 300 pairs beginning in October. A small pile of stones or a heap of grass with a shallow depression on top serves as a nest. The incubation of one egg lasts for 8 to 9 weeks, and the nestling is looked after for another 13–19 weeks. They feed mostly on seal and penguin carrion although they also kill young penguins and albatrosses.

Daption capense

CAPE PETREL　　　　**AF AU NT AN**

Its wingspan of 2.6–3ft/80–90cm puts this bird among the smaller species. It is abundant in seas and oceans south of the Tropic of Capricorn. The upperparts, checkered with white and blackish brown patches of various sizes, make the bird unmistakable. It feeds mostly on crustaceans and fish. Hundreds of birds often follow trawling fishing boats. They nest alone or in colonies of thousands of birds on rocky slopes.

Daption capense

Puffinus tenuirostris

SHORT-TAILED SHEARWATER   **AU**

The bird is overall brown with a paler underwing. It is 15.5 to 17.7in/40 to 45cm long, with a wingspan close to 40in/100cm. It breeds in colonies while nesting in burrows on the shores of South Australia and Tasmania. It is a transequatorial migrant that moves as far north as the Bering Sea. Short-tailed shearwaters are among the most abundant species. The total population is about 23 million birds at 160 breeding sites. More than 5.5 million pairs nest in Tasmania alone.

Pelecaniformes

TROPICBIRDS AND PELICANS

Members of this order typically feature short legs with all four toes set forward and connected together by webs. These are effectively used as paddles. There are 60 species on the earth whose sizes range from 55 to 180 cm. All of them feed on fish though their fishing techniques often drastically differ. Nostrils and tongue are underdeveloped, while the gullet and stomach are flexible and capable of taking in large quantities of food.

They mostly nest in colonies. Because pelicans have no brood patch, they have to use their exceedingly vasculated webs of the feet to incubate eggs. The breeding chicks are predominantly hatched blind and naked. When being fed, they place their head in the parent's gullet.

Phaethon aethereus

RED-BILLED TROPICBIRD   **AF NA NT**

All three tropicbird species spend most of their time flying over the tropical and subtropical oceans. Their bodies are about the size of a pigeon. The wedge-shaped tail is by far exceeded by outstanding central rectrices. They feed mostly on flying fish, catching them right in the air. They often charge at their prey from heights and thus are able to dive several meters deep. Tropicbirds nest in rather small, loose colonies on oceanic islands. A female lays a single egg on bare ground. Both partners participate in the incubation and feeding of the chick which hatches covered with dense down. Unlike other Pelecaniformes, it is the adult that puts its bill into the chick's bill during feeding. The Red-billed is the largest tropicbird. It is mostly white with dark colored bars on

its back. The tips of its wings and its eye-stripes are also black. Its bright red bill is conspicuous. The bird is about 3.3ft/1m long from its beak to its tail though a good half of this length is made up of the central tail streamers. Its wingspan also approaches 3.3ft/1m. It inhabits extensive areas from the East Pacific through the Caribbean to the Red Sea.

Phaeton rubricauda

RED-TAILED TROPICBIRD   **PA AF AU**

Its habitat spans from the eastern part of the Indian Ocean to many Pacific islands. It is mostly white with a black eye-stripe and black stripes on primaries and tertials. The red bill provides a perfect contrast as do long, narrow tail streamers of the same color, overlapping the tail by as much as 14in/35cm. It nests in colonies in rocky cracks or on the ground sheltered by vegetation.

Pelecanus onocrotalus

Pelecanus onocrotalus

GREAT WHITE PELICAN   **PA AF OR**

A distinctive feature of all pelicans is a long bill with the enormously distendable pouch underneath, which serves as a kind of landing net. Since pelicans are among the heaviest flying birds in the world, they need a longer run over the surface of the water in order to take off successfully. They fly with grace and confidence, flapping actively or gliding on large, broad wings. Often they exploit thermals to spiral upwards. While flying, they keep their neck retracted in a way similar to egrets. Pelicans are gregarious birds that fly in flocks, and breed in colonies. Some of them even practice communal fishing. Usually a group of pelicans creates a horseshoe formation in which they beat the water with their wings in order to drive the fish towards shallow water where they can catch them in their capacious throat pouches. Seven pelican species occupy all of the zoogeographic regions. The Great White pelican is all white with a pinkish tint and blackish flight-feathers. Its breast, the pouch under its lower mandible and the area around its eyes are yellow. It breeds in southeastern Europe, Asia, tropical and subtropical Africa. Wintering grounds are located in Africa and southern Asia. Breeding colonies can mainly be found in extensive reeds close by open water surfaces. Chicks hatch black and naked. They have to reach for food in the parent's gullet. Some feeding grounds may be fairly remote from a breeding-site, and birds then have to commute as much as 62 miles/100km. The chicks are fully fledged at 12 to 15 weeks and attempt to fish themselves.

Pelecanus rufescens

PINK-BACKED PELICAN   **AF**

This pale gray tinted pelican with pinkish back and underparts is abundant in Africa south of the Sahara Desert. It prefers freshwater lakes and rivers. Its body reaches a length of 4.3ft/130cm, a weight of 8.8–15.4lb/ 4–7kg, and a wingspan nearing almost 10ft/3m. It is a tree-nester that breeds in colonies of 20–500 pairs.

Pelecanus rufescens

Pelecanus crispus

Pelecanus conspicillatus

AUSTRALIAN PELICAN   **AU**

This large species breeds solely in Australia and Tasmania. In non-breeding times, it is also regularly observed in New Guinea. Its body is white, the wings and tail mostly black, and the legs dark grayish blue. It frequents large lakes and rivers and their estuaries, coastal lagoons, etc. Nesting takes place along the shores of oceans, lakes, and marshes, or on small sandy islands. Unlike other pelicans, its diet does not depend only on fish. It also eats insects, crustaceans, and occasionally even birds, reptiles, and amphibians.

Pelecanus crispus

DALMATIAN PELICAN   **PA**

The Dalmatian pelican is only slightly bigger than the Great White pelican. Its body size is somewhere between 5–6ft/160–180cm, with a weight of 22–28lb/ 10–13kg, and a wingspan of 10–11ft/310–350cm. It feeds mostly on carp, perch and rudd, and also eel and pike up to 50cm. Its daily feeding requirement is about 2.5lb/1.2kg of fish. Nests of reeds, grass and twigs are placed on the ground or on floating islands. They are frequently 1m high and 60cm wide. Nowadays, the Dalmatian pelican unfortunately belongs among the endangered species. The breeding area, spanning from the Balkans to China, contained only 21–22 breeding colonies in 1991. The maximum total population was estimated at 2,700 pairs. The main reason for the catastrophic decline is the loss of suitable habitat and the disturbance of breeding colonies.

Pelecanus conspicillatus

29

Pelecanus erythrorhynchos

Pelecanus erythrorhynchos

AMERICAN WHITE PELICAN   **NA**

Its coloration and size are quite similar to the Great White pelican. Its upper mandible, however, features an identifiable knob. It is distributed inland in the northern parts of North America. Breeding colonies of as many as 5,000 pairs can be found nearby lakes and rivers and at the sea coast. Besides fish, it also consumes salamanders and crayfish. It is known to live up to 34 years in captivity.

Pelecanus occidentalis

BROWN PELICAN   **NA NT**

It differs from other pelicans in many ways. First of all, it is a truly marine bird that adopted a method of fishing unusual for pelicans: plunge-diving from heights of 33–66ft/10–20m. The main prey are anchovies and sardines. It is the only pelican with all dark plumage. It breeds mostly on the ground, but also sometimes on cliffs and occasionally in small trees and bushes. The clutch usually consists of 3 eggs; the incubation takes about a month. The chicks are fed for the following two months after hatching. The birds reach sexual maturity at 2 to 5 years. The Brown pelican is the most abundant pelican species. Just the Peruvian colonies consist of up to a million birds.

Sula bassana

NORTHERN GANNET   **PA NA**

A robust body, long narrow wings and the conical bill enable gannets and boobies to perform a highly distinctive method of fishing. A bird plunge-dives from a height of 33–99ft/10–30m above the sea gaining a speed of up to 62mph/100kph, it dives 33ft/10m deep and captures a fish which is swallowed immediately. Gregarious birds, sulids often forage in groups. They nest in colonies, preferably on flat shores, rock cliffs, and some species also nest in trees. Like most of the other Pelecaniformes, they lack brood patches, and so the adults warm the eggs with the highly vasculated webs of their feet. Most of the nine existing sulid species inhabit tropical and subtropical seas; only a few

Pelecanus occidentalis

of them live in temperate and cold zones. One of these is the largest Northern gannet of the North Atlantic. It reaches approximately the size of a goose with a wingspan of about 5.7ft/175cm. It flaps quickly and then glides in flight during which its long, wedge-shaped tail is very noticable. Adult birds are white with black tips on the wings, black legs and pale cream head and neck. They form large colonies on steep slopes. A female lays one egg in a large nest of seaweed, grass, earth and other material which is cemented together by droppings. For about 6 weeks, the parents share the incubation duties. They take turns which involve specific movements and rituals. The newly hatched chicks are born black, naked and blind. The adults have to brood them with their webs until a down grows. After 10 weeks of feeding, the young weigh about 8.8lb/4kg (i.e., 2.2lb/1kg more than the adults). At this time they quickly move to the sea and spend a week on the water surface. Only after that are they fully capable of flying and functioning as adults.

Sula leucogaster

BROWN BOOBY	AF OR AU NA NT

All its body is uniformly dark except for white underparts and yellow legs and bill. It lives near tropical and subtropical seas all around the world. The main prey is flying fish and squid which average about 4in/10cm in length. The Brown booby nests on the ground in small colonies. The usual clutch is two eggs. It is probably the most abundant of all sulids–the total population amounts to several hundred thousand pairs.

Sula bassana

Sula leucogaster

Phalacrocorax olivaceus

Phalacrocorax olivaceus

NEOTROPIC CORMORANT   NT

Cormorants are medium to large-sized waterbirds with long necks, and typically dark plumage. Their long slender bills are hooked at the tips. Their legs are set well back on the body and come in handy as paddles when the birds are diving. Cormorants are able to reach depths of 165ft/50m and stay submerged for as long as 90 seconds. They are quite skillful fishers. In order to swallow the captured prey, they have to rise to the surface. They complement their fish diet with crus-

taceans, cephalopods, mollusks and annelidans. Their plumage gets thoroughly soaked when the birds enter the water so the birds have to rest for a long time on branches or rocks with their wings held half-open to dry out before flying out. They are sociable birds, and their nests can be found on the ground, rocky cliffs, or in bushes and trees. The clutch usually consists of 2 to 6 eggs that are pale green or blue. Most of the 37 species are distributed around the Southern Hemisphere where they use inland waters as well as sea coasts.

The Neotropic cormorant belongs amongst smaller species with its wingspan of 3.3ft/1m and weight of 4.4lb/2kg. It is all black except for a white area around the base of the bill. It occupies sea coasts, estuaries, rivers and lakes. It often forages in groups, even on fast-flowing rivers. Its main prey are small fish, frogs, crustaceans and aquatic insects. It inhabits the whole of South and Central America as well as the southern parts of North America. The cormorants often form mixed colonies with egrets, spoonbills, darters, or gulls that may consist of thousands of nests.

Phalacrocorax carbo

GREAT CORMORANT   PA AF OR AU NA

It can be found on all the continents except South America. It nests in colonies on the cliffs of rocky seashores, and also inland in tree tops nearby freshwaters abundant with fish. Adults are almost all black except for the clearly white face and throat, and a white patch on the thighs. Like other cormorants, it swims quite low in the water and dives with great ease. Its daily consumption is close to 2.2lb/1kg of fish. When threatened, only its

Phalacrocorax carbo

Phalacrocorax varius

head protrudes from the water. It flies fast and direct, resembling a "cross" with its long tail and neck outstretched. Flocks travel in V-formation or in a line.

Phalacrocorax varius

PIED CORMORANT   **AU**

The Pied cormorant inhabits Australia and New Zealand. Its coloration is significantly lighter. All the underparts from the belly to cheeks are clearly white. The upperparts from tail to crown are dark, and there is a dark yellow patch between its eyes and the bill. It prefers seashores but often occurs in inland lakes and rivers with constant water level. Colonies may be comprised of several thousand nests, placed mostly on trees or bushes. Three eggs are warmed by both partners who take stints for about 4 weeks. Adults look after their young that hatch naked and blind for about 7–8 weeks in a nest, and then perform post-fledging care for at least an additional 11 weeks.

Phalacrocorax melanoleucos

LITTLE PIED CORMORANT   **AU**

This bird has distinctive pied plumage with a clear demarcation between white and black. Its length of 20–25in/55–65cm puts it among the smallest cormorant species. Their vast territory spans from eastern Indonesia down to New Zealand. As for the habitat, it is fairly flexible. However, they prefer fresh waters with periodic floods. It nests on trees and bushes in smaller colonies, often together with other waterbirds. It feeds on various fish and aquatic invertebrates including freshwater crayfish. The adult birds are sedentary but the young birds engage in the extensive dispersal.

Phalacrocorax melanoleucos

Phalacrocorax africanus

Phalacrocorax africanus

LONG-TAILED CORMORANT   AF

This bird is another small cormorant that is basically all dark with pale upperparts. It occupies mainly inland waters in Africa south of the Sahara, and Madagascar. It readily moves to flooded areas. During draughts it concentrates by fresh water, especially large rivers. It fishes individually for fish of up to 8in/20cm long and frogs. The nest, which is built of thin sticks and lined with grass and leaves, is placed in trees, reedbeds or on ground. A clutch consists of 3–4 eggs.

Phalacrocorax pygmaeus

Phalacrocorax pygmaeus

PYGMY CORMORANT   PA

Thy Pygmy cormorant nests in a rather small area between the Balkans and the Aral Sea. It is about the size of the Wood Pigeon. The adult's breeding plumage is black with frequent white dots, and the head and neck are chestnut brown. This species frequents freshwater lakes and slow-flowing rivers. It forms common colonies with the Great cormorant, herons, and egrets on trees, bushes or reedbeds. Its population is steadily decreasing.

Anhinga anhinga

ANHINGA   NA NT

Darters feature long thin bodies and necks which are bent back in an S-shape. Their pointed, straight bills have a harpoon-like shape and are actually used the same way. Darters forage mainly in shallow waters where they dive with only the head and neck above the surface and spread their wings in order to attract fish into the shade. Using a rapid jab forward of its neck, the darter stabs its prey with its bill. They are monogamous and form pairs that remain together for a number of years. They nest individually, in small groups or numerous colonies in trees or bushes. A platform-like nest is built of sticks and leaves above water. They breed on all the continents except Europe and Antarctica.

The Anhinga is one of the two existing species. Its body with tail reaches 32–35in/80–90cm, and it has a wingspan of about 4ft/120cm. The male is all black with silvery stripes on the upperwing-coverts and an erectile crest on its nape. Females are brown. The anhinga in-

Anhinga anhinga

habits mainly shallow inland waters in the southern part of North America, and all of Central and South America. It can less frequently be found in estuaries and coastal areas with lagoons and mangroves. Its main diet is fish, but it also eats amphibians, snakes, newly born alligators, crustaceans and other invertebrates.

Fregata magnificens

MAGNIFICENT FRIGATEBIRD   **NA NT AF**

The small family of frigatebirds includes 5 tropical marine species that feature very long wings, a deeply forked tail, and a long bill hooked at the tip. Their relatively large body is very light in weight due to immense bone pneumatization, with bones amounting to only 5% of the total weight. This is a critical characteristic of these birds who spend most of their time in the air. They are expert gliders, able to cover considerable distances above the ocean. They are keen on flying fish but also pick other fish swimming close to the surface. They are notorious for being piratical kleptoparasites, harassing other birds to make them disgorge their prey which they are dexterously able to catch while still in the air. Robbing nests of breeding seabird colonies is another source of food for them. In breeding season, males of all frigatebird species inflate the carmine gular pouch in order to attract females.

The Magnificent frigatebird inhabits seas of tropical and subtropical zones from California to western Africa. It is the largest frigatebird, measuring 3–3.8ft/ 90–115cm. Its wingspan approaches almost 8ft/2.5m, and its weight ranges between 2.4 and 3.5lb/1.1 and 1.6 kg. It nests on coasts or small islands, often in mangroves, bushes and, in the Galapagos, also on cacti. If there is no other choice, it would nest on ground, too. A female lays just one egg. The naked chick hatches after 7 weeks of incubation and is looked after mostly by a female for quite a long time. It stays in the nest for as long as 24 weeks, and the post-fledging care takes an additional 5–7 months. For this reason, a female breeds only once in two years while the male mates annually.

Fregata magnificens

5. Wading birds and Flamingos

The two groups are related and have many similar characteristics. Because their long slim legs are ideal for wading in shallow waters, most of these birds require a close proximity to water where they forage.

Ciconiiformes
WADING BIRDS

Middle to large-sized birds of a unified look belong to this order. Most of them have long legs, neck and a bill. They live practically all around the world except for the coldest and driest places. All of them are carnivorous, and they chiefly feed on aquatic animals from insects to fish and other vertebrates. One hundred and thirteen living species of 5 families have been described so far: Herons *(Ardeidae)*, the Hamerkop *(Scopidae)*, Storks *(Ciconiidae)*, the Shoebill *(Balaenicipitidae)*, and Ibises and Spoonbills *(Threskiornithidae)*.

Herons include 60 species that are spread out almost all over the world. Their long neck is folded back into the body in flight. They preen their plumage using a powder that is picked from the breast and rump in order to powder-down patches. They catch prey in shallows or on the ground either while lying patiently in wait or by slowly walking about, with their neck retracted and sharp bill pointed ahead. When a suitable prey appears, they thrust the neck forward and harpoon it with the bill. Small species feed on insects, crustaceans, larvaes of amphibians or small fish, larger species on fish, adult amphibians, snakes, little mammals and birds. They nest mostly in colonies in trees or in wetland vegetation.

Storks are large birds that extend their long neck in active flight or soaring. Most of the 19 species are distributed throughout the tropical zone. They breed alone or in colonies.

Ibises are medium-sized to large birds that breed in colonies and are found on all continents except Antarctica. The family has 32 species. Most of them live in the tropics. They mainly occupy various types of wetlands. Their bill is either long and decurved (ibises) or long, straight, and flattened with a spoon-like broad end (spoonbills).

Left: *Egretta thula*

Ardea cinerea
GRAY HERON   PA AF OR

Grayish coloring predominates although any tones ranging from white to black can be found. The body is about 3.3ft/1m long, and the wingspan can reach almost 6.6ft/2m. The Gray heron is common in Europe, Asia, and Africa. It is partly migratory. The bird can mostly be found in areas with plenty of waters rich in fish. Its diet consists mainly of fish 4–8in/10–20cm long with a daily take of 1.1lb/0.5kg. Besides fish, it also eats frogs and is able to catch minor mammals and larger insects on land. Dense breeding colonies that often consist of hundreds of platform nests of sticks are situated in the tops of tall trees. The full clutch is comprised of 3–5 pale blue and green eggs. The incubation as well as the feeding of the loud and cantankerous chicks is performed by both sexes. After several years of supporting such a colony, the

Ardea cinerea

Ardea purpurea

trees with nests die because of overly abundant nutriments from piled bird droppings.

Ardea purpurea

PURPLE HERON   PA AF OR

The Purple heron is similar to the Gray heron though it is a bit smaller and has chestnut brown neck and underparts. The bird requires extensive dense reedbeds where it builds its nest on broken reeds. The clutch of 3–5 pale blue eggs is warmed by both parents for 4 weeks. After hatching, they are fed for an additional 6–8 weeks with food brought in a throat pouch from which the chicks pick themselves. The chief prey are fish up to 6in/15cm. After it is stabbed, a fish is shaken off the bill and swallowed head first. The breeding territory of the Purple heron is Europe, South Asia and Africa. European populations migrate to winter in areas south of the Sahara.

Ardea goliath

GOLIATH HERON   AF

The largest heron is over 4.6ft/140cm long with a wingspan reaching 6.9–7.6ft/210–230cm. Its very long legs are conspicuous. Gray and chestnut brown prevail in rather dark plumage coloration. Its territory spreads out throughout sub-Saharan Africa. The adult Goliath heron is sedentary. However, the immature birds are quite active, frequently taking flight over the nesting and feeding areas. Any shallow waters, fresh or salt, provide suitable habitat as long as they are abundant in larger fish, frogs, reptiles or crabs. The bird is able to swallow

a fish as heavy as 2.2lb/1kg. It also feeds on the floating carrion of large animals. It nests alone or in small colonies, especially during rains.

Ardea goliath

Egretta alba

Egretta tricolor

Egretta alba

GREAT WHITE EGRET   **PA AF OR NA NT**

With a wingspan of 5.6ft/170cm and length of 3ft/90cm, the Great White egret comes close to the Gray heron in size. The plumage is always snow-white. The bill is black except for a yellow base during the breeding season, while juveniles and non-breeding adults have a yellow bill. Breeding plumage features a 20in/50cm long veil of ornamental plumes which flows down from the scapulars. Their habitat is fairly extensive and reaches all the continents except Antarctica. The Great White egret prefers densely overgrown swamps and shallow waters along river banks. In Europe, it breeds individually or in small colonies in inaccessible parts of vast reed beds. Elsewhere in the world, however, it also builds nests in tall trees. The Great White egret enjoys fishing in still water shallows, rice fields or wet meadows. In breeding season they often fly 6.2–9.3 miles/10–15 km for food.

Egretta tricolor

TRICOLORED HERON   **NA NT**

When looking at this generally dark egret, a bird watcher would be sure to notice an extremely long and thin bill and neck, together with a white crest and belly. The bird frequents coastal areas of the New World. It prefers mangrove growths and mudflats. It breeds in numerous colonies of hundreds of nests that are placed on the ground, in bushes or in low trees.

Egretta caerulea

Egretta thula

SNOWY EGRET   **NA NT**

This snow-white egret features a striking contrast be-tween black legs and yellow toes as well as between the black bill and its yellow base. Breeding plumage features a bushy crest. The species inhabits various kinds of wetlands from the United States to Chile. It captures shrimp, small fish, frogs, molluscs, aquatic in-sects, lizards, snakes, and grasshoppers. Various for-aging techniques are carried out, including catching insects in the air. It often follows grazing cattle and preys on the disturbed insects.

Egretta thula

Egretta caerulea

LITTLE BLUE HERON   **NA NT**

This dark gray heron resides especially in still fresh-waters of the tropics and subtropics of the New World. In the Andes, it can be found at the considerable alti-tude of 8,200–9,850ft/2,500–3,000m and occasional-ly even up to 12,300ft/3,750m. It feeds mainly on in-sects and other arthropods, capturing them while walking slowly. After fledging the juveniles migrate northward, some of them even reaching Canada and Greenland.

Egretta garzetta

Egretta garzetta

LITTLE EGRET   **PA AF OR AU**

As for the size and coloring of the Little egret, there is a conspicuous resemblance to the Snowy egret. Its territory, however, includes Eurasia, Africa and Australia. It can be distinguished from the Snowy egret by a thinner crest and a brighter yellow base of the bill. A dark morph with a white throat can sometimes be found, especially in tropics, as can also a race *E. g. schistacea*, living in areas from East Africa to India, and features a yellow bill. The Little egret inhabits all different kinds of wetlands with shallow water: edges of rivers and lakes, rice fields, flooded areas, sand beaches, mangroves, occasionally even dry areas like pastures where it follows grazing livestock. It occurs on inland savannas in South Africa. It can usually be found in lowlands, though in Nepal it inhabits areas up to 4,600ft/1,400m, and even up to 6,600ft/2,000in Armenia. Its nests are placed on the ground, in reedbeds, bushes or trees. It breeds alone or in numerous colonies of several thousand pairs.

Bubulcus Ibis

CATTLE EGRET   **PA AF OR AU NA NT**

Unlike other herons, the Cattle egret is plumper and has a shorter bill. It is a part of the fauna of all the continents except Antarctica. Race *B. i. coromandus*, living in southeastern Asia, Australia and New Zealand, is larger. Its whole head and neck are rusty buff, and it features a stronger bill and longer legs. Of all the herons, the Cattle egret is associated with an aquatic habitat the least–it shows preference for steppes, meadows, freshwater swamps, rice fields, etc. It can remain in dry places without any water for a fairly long time. Occasionally, it even appears in towns. Insects prevail as its diet, but small vertebrates are not rejected either. It picks food while walking slowly following cattle, great mammals or a tractor. Breeding colonies of various sizes, from several dozens to thousands of nests, may be on the ground or in bushes or trees.

Bubulcus ibis

Ardeola ralloides

SQUACCO HERON   **PA AF**

The adult birds of this smaller, rusty-red and white heron feature long flowing feathers at their nape. Non-breeding birds and juveniles are brownish, spotted dark and light. They feed mostly on insect larvae. They breed in small to huge colonies in reeds or low in trees near water.

Nycticorax nycticorax

BLACK-CROWNED
NIGHT-HERON   **PA AF OR NA NT**

Among the significant characteristics of the night-herons are a rather big head with a robust bill, and a crouched bearing. The adults are strikingly elegant. A black back and cap are accompanied by bright white underparts and several fairly long and thin nuchal plumes. The chicks are dark brown with yellowish spots. During the day the bird roosts motionless on branches. It is predominantly active around dusk, although it also travels with its inaudible "owl-like" flight at night. In the breeding season, it is also active during the day. It prefers to occupy waters that are densely overgrown with vegetation or forest margins skirting shallow rivers. Various prey is caught mostly by a method that involves standing and sudden attack. It nests in colonies of up to several thousand nests, mostly in trees or bushes.

Ardeola ralloides

Nycticorax nycticorax

Ixobrychus minutus

LITTLE BITTERN   **PA AF OR AU**

The Little bittern belongs among the smallest herons. In their coloration, a significant sexual dimorphism has evolved. The male shows a contrasted dark, cream and brown plumage, while the female is an inconspicuous streaky brown. The Little bittern lives in dense aquatic vegetation. Its movement is skulky with the bird being typically crouched. It often climbs reeds very skillfully. It flies only for short distances just above the reeds or very low above the water surface and soon returns to cover. When disturbed, it moves off rather swiftly instead of taking off. It commonly breeds alone or in loose colonies. Populations from Europe and Asia migrate towards Africa south of the Sahara, and to northern India.

Botaurus stellaris

EURASIAN BITTERN   **PA AF**

The Eurasian bittern's territory spreads out mainly through Eurasia. From here, the birds migrate to Africa and southern Asia. There are sedentary populations in the southernmost part of Africa. Even though it is a large bird, weighing up to 4.2lb/1.9kg with a wingspan of 4.1–4.5ft/125–135cm, it usually passes completely unnoticed. Shadow-like, it skulks through extensive, thick reedbeds to which it is exceptionally well adapted by its coloring and living habits. Protective pale brown plumage is dark mottled

Ixobrychus minutus

and barred. When disturbed, the bird remains motionless with its body and head stretched and the bill pointed vertically in order to blend perfectly with the surroundings. Its flight on short, broad wings just above the reeds or the water surface is extraordinarily quiet. The bird's most distinctive manifestation is a booming sound produced by a resonance of its oesophagus, which is inflamed during the breeding season. At night the sound may be audible for several kilometers.

Botaurus stellaris

Scopus umbretta

Anastomus lamelligerus

AFRICAN OPENBILL   **AF**

The bird is black overall with greenish and purple iridescence. Feather webs at neck, breast and thighs are prolonged to form long and narrow horny scales. The long bill has a unique structure. Its upper and lower mandibles, flattened at the sides, touch only at the bill's end and base, creating a gap in the middle. The African openbill inhabits freshwater wetlands. Freshwater mollusks are the most common item in its diet due to the fact that it is able to get inside their shells with the help of its unusually shaped bill. It nests in colonies in trees.

Balaeniceps rex

Scopus umbretta

HAMERKOP   **AF**

The hamerkop is the only member of the *Scopidae* family. The medium-sized, completely brown body is accompanied by a pronounced backward-pointing crest, strong bill and short legs. The bird prefers forested margins of waters located south of the Sahara and on the island of Madagascar. A significant part of its diet consists of frogs that are caught mostly at dawn and dusk while the bird is wading in different types of shallow waters. Roofed, sheltered nests of 5–6.5ft/ 1.5–2m in diameter are built by individual pairs in major forks of huge trees. The structure is a mass of sticks and grass connected by mud. The nest is entered from below.

Balaeniceps rex

SHOEBILL   **AF**

The shoebill is an interesting bird whose membership as a wader is sometimes doubted. DNA analysis associates it with pelicans. It differs from the other waders due to its robust bill which has sharp edges and ends in a nail. Its shape and size resemble a wooden shoe. When resting, the shoebill leans its bill against its craw. The bird prefers a solitary life and lives in heavily overgrown swamps in eastern tropical Africa. It particularly favors papyrus swamps. Using a method of waiting and suddenly striking, it captures fish, amphibians and water turtles in shallow water. The nest is a flat pile of sticks and reeds in which a female lays 2 eggs. The chicks hatch after a month-long incubation. The adults may shower them up to several times daily with water from their bills in order to cool them down.

Ciconia nigra

BLACK STORK   **PA AF**

The Black stork really is all black with largely white underparts. It nests in woodlands rich in water and streams where it can feed on fish and also on other small vertebrates and invertebrates. Unlike the White stork, its close relative, it remains shy and avoids humans. Its nest is built 33–66ft/10–20m up in trees. In the past decades, an intensive westerly movement of the Black stork has appeared in Europe. While the Eurasian populations are migratory, there are sedentary populations living in southern Africa.

Anastomus lamilligerus

Ciconia nigra

Ciconia abdimii

Ciconia ciconia

Ciconia abdimii

ABDIM'S STORK AF

The Abdim's stork is quite similar to the Black stork, though considerably smaller. Facial skin is bluish with a red patch near the eye and on the chin. The bill is brownish with a red tip. Nesting territory spreads in Africa between the equator and the Sahara. Its suitable habitat is formed by open, dry grassland, mostly near water. It breeds at the beginning of the rainy season in colonies in rock cliffs and trees. It feeds almost exclusively on large insects. Non-breeding time from November to March is spent in tropical areas south of the equator.

Ciconia ciconia

EUROPEAN WHITE STORK PA AF

Probably the most popular bird of all nests chiefly throughout Europe, though its territory reaches as far as Central Asia. Winter habitats include India, Arabia, and Africa where a sedentary population can be found on the southernmost tip of the Cape. Today White storks mostly place their nests on buildings, but once they nested in tall trees and often formed loose colonies. The nest is re-used for many years. The most important condition for the storks presence is the abundance of suitable food. Their prey includes small vertebrates and larger invertebrates. When foraging, the White stork walks deliberately about and as soon as a suitable prey is spotted, the bird kills it with its bill and swallows it immediately. The storks' vocal repertoir is not very rich; it is mostly limited to hissing and bill-clattering. Storks are long-lived and zoo records suggest that they can live 30 years or more.

Ciconia boyciana

ORIENTAL WHITE STORK PA

The Oriental White stork is distinguishable from the European White stork only by a grayish black heavier bill and darker red legs. The species breeds in southeastern Siberia and in parts of northeastern China and migrates for winter to southern and southeastern of China. It lives in a similar way as the White Stork, though it is more reluctant to get close to human sites. Its present population does not exceed 3,000 birds which places it amongst endangered species. It formerly lived in Japan and on the Korean Penninsula, too.

Ciconia boyciana

Ephippiorhynchus asiaticus

BLACK-NECKED STORK   **OR AU**

Black plumage with metal iridescence on the neck and head makes the bird essentially different from the European White stork. Even less significant differences can naturally be found. For example, it has a larger share of black coloring on the wings and brighter red legs. The Black-necked stork is at home in India and northern Australia where it solitarily frequents freshwater wetlands including swamps and areas near lakes and rivers. It often visits wet meadows and drier grassland. The main part of its diet consists of fish, although no food of animal origin is rejected, either.

Leptoptilos crumeniferus

MARABOU   **AF**

It is about 50% larger than the European White stork, reaching the weight of 8.8–19.8lb/4–9kg and a wingspan of almost 10ft/3m. Its smooth flight resembles more that of a vulture than a stork. Its head and neck are sparsely feathered with hairy feathers. It is distributed in sub-Saharan Africa in savanna-like landscapes, often close to human settlements. It feeds on carrion, and various food discarded by man. It also actively captures smaller vertebrates and larger insects. The marabou regularly waits together with hyenas for what food remains after a feast by large predators. The nest of sticks is built high up in tree tops. It breeds gregariously; a colony may comprise dozens as well as thousands of pairs. It is known for its longevity, and has been reported to live for 41 years in captivity.

Leptoptilos crumeniferus

Threskiornis aethiopicus

Threskiornis aethiopicus
SACRED IBIS   AF PA

Clear white prevails in the coloring of this African in-habitant. Only its head, neck, legs and tips of primaries and secondaries are black as are also the longish orna-mental plumes growing out of the scapulars. In ancient Egypt, it was acknowledged as a sacred bird and mum-mified in great numbers. It prefers marshy areas abun-dant in suitable prey which consist of insects and small vertebrates. The breeding begins during rains or short-ly afterwards except for the areas with plenty of water where breeding can take place during a draught, too. It nests in colonies ranging in size from several dozen to two thousand pairs, together with other wading birds. Its nest, a large platform of branches, is placed in trees, bushes, or on the ground.

Geronticus eremita

Geronticus eremita
NORTHERN BALD IBIS   PA AF

The bird has a red bare head and bill, while the rest of its body is dark with elongated nape feathers. It is one of the most endangered birds of the world. The last colonies counting several dozens of pairs breed in the Atlas Mountains in Morocco. The species used to nest in Switzerland, Austria and Hungary until the end of the 17th century, but then it disappeared from Europe. At present, captive bred birds are being released there in an attempt to return them to the wilderness. For breeding, the Northern Bald ibis picks inaccessible places in the mountains, formerly often used nesting sites in castle ruins and abandoned human structures. From there, it flies to open grasslands and fields to feed mainly on grasshoppers and other arthropods.

Geronticus calvus

Geronticus calvus
SOUTHERN BALD IBIS   AF

The Southern Bald ibis' dark plumage has a metallic sheen, but the most distinctive characteristic is its bald head with the bright red crown and bill. Less than 10,000 pairs live in a fairly restricted territory in southern Africa. High altitude grasslands at 3,400–6,100ft/1,200–1,850m constitute a suitable habitat. It nests on mountain cliffs, mostly close to water. The beginning of breeding occurs during July, during winter in the Southern Hemisphere. This al-lows a pair to rear their young when grass is growing and food is plentiful. The main part of their diet con-sists of terrestrial invertebrates.

Bostrychia hagedash

HADADA IBIS   **AF**

This African bird is a true gem among ibises. It displays green and blue sheens on its back and upperwing plumage. It occupies grasslands and savannas, primarily along rivers lined with trees. Often it can be spotted in town parks or cemeteries. When disturbed it produces an unpleasant shriek. It builds a poor tree nest of twigs on horizontal branches, usually 10–20ft/3 to 6m above the ground. The incubation of 2–3 eggs lasts for 4 weeks. The parents then have to feed the chicks for the next 7 weeks until they fledge.

Theristicus melanopis

BLACK-FACED IBIS   **NT**

Its head and neck are a deep ochre, while the belly, cheeks and chin are dark; upperparts are gray and legs are reddish. It inhabits the open landscape in western and southern South America. In some locations it is found at heights of 9,850–16,400ft/3,000–5,000m. The Black-faced Ibis breeds in colonies of up to 50 pairs, in reeds or on the ground. The southern populations migrate further north for the winter.

Bostrychia hagedash

Theristicus melanopis

49

Eudocimus albus

Eudocimus albus

AMERICAN WHITE IBIS   **NA NT**

The American White ibis is distributed from California and Florida to Venezuela and northwestern Peru. It is all white except for its bill, bare face and legs. It inhabits any kind of wetlands with shallow water abundant in crustaceans, fish and other suitable prey. Breeding colonies can be comprised of as many as thousands of pairs. Platform nests of branches and leaves are usually situated 6.5–11.5ft/2–3.5m above the mud or water, only occasionally are they built on dry ground. Incubation of the clutch of 2–3 eggs takes about three weeks, and the chicks are looked after for almost two months. Even though the bird is sedentary, it occasionally migrates to richer feeding grounds. Flocks fly in a straight line or in a V-formation.

Eudocimus ruber

Eudocimus ruber

SCARLET IBIS   **NT**

The Scarlet ibis is relatively numerous in the northern areas of South America. It is overall bright red with the exception of dark eyes, bill and legs. Crossbreeding may occur in shared habitats in Venezuela with the closely related American White Ibis. It frequents mangrove wetlands and muddy estuaries but also can be found in shallow freshwater lakes, floodplains, fish ponds and paddyfields. 30 to 70 birds gather for foraging, probing in the mud and shallow water with their bills. Crabs are the main source of food, followed by molluscs, insects and small fish.

Plegadis falcinellus

GLOSSY IBIS   **PA AF OR AU NA NT**

In the breeding season, the adult's entire body is reddish brown with a metallic sheen on various areas. During flight, rapid wingbeats are alternated with long glides. When flying in a group, they tend to form oblique lines. At present, Glossy ibis enclaves can be found on all continents, but their populations are steadily declining. The main cause is the disappearance of suitable habitats–shallow lakes, swamps and other wetlands with plenty of insects and other animals. They pick prey from mud, shallow water or water surfaces while walking about slowly. They mostly breed in closed colonies of up to 1,000 nests together with spoonbills, herons and pelicans. These colonies can be found in large reedbeds with tall, dense vegetation. Occasionally, nests are built in trees or bushes just above the ground or water. Both parents sit on a clutch of 3–6 dark blue-and-green eggs for 3 weeks. The chicks are fed for about 4 weeks, inserting their head into the adult's mouth to obtain food from the gullet.

Platalea leucorodia

EURASIAN SPOONBILL   **PA AF OR**

Spoonbills are distinguishable from any other bird due to the shape of their bill which is elongated, flattened, with the broader distal end of a spoon-like shape. The Eurasian spoonbill is all white with black legs and a bill with a yellow tip. The breeding plumage draws attention because of the occipital crest of elongated feathers and an ochre stripe at the base of the neck. It is a rather large bird, almost 3.3ft/1m long, weighing 2.5–4.5lb/1.2–2kg, with a wingspan of 3.7–4.3ft/ 115–135cm. Nesting sites include southern Europe, Asia and northern Africa. It requires still shallow waters or slow-flowing rivers with shallows and a muddy bottom. It usually forages in small flocks, swinging its slightly open bill from side to side while wading through water in a manner similar to ducks. Captured prey is then swallowed, whether it is insect larvae, annelidans, crustaceans, small fish and frogs or even

Plegadis falcinellus

parts of aquatic plants. Spoonbills breed mostly in monospecific and sometimes mixed colonies in reedbeds or trees and bushes. They tend to nest apart from other types of birds in mixed colonies.

Platalea leucorodia

Platalea alba

AFRICAN SPOONBILL   AF

This African inhabitant with a short nuchal crest is all white; only its legs and bare face are red. It haunts large inland shallow waters, and, to a lesser extent, coastal lagoons and estuaries. It breeds in colonies of up to 250 pairs, often with other waders, cormorants or darters. A female usually lays 2–3 eggs in a flat nest of sticks and reeds that is often placed in the top of a partially submerged tree or bush. Incubation lasts 4 weeks, and fledging of chicks about 7 weeks.

Platalea alba

Platalea ajaja

ROSEATE SPOONBILL   **NA NT**

The Roseate spoonbill is the only spoonbill species with pinkish plumage. In addition, it features a bare head and neck. It is mainly distributed throughout subtropical and tropical zones of the New World. It is primarily found in salt and brackish wetlands near the sea coasts. Less often, it can be found near inland fresh-waters. Its main diet includes little fish, crustaceans, and other invertebrates, captured the same way as by other spoonbills. It breeds in wetlands and on coastal islands–the nests are built on low trees, thick bushes, mangroves, and occasionally on the ground.

Phoenicopteriformes

FLAMINGOS

All of the five known species of flamingos have an ex-tremely long neck and notably long, thin legs with web-like toes. A small head carries the strong down-curved bill that features special lamellae which serve to catch tiny particles of plankton. While feeding in shallow water, the bill is submerged with the upper mandible down, while the fleshy tongue functions as a pump. Plumage of all the flamingos has reddish col-oration owing to carotenoid pigments contained in their food. In flight, their neck is stretched out. Flamingos are highly gregarious, and their breeding colonies may number as many as hundreds of thou-sands of pairs. Their nest, a scraped 12–20in/30–50cm high pile of mud with a depression on the top, is built on shore or in shallow water. A female usually lays one egg there which is, by turns, incubated by both partners who accomplish this task by folding their legs underneath the body. Chicks, hatched after 4 weeks, leave their nest after about a week to assemble in creches together with the other young. Parents feed them with a special red liquid secretion which main-ly consists of blood and carotenoids. Within about two weeks, their straight bill starts to curve to aquire the adult's shape, and they slowly begin to obtain their own food. Fledging is completed when they are 10 weeks old. Flamingos are resident in Central and South America, Africa, southern Europe, and south and Central Asia.

Phoenicopterus ruber

GREATER FLAMINGO   **PA AF OR NT**

These flaminges comprise the largest species. Their bodies reach a length of up to 4.75ft/145cm, a weight of 4.4–8.8lb/2–4kg, and a wingspan of 4.5–5.4ft/140–165cm. The largest number of them are dis-

Phoenicopterus ruber

tributed in the Old World where its population approaches 1 million birds. It can also be found in Central America, in the northern areas of South America and in the Galapagos, although different sub-species are found here as well. A suitable habitat is created by ocean lagoons and also by large inland salt lakes. The birds form dense colonies of up to 200,000 nests. The Greater flamingo is long-lived. Wild, tagged birds have shown a life span of 33 years and they may live up to 44 years in captivity.

Phoeniconaias minor

LESSER FLAMINGO   **AF OR**

The Lesser flamingo is apparently the most numerous flamingo with a population that reaches 6 million birds. It mostly frequents salt and alkaline lakes as well as coastal lagoons in the eastern areas of tropical Africa. Smaller numbers live in southern Africa and on the border between India and Pakistan. It is about a quarter to a third smaller than the Greater flamingo. It breeds in remarkably numerous colonies of as many as 1,100,000 pairs, on mudflats, often far from water. Its diet requirements are quite specific and focused on microscopic blue-green algae and diatoms.

Phoeniconais minor

6. Wildfowl – screamers, ducks, geese, swans

Anseriformes constitute a relatively numerous order of chiefly aquatic birds which includes two families and 152 species distributed all over the world. Their common features include large swimming webs between the three front toes of their short legs, and a strong bill covered with tender skin, as well as a special, hard, spiked plate called the "nail" at its front part. There are rows of serrated lamellae along the bill edges which interlock when the bill is closed. The bird's thick plumage is very efficient for insulating its body from cold water. Wax-like secretion from the highly developed uropygial gland, which the bird applies with its bill, assures that the plumage will be waterproof. Sexual dimorphism is well developed in many species. Males are often a profusion of color, while the females, who usually undertake all the duties concerning the incubation of eggs and chick rearing, are fairly inconspicuous. The nest is usually placed on the ground. The nesting pit is lined with down which the female plucks from its breast. The female does not sit on the nest until the last egg is laid, and the chicks therefore hatch virtually at the same time. After drying out from hatching the chicks have dense down and are very independent. They leave the nest accompanied by one of the parents and never return to it. After breeding, the adults moult all their flight-feathers and become flightless for some time. During this period they stay under cover in thick reeds. Anseriformes are generally good and fast flyers.

Chauna torquata

SOUTHERN SCREAMER   NT

The Southern screamer represents one of the three species that form the family *Anhimidae* (Screamers). All of them inhabit South America. With middle-sized, sturdy legs and a small head, they rather resemble Galliformes. They feature two long sharp spurs at the bend of the wings which they use for defending themselves. They live close to still waters, and their long toes that are not webbed prove useful for walking on the aquatic vegetation. The sexes are hardly distinguishable. The Southern screamer is the largest species, weighing up to 10lb/4.5kg. Of all the screamers, it is the least bound to marshy areas and often appears in agricultural areas. It feeds mostly on green parts of succulent and aquatic plants and also on the seeds, leaves and stems of agricultural crops. The bird is called "Chajá" in South America thanks to a ringing call of a similar sound which is often voiced during the flight and heard as far as 1.9 miles/3km away. It nests alone in wetland vegetation.

Left: *Cygnus atratus*
Chauna torquata

Anseranas semipalmata

Dendrocygna viduata

Anseranas semipalmata

MAGPIE GOOSE   **AU**

The Magpie goose is the first representative of the *Anseridae* family. It lives in floodplains of large rivers in northern Australia and southern New Guinea. It used to nest in other parts of Australia, too, but disappeared due to drainage of wetlands and intensive hunting. A combination of a typically goose-shaped body and yellow legs featuring long toes with only vestigial webs makes it look rather awkward. The bird can be found mainly in swamps and shallow waters. It nests in larger groups. The male usually has two or more females that lay eggs in one nest. The male actively helps with incubating. All the *Anseriformes* have nidifugous nestlings that find their own food, the parents do not have to feed them. The only exception is the Magpie goose.

Dendrocygna viduata

WHITE-FACED WHISTLING-DUCK   **AF NT**

The home of this multicolored duck is partly in sub-

Cygnus olor

Cygnus atratus

Saharan Africa and Madagascar and partly in Central and South America as far south as northern Argentina. It has managed to adapt well to populated areas and causes substantial losses to crops in rice fields. In places its population is abundant, and there are 1–2 million birds living in eastern and southern Africa.

Cygnus olor

MUTE SWAN   **PA AF AU NA**

With its length of 5ft/1.5m and weight of up to 33lb/15kg, the Mute swan is among the largest flying birds. It looks quite distinctive in flight with its out-stretched neck and considerable wingspan (up to 8ft/240cm). It is easily distinguished from other swan species by the black knob on the base of the bill which in males is greatly enlarged during the breeding season. The Mute swan first inhabited northern parts of Europe and Asia. Its graceful appearence and majestic behavior always attracted people who reared the bird in park lakes. It was successfully introduced into North America, southern Africa, Australia and New Zealand. Thanks to consistent protection and winter feeding, it has spread to Central Europe during the last few decades. The main diet of Mute swans is aquatic vegetation. It breeds near water or in reeds. The male vigorously defends the nesting territory not only against its own kind, but also against various intruders including humans.

Cygnus atratus

BLACK SWAN   **AU**

The bird is really all black except for the red bill and white tips of primaries and secondaries. Its behavior is very similar to the more common Mute swan. It is

a bit smaller and its neck is longer than that of the Mute. Its original homeland was in Australia and Tasmania, but it was introduced with success in many places. It is quite prevalent on suitable water bodies and rivers and can cause damage to the surrounding agricultural land.

Cygnus melanocorypha

BLACK-NECKED SWAN   **NT**

The overall white coloring of this swan is disrupted by its black neck and head, and in adults, also by a red knob at the base of the gray bill with a yellow tip. It nests on lake shores in South America from Paraguay to the Falkland Islands. The chicks hatch in white down and grow extremely fast, reaching almost the adults' size by the autumn of their first year. After breeding, the birds congregate in large flocks and move further north. The Black-necked swan is often reared in zoological gardens due to its decorative character.

Cygnus melanocoryphus

Cygnus cygnus

Cygnus cygnus

WHOOPER SWAN   **PA**

The nesting region of the Whooper swan spans from Scotland to the Chukotski Peninsula. It migrates south for the winter. Its body and wingspan are somewhat smaller than the Mute's. The entire plumage is snow-white, while the legs, upper part and tip of the bill are black, and its base yellow. It produces loud, trumpeting calls, especially in flight. The birds form breeding pairs while still on the wintering grounds. Breeding begins by the end of May or the beginning of June. Its typical habitat consists of densely overgrown lake shores and shallow ocean bays. An extensive heap of withered vegetation on small islets, in shallow water or reedbeds serve as a nest. The female warms the clutch of 4–6 eggs for 5 weeks while the male is on guard. The chicks are raised by both parents.

Cygnus buccinator

TRUMPETER SWAN   **NA**

The Trumpeter swan breeds on wetlands of boreal coniferous forest zone in North America. It is closely related to the Whooper swan and is sometimes considered to be its subspecies. It is distinguished by a rather longer black bill. The total feral population is estimated at 6,000 pairs with about the same number of birds living in captivity.

Cygnus columbianus

TUNDRA SWAN   **PA NA**

The Tundra swan is very similar to the Whooper swan though distinctively smaller, and the yellow of the bill is limited just to small patches at its base. Its voice is quieter and deeper. It nests only in very northernmost parts of Europe and Asia. In winter, the European birds congregate in Great Britain, France and the Netherlands. Shallow freshwater lakes and swampy tundra constitute its breeding habitat. The complete clutch consists of only 3–4 eggs that are incubated by a female for a month. Newly hatched chicks are covered in pale gray down. They grow very fast and are already able to fly when they are 45 days old. The winter arrives in the Arctic breeding grounds in September, forcing the swans to migrate south.

Anser fabalis

BEAN GOOSE   **PA**

Geese of the *Anser* genus have a number of common features. The upper part of the bill is conical while the lower is flat. The bill is fairly thick at the base and narrows at the tip. There are hard lamellae along its edges that help to pluck grass. There is almost no difference between males and females, and their pair bonds are permanent. They walk on dry land easily and spend more time there than most of the other wildfowl. The Bean goose breeds in the Eurasian taiga and tundra zones. Several subspecies are distinguishable by markings on their bills. In the fall, large flocks migrate to more southerly wintering grounds. Once there, they roost on larger water bodies and graze on nearby pastures and fields during the day. In flight, they produce a loud, distinctive "ung-unk" call.

Cygnus buccinator

Cygnus columbianus

Anser albifrons

Anser albifrons

GREATER WHITE-FRONTED GOOSE **PA NA**

The Greater White-fronted goose has an overall dark coloration. There is a characteristic white patch around the base of its pink bill which does not reach all the way to the eyes. Adults have conspicuous dark blotches on their underparts. Nesting grounds are spread in the tundras of Europe and Asia. The breeding does not take place until the second half of June and July. A simple nest is often placed on elevated ground. The female sits on the nest of 4–7 eggs while the male guards it from a distance. Hatched chicks are raised by both parents. They fledge by the end of August, form large flocks together with the adults and then move to fairly distant wintering sites around the North, Caspian and Black Seas.

Anser fabalis

Anser erythropus

Anser cygnoides

SWAN GOOSE   PA

The Swan goose's back, the hind side of its neck and its cap are dark brown, while its underparts are pale brown, and its cheeks and frontneck are white. It breeds in the southern parts of eastern Siberia, northern China and Mongolia. It migrates to eastern China. Its population is declining at an alarming rate and presumably does not exceed several tens of thousands of birds. It was domesticated in China more than three thousand years ago and is bred for its meat. Its coloration is the same as the wild ancestors' but unlike them it features a high fleshy caruncle on the upper mandible.

Anser anser

Anser erythropus

LESSER WHITE-FRONTED GOOSE   PA

It noticeably resembles the Greater White-fronted goose, but is distinguished by its considerably smaller size and short, high head with a minor bill. The white on the adult's forehead extends higher on the crown. It breeds in Eurasia near the northern forest boundary, i.e. slightly further south than the Greater White-fronted goose, but usually at higher altitude. The nest, lined with moss, is placed among shrubs, usually not far from a lake. The young are fledged when they are less than 4 weeks old. The wintering grounds can be found around the Black and Caspian Seas, and in the Balkans and China.

Anser cygnoides

Anser anser

GRAYLAG GOOSE   PA

The male Graylag goose is slightly larger than female. The bill is pinkish or deep orange with a white nail. Due to the debilitating effects of human activities, it breeds in Europe only in isolated areas. However, it has been protected throughout Western Europe in the last decades, which is positively reflected in its growing population. In Asia, its region extends to the Far East. The original habitat included lakes surrounded by reeds, although now it also breeds on fish ponds. The breeding season starts in March. The female builds a nest of 20–30in/50–80cm in diameter in off-shore vegetation or on islands, always making sure that the nest has good visibility so she will have time to spot any possible intruder during incubation. The chicks are raised by both parents.

Anser indicus

BAR-HEADED GOOSE　　　　　　　　　**PA**

The goose inhabits the surroundings of steppe lakes and rivers in Central Asia at altitudes of 13,000–16,400ft/4,000–5,000m. It nests on rocky crags, either alone or in loose groups. The complete clutch consists of 4–6 eggs. Two dark bars on its white head are its most conspicuous markings. Long legs enable it to move easily on dry land. The mass wintering grounds are located in lowland swamps in the north of India. There is a small, non–indigenous population of the Bar-headed goose currently living in northern Europe.

Anser indicus

Anser caerulescens

SNOW GOOSE　　　　　　　　　**NA**

The species is only slightly smaller than the Graylag goose. Adults are snow-white except for black-tipped wings; juveniles are grayish-white. It inhabits the tundra region of North America, western Greenland and Wrangel Island. Its main diet consists of grass and the roots of marshy plants which the bird is able to dig out of the partially frozen soil with its short, strong bill. It breeds in colonies in dry places near lakes and rivers. The nest is a mere depression lined with grass and down. It is frequently hunted during migration and on its wintering grounds in Mexico. Besides humans, the Arctic fox is considered its main enemy.

Anser caerulescens

Branta sandvicensis

HAWAIIAN GOOSE　　　　　　　　　**NA**

Unlike the other "black geese," the Hawaiian goose features partly reduced webbed feet as a result of living on dry land. It inhabits lava flows on the Hawaiian Islands at altitudes of 4,900–8,200ft/1,500–2,500m. Succulent plants constitute the core of its diet. The individual pairs nest in cracks between the lava slabs. The species was at the edge of extinction by 1950. However, programs of consistent protection, captive breeding and introduction of the bird into the wild have resulted in its survival.

Branta sandvicensis

Branta canadensis

Branta canadensis

CANADA GOOSE   **PA NA**

The Canada goose is easily distinguished by a black neck and head with a pure white patch from throat to cheek. Its habitat encompasses almost all of North America where several different-sized subspecies live. Their body lengths range from 55 to 110cm, wingspan is 1.2–1.8m, and the weight is 2–6.5kg. It was quite successfully introduced into Great Britain, north-western Europe and New Zealand. It is an important gamebird in its homeland. During the annual hunting season, more than 400,000 birds are killed.

Branta leucopsis

BARNACLE GOOSE   **PA NA**

The Barnacle goose is a medium-sized goose, reaching the weight of only 2.9–4.4lb/1.3–2kg. It resembles the Canada goose, though the white patch on the head is larger and stretches across its face, forehead and throat. It nests only in eastern Greenland, Spitzbergen and Novaya Zemlya. Breeding colonies are found on cliffs and rocky outcrops in Arctic tundra, usually not far from the water. The complete clutch consists of 4–5 eggs. The prime wintering grounds are in Great Britain and northwestern Europe.

Branta bernicla

BRENT GOOSE   **PA NA**

It is the smallest of the "black geese." Its head, neck and back are dark or black, and there is a white ringlet on the adult's neck. The nesting colonies are set up far north in Arctic tundra near the ocean coast. The winter is spent along southern sand beaches and estuaries. On breeding grounds, it feeds on grass, moss, lichens and aquatic plants; on wintering sites, it mostly eats marine algae and seaweeds. The total population of the Brent goose reaches 400–500 thousands, but there is a great fluctuation in numbers every year depending on the breeding success.

Branta leucopsis

Branta bernicla

Branta ruficollis

Cereopsis novaehollandiae

Branta ruficollis

RED-BREASTED GOOSE   **PA**

Owing to a contrasting combination of black, white and chestnut colors, the Red-breasted goose cannot be mistaken for any other species. It belongs among smaller *Branta* species and is only slightly larger than the Mallard. Its breeding territory is limited to the Taymyr, Gydan, and Yamal peninsulas of northern Siberia. Tundra with shrubs and lichens, not far from water, constitute the breeding habitat. It nests in loose groups. The nest itself is a shallow depression in sloping terrain, lined with down, often close to a nest of the Rough-legged buzzard or Peregrine falcon. This way, the geese are protected from Arctic foxes which are the biggest threat to them. Its wintering grounds have changed from western and southern parts of the Caspian Sea to the areas north-west and west of the Black Sea over the last few decades.

Cereopsis novaehollandiae

CAPE BARREN GOOSE   **AU**

The 2.5–3.3ft/75–100cm long and 7–15lb/3.2–6.8kg body of the Cape Barren goose has quite a peculiar shape. It has a small head on a rather short neck. The head features a short, high bill which is covered with a yellow-green nail almost all the way to the tip. Long, red legs feature short, black toes with dwarfed webs. It lives on dry land in southern Australia and in Tasmania. Except for chick rearing periods, it avoids water altogether. It is often adopted by zoological gardens, even though it is highly intolerant of other birds.

Chloephaga melanoptera

ANDEAN GOOSE   **NT**

The Andean goose is all white except for its dark tail and wings. Both sexes show the same coloring, but the female is a bit smaller. The weight ranges between 6–7.9lbs/2.7–3.6kg. It inhabits the Andes from Peru to Argentina at altitudes above 11,000ft/3,300m, frequenting lakes and wetlands surrounded by grassland. It feeds principally on grass and succulent aquatic vegetation. Breeding begins in November. The female lays 5–10 eggs which are incubated for 4 weeks in a shallow ground nest lined with vegetation. Newly hatched chicks have white down with three black stripes on their upperparts. The adults lead them for about 12 weeks. Sexual maturity is reached at 3 years of age. The birds move to lower altitudes for winter.

Chloephaga melanoptera

Alopochen aegyptiacus

Alopochen aegyptiacus

EGYPTIAN GOOSE   **AF**

The Egyptian goose belongs amongst the most numer-ous representatives of *Anseriformes* in sub-Saharan Africa. It formerly nested on the Danube river and also in Palestine prior to 1930. It was successfully introduced into England. It has a slim body with a thin neck and a big head. Yellow-and-brown dominate the plumage coloring. The eye patch is dark brown and there are black, green and white feathers on its wings. It occupies various kinds of wetlands. It feeds on grass, seeds, leaves and stems of plants, and to a lesser degree on in-vertebrates, such as grasshoppers and annelidans. It grazes in fields and grasslands or forages in shallows with its head immersed in the water. It is an excellent swimmer, able to dive swiftly when necessary and to re-main under water for a long time. The pair breeds alone with their nest built on the ground, in trees or in holes in trees.

Tadorna ferruginea

Tadorna ferruginea

RUDDY SHELDUCK   **PA AF OR**

The Ruddy shelduck is mostly orange-brown with a paler head. The bill, tail and wing-feathers are black. In flight, the white parts of its wings and its deep green speculum are very noticable. A courting male features a darker head and a narrow, black neck-ring. It inhab-its Eastern Europe, Asia, and Africa, nesting primarily in freshwater or brackish lakes in open country. It can be found at high altitudes up to 15,750ft/4,800m in Cen-tral Asia. It also consumes small terrestrial and aquatic animals as well as plants. The nest, lined with down, is placed in various ground or tree holes. It is often reared in zoological gardens.

Tadorna tadorna

Tadorna tadorna

COMMON SHELDUCK   **PA**

The Common shelduck breeds along European coasts and inland in Eastern Europe and Asia. It prefers a habi-tat with salt or brackish water. Its colorful plumage is complemented by a rich red bill. Breeding males display a prominent knob at the base of the bill. The Common shelduck is about the size of a mallard. Its main food consists of aquatic invertebrates. The nest is often placed in rabbit, badger or fox burrows, and only rarely does the duck scrape a hole in the sand itself. The nest is often 10–13ft/3–4m under the ground. The complete clutch usually consists of 8–10 eggs. The chicks hatch after a month, and both parents raise them for another month and a half. In summer, the shelducks move to common moulting sites where they simultaneously lose both their flight and tail feathers and thus become flight-less during this time period.

Tachyeres brachypterus

Plectropterus gambensis

Tachyeres brachypterus

FALKLAND STEAMERDUCK   NT

The Falkland steamerduck is gray with a paler head, white belly and a wing speculum. The massive bill and legs are yellow. It belongs among the three flightless species of this genus. Distribution is limited to the Falkland Islands. The greatest numbers occupy small islands and sheltered bays. It feeds mostly on ocean mollusks and crustaceans, diving expertly in order to obtain them. Breeding takes place from August till December on ground sheltered by vegetation or in penguin burrows not far from water. Many ducklings are prey to skuas and gulls.

Plectropterus gambensis

SPUR-WINGED GOOSE   AF

This sturdy bird is up to 3.3ft/1m long and can weigh almost 15lb/7kg. Its underparts and cheeks are white, the bill and legs are red, while the rest of the body is black. The male is larger than a female and has a more prominent bill caruncle. It lives near standing or moving waters surrounded by grasslands with scattered trees. It is exclusively vegetarian, grazing mostly on grass and seeds. On rare occasions, it might also find and swallow small fish. It builds its nest either in abandoned nests of other birds found in trees or on the ground.

Cairina scutulata

WHITE-WINGED WOOD DUCK   OR

The duck is mostly dark except for the white head with fine, black mottling. It inhabits the waters of the undamaged, swampy tropical forests of southeastern Asia. It belongs among scarce species today with a total population probably not exceeding 1,000 birds. The main reason for this catastrophic decline is the destruction of suitable habitat. It is chiefly nocturnal. It feeds on water plants and their seeds. It nests in tree holes, in old tree nests of other birds or on the ground.

Cairinia scutulata

Nettapus pulchellus

Callonetta leucophrys

Nettapus pulchellus

GREEN PYGMY-GOOSE   **AU**

Members of the *Nettapus* genus are tiny in size and feature sexual dimorphism. The males are usually more colorful. The male of the Green Pygmy-goose has neck and upperparts which are deep green, while the belly and cheeks are white and the flanks and breast are mottled with wavy lines. It occupies the northern areas of Australia and New Guinea. It seeks tropical lowland lagoons and lakes with lush vegetation of aquatic plants for its habitat. It particularly likes water-lillies, consuming their leaves, flowers and seeds. Nests can be found in tree-hollows.

Nettapus auritus

AFRICAN PYGMY-GOOSE   **AF**

The bird has quite striking looks. Its white cheeks, foreneck and belly are complemented with bright orange breast and flanks as well as a black–edged pale green patch on the sides of the neck. Similar to the previous species, its diet is also dependent on water-lilies. It is distributed throughout Africa south of the Sahara and Madagascar.

Callonetta leucophrys

RINGED TEAL   **NT**

The Ringed teal belongs amongst the smallest wild-fowl. Its body is only 13.5–15in/35–38cm long and it weighs just 0.4–0.8lb/190–360g. The male possesses colorful plumage. It inhabits tropical swampy forests. It breeds in tree-holes or in abandoned tree nests of other birds.

Aix sponsa

AMERICAN WOOD DUCK   **NA**

This smaller North American species was endangered in the 1930s due to excessive hunting. However, protective measures, including placing of man-made nests, bore fruit, and by the mid-70s its population exceeded a million birds. The male is very decorative with a smart, drooping nuchal crest. It frequents fresh-water wetlands, lakes, fish ponds and slow-flowing rivers surrounded with deciduous forest. The nests are situated in natural or artificial cavities. Only the female takes care of the incubation of eggs and rearing of the chicks. The American Wood duck is often bred for ornamental purposes. In Great Britain, it was successfully introduced into the wild.

Nettapus autirus

Aix sponsa

Aix galericulata

MANDARIN DUCK   **PA**

The male Mandarin duck is extremely decorative owing to highly colored plumage and feather trimming of various shapes. As a result of both hunting and thoughtless habitat destruction, this bird is rare in its original homeland, namely northeastern China and Japan. It frequents rank, overgrown waters in wooded country. It is very skillful in moving on tree branches and flying through the tree tops. It feeds on seeds, aquatic plants and invertebrates. Nesting takes place in tree-holes as high as 33ft/10m above the ground. Right after hatching, the chicks jump down from the nest and follow their mother. The Mandarin duck is often bred in captivity. It was successfully introduced

Aix galericulata

into the wild in Great Britain, resulting in more than 7,000 birds living there today.

Chenonetta jubata

MANED DUCK   **AU**

The Maned duck is another colorful species which calls Australia and Tasmania its home. When disturbed, the male erects elongated occipital and neck feathers on its dark brown head and neck to form a sort of mane. It frequents densely overgrown fresh waters in close proximity to open deciduous forests. Dry land vegetation forms the main part of its diet. In winter, aquatic vegetation is also added. Nesting in tree-hollows usually begins in August.

Chenonetta jubata

Anas penelope

EURASIAN WIGEON   **PA**

This predominantly northern Eurasian duck requires shallow lakes with densely overgrown aquatic vegetation for breeding. Wintering grounds can be found along the sea coasts of Europe, Asia, and Africa, and on larger inland bodies of water. The male is easily distinguished by a creamy crown on a round, reddish head with a short bill. Melodic whistling is produced in flight. The mating pairs are formed on the wintering grounds or during the spring migration. It constructs its nests on the ground. The female duck lines the nest with down and carefully covers the clutch with the down any time it leaves the nest.

Anas penelope

67

Anas sibilatrix

Anas sibilatrix

CHILOE WIGEON   **NT**

The body of the Chiloe wigeon weighs less than a 2.2lbs/1kg and features mostly black, gray, white and orange plumage. It is distributed in the southern areas of South America and the Falkland Islands on lakes, lagoons and slow-flowing rivers surrounded by sparse forests. The nest is placed on the ground amongst vegetation.

Anas strepera

GADWALL   **PA NA**

The gadwall is only slightly smaller than the Mallard. The differences in coloring between males and females are not as pronounced as in other ducks. Both sexes can be well distinguished by a white speculum. It lives in Eurasia and North America on shallow lakes and fish ponds with heavy vegetation along the banks. Most of the populations move further south for win-

ter. Seeds, leaves, stems and roots of aquatic plants dominate its diet. These are often obtained by "upending" in shallow water, a process during which the duck immerses the front part of its body deep in the water, while the rear part projects vertically out of the water.

Anas formosa

BAIKAL TEAL   **PA**

Unlike the entirely inconspicuous female, the male is the truly beautiful specimen. A combination of sharply edged yellow and metalic green areas on its head is particularly striking. The nesting takes place in northeastern Asia. Its most suitable habitat lies in freshwater bodies in wooded country or in the Arctic tundra. It moves to the swamps and floodplains of southern China and Japan for the winter. Because of its attractive coloration, it is often reared in zoological gardens.

Anas crecca

COMMON TEAL   **PA NA**

The Common teal is an Eurasian and North American duck that prefers shallow and densely overgrown waters. In certain areas of Central Europe, its population has dramatically declined as a result of the depletion of suitable wetlands. The male in breeding plumage is easily recognized by its chestnut head and deep green patch across its eye as well as by the bright yellow patch beneath its tail. Limited mating activites begin as early as the autumn. However, full courting and action display begin in earnest in the springtime. The female builds a ground nest under cover of dense vegetation, often fairly far from the water. During breeding, she gradually fills the nest with down.

Anas strepera

Anas formosa

Anas platyrhynchos

MALLARD   **PA AU NA**

The mallard was originally found in Eurasia, northern Africa and North America. It has also been successfully introduced into New Zealand and southeastern Australia. The body measures 20–26in/50–65cm and reaches 1.7–3.3lb/0.75–1.5kg in weight with a wingspan of 2.5–3.3ft/75–100cm. The male shows his colorful breeding plumage for most of the year. The central tail feathers are wound up to form a typical crest. The female is unobtrusively brownish. A purple wing speculum with white margin is a common feature of both sexes. The mallard is fairly numerous and adapts well to the close proximity of humans. Despite intensive hunting, its winter populations in Europe are estimated at 8 million, in North America at as many as 17–18 million, and in New Zealand at more than 5 million birds.

Anas platyrhynchos

Anas crecca

Anas luzonica

Anas versicolor

Anas luzonica

PHILIPPINE DUCK   **OR**

This unimpressive brownish duck is distributed on several islands of the Philippines. It inhabits various wetlands from mountain lakes and rivers to coastal waters. It is a sedentary bird which suffers from constant pressure due to hunting and changes in the environment. However, it is not yet endangered, and is even numerous in places.

Anas acuta

Anas acuta

NORTHERN PINTAIL   **PA NA**

The Northern pintail is more slender than the mallard and has a considerably longer neck which is frequently stretched. The male's breeding plumage is strikingly elegant. The dark brown head contrasts with the clear white neck and the narrow white streak that runs up its sides. Fairly elongated tail feathers form a pointed tail. An extensive breeding region includes a sizable part of Eurasia and North America. Most populations are migratory.

Anas versicolor

SILVER TEAL   **NT**

The Silver teal inhabits South America from Peru to Tierra del Fuego and the Falkland Islands. Only the most southern populations are migratory. The bird's coloring is brownish overall with a conspicuous dark crown, pale cheeks and a blue bill with a yellow base. Its breast and flanks feature dark blotches. It occupies shallow lakes, swamps and fish ponds with plentiful offshore vegetation. In the Andes, it can be found at altitudes up to 15,000ft/4,600m. It feeds on seeds, water plants and aquatic insects.

Anas querquedula

GARGANEY   **PA**

This small Eurasian duck measures only 14.5–16in/ 37–41cm and reaches a maximum weight of 1lb/0.5kg. The most conspicuous sign of the male is a pronounced white stripe above its eyes. The bird is strictly migratory. European populations winter in sub–Saharan Africa, Asian ones mainly in the West and East Indies. The prime nesting habitat is made up of

Anas querquedula

marshy meadows, flooded fields and small, shallow water bodies with rich, offshore vegetation. Aquatic invertebrates, small fish, amphibians and various parts of marsh and water plants form key portions of its diet.

Anas smithii

CAPE SHOVELER AF

This generally brown duck with a paler head and dark bill lives only in southern Africa, the Cape in particular. It prefers large, shallow, freshwater lakes and brackish waters abundant with zooplankton. The nest is usually well hidden in dense off-shore vegetation.

Anas smithi

Anas clypeata

NORTHERN SHOVELER   **PA NA**

Besides truly colorful plumage, this duck is also distinguished by, and named for, a broad, spoon-like bill. The bill is helpful in filtering a surface layer of shallow waters or fine mud and thus catching tiny invertebrates and seeds. The Northern Shoveler's nesting region spreads through Eurasia and North America. It migrates to areas situated further south and congregates mainly on brackish lagoons and along muddy coastal waters.

Malacorhynchus membranaceus

PINK-EARED DUCK   **AU**

Its coloration is generally brownish. A dark brown patch around the eye provides a contrast, as does its dark back in comparison with its paler body parts. Its breeding habitat involves shallow saline and brackish waters in inland Australia. The nest is situated in old tree nests of other birds or in tree-holes mainly above the water surface. Thanks to the fine lamellae in the bizarre-shaped bill, the duck is able to catch microscopic algae, seeds and tiny animals through water filtration.

Marmaronetta angustirostris

MARBLED TEAL   **PA**

Hunting, combined with the disappearance of shallow, overgrown waters in otherwise dry areas, has caused a catastrophic decline of this inconspicuous brown duck. Today, it breeds in several places from Spain to Central Asia. The total population does not exceed 20,000 birds.

Netta rufina

RED-CRESTED POCHARD   **PA**

The reddish head with high forehead, black breast and neck, and red bill are the most significant features of the male of this species. The female is drab brown with a dark crown and pale cheeks and neck. It is distributed in isolated areas from eastern Spain to northwestern China. It prefers rather large and deep freshwater lakes with dense, off-shore reeds. It particularly feeds on roots, seeds and leaves of aquatic plants, and to a smaller extent on invertebrates and small fish.

Malacorhynchus membranaceus

Marmaronetta angustirostris

Netta rufina

Aythya collaris

Aythya ferina

COMMON POCHARD **PA**

The most prominent feature of the male is its chestnut head in combination with its black breast and gray back. The female is unremarkably brownish. The Common pochard originally occupied brackish and salt lakes in the steppe zones of Eastern Europe and Central Asia. During the last century, it has since spread to almost all of Europe, becoming the most populous duck in many areas. It nests on freshwater bodies like fish ponds or lakes that may have a low food supply. Pochards can consume both vegetation as well as small fish and insects. The variability of its diet depends on the food supply available. The female alone builds the nest in dense vegetation at the very edge of the water. Also the responsibility for incubating the eggs and raising the chicks is left entirely to her.

Aythya collaris

RING-NECKED DUCK **NA**

The male is black and white, while the female is brownish. The nesting region includes northern parts of the North American continent. The prime breeding habitat is formed by still bodies of fresh water that have surfaces partly overgrown with floating vegetation. Most of the Ring-necked ducks migrate to southern wintering grounds with large bodies of water.

Aythya ferina

Aythya nyroca

Anthya fuligula

Somateria mollissima

Aythya nyroca

FERRUGINOUS DUCK   **PA**

The male Ferruginous duck is dark chestnut brown with a white belly and a white patch under the tail coverts. The birds nest in scattered areas throughout Europe, Central Asia, and northern Africa. Recently, decreasing numbers on the wintering ground suggests a considerable decline in the population. It readily dives for vegetable food.

Aythya fuligula

TUFTED DUCK   **PA**

The bird originally nested only in northern Europe and Asia. During the 20th century, the breeding region was expanded to Central and Western Europe and, in the newly inhabited areas, the Tufted duck often became the most frequent of the duck species. The male's breeding plumage is black and white with marked occipital crest, while the female is brownish with a white patch at base of its bill. The Tufted duck is a typical diving duck. It is able to remain underwater for up to 40 seconds and dive as deep as 33ft/10m. It feeds on vegetables as well as on small fish and insects. The nest is built by the female in close proximity to water or even more preferably on an islet. The clutch of 8–11 eggs is warmed for 23–28 days.

Somateria mollissima

COMMON EIDER   **PA NA**

The Common eider cannot be mistaken for any other species because of the distinctive plumage of the male. Its head, neck, breast and back are white, while its crown, belly and flanks are black. There are mossy green patches on its nape and sides of the neck. The female is uniformly brown. Their common features include the flatter profile of the head and a characteristic wedged bill, feathered on the sides. The Common Eider is easily distinguished by its manner of flying. Unlike other duck species that exhibit sustained wing flapping, the Eider glides. Its homeland is in the northern areas of Eurasia and North America. It nests alone on the ground, but also in very dense colonies near water. The nest is usually heavily lined with fine down that locals traditionally collect and use for filling sleeping bags and winter jackets. When foraging for food that consists mostly of mollusks, these sea-ducks dive as deep as 80ft/25m.

Histrionicus histrionicus

HARLEQUIN DUCK   **PA NA**

The male's breeding plumage is blue-gray with white and rusty patches of various sizes. The female is all brown except for the trio of white spots on her face. The Harlequin duck lives in the northern regions of North America, in Greenland, Iceland and northeastern Siberia. It breeds on swift rivers with rapids and waterfalls. The nest is usually well hidden in thick shrubs, rocky clefts or even behind the waterfalls. While in breeding quarters, it consumes mostly larvae of mosquitos and other insects *(Trichoptera)*. The winter is spent along rocky coasts where the bird is capable of diving for crustaceans, even when rough surf is breaking upon the rocks.

Clangula hyemalis

LONG-TAILED DUCK   **PA NA**

The combination of white and dark areas with remarkably long central tail feathers is the most striking feature of the male. Non-breeding plumage is considerably darker. The female is paler brown and white with no elongated tail. Its region includes the northern areas of Eurasia and North America. It breeds on small lakes in tundra, on peat-bogs, rivers and coasts where it feeds on aquatic insects, larvae and more delicate aquatic plants. It stays on the open sea in non-breeding season, often far from the shore, and also on large, deep lakes. It dives as deep as 100ft/30m for its favorite lamellibranches and crustaceans. Like the auk, it holds its wings half open when diving. It be-

Histrionicus histrionicus

longs among common ducks and is abundant in places. Its population is estimated at about 10 million birds.

Clangula hyemalis

Bucephala albeola

BUFFLEHEAD   **NA**

This small North American diving duck nests on freshwater lakes, fish ponds and rivers in the northern parts of the continent. It winters along the coast and on more southern larger lakes. The male has mostly white plumage except for its dark back and head. The head features a large white patch spreading out from the eyes. The darker female has a white patch on the cheeks of its otherwise brown head. It nests in tree-holes and, if necessary, also in ground holes found in the banks of sparsely vegetated waters. Three fourths of the Bufflehead's diet consists of aquatic invertebrates.

Bucephala islandica

BARROW'S GOLDENEYE   **PA NA**

The Barrow's goldeneye is very much like the Common goldeneye. However, spotting found on the male's back and wings is less uniform. The dark head is glossy purple and features a larger crescent-shaped white patch between the bill and eye. The female's bill is mostly yellow. While Icelandic populations are sedentary, North American and Greenland birds migrate for winter from inland waters to the sea coasts.

Bucephala islandica

Bucephala clangula

COMMON GOLDENEYE   **PA NA**

The duck lives in Eurasia and North America, primarily in the coniferous forest zone. Unlike the somewhat larger Barrow's goldeneye, the male shows a greater amount of white on its back. The dark head is glossy green, and there is a smaller oval white spot at the base of its bill. It is migratory with a few exceptions. The wintering grounds are adjacent to the southern edge of the nesting region. The pair breeds alone in holes in trees skirting still or slow-flowing waters. It readily accepts man-made nesting boxes too. The complete clutch consists of 8–11 eggs. Black and white chicks hatch after 30 days. They spend just one day in the nest, then climb to the entrance hole aided by their sharp claws and boldly jump down to their calling mother.

Mergus cucullatus

HOODED MERGANSER   **NA**

The mergansers' bill is long and slim with a sharp, hooked nail. Edges of the upper and lower mandible feature horny teeth. These adaptations help during fishing, as fish constitute the main part of their diet. Typically, the "saw-bills" nest in hollows. The Hooded merganser is a beautiful North American species. This is mostly true for the markedly more colorful male which has a large crest with a white patch on its black head. The Hooded marganser occupies various smaller bodies of water in wooded areas. The winter is spent primarily on larger inland waters south of the breeding region.

Bucephala clangula

Mergus cucullatus

Mergus serrator

Mergus albellus

SMEW **PA**

The shape of its body and a short bill largely resemble some diving ducks. In breeding season, the male is predominantly pure white with a black eye-patch. Also the back is black, as is a good part of the wings. The female is grayish with a chestnut cap. It nests in hollow trees near lakes and rivers in the Eurasian taiga. It also uses man-made nesting boxes. It winters further south, mostly in freshwater bodies and estuaries.

Mergus merganser

Mergus serrator

RED-BREASTED MERGANSER **PA NA**

The characteristic feature of this duck is the double occipital crest of delicate feathers. The more colorful male has a black head with a greenish metallic sheen, while the female's head is rusty brown. The Red-breasted merganser inhabits the northern regions of Europe, Asia and North America. It nests alone or in small loose groups on the ground, in depressions under rocks or in ground hollows. It is chiefly maritime in winter. It forages mostly for fish with its head submerged underwater similar to other mergansers.

Mergus albellus

Mergus merganser

GOOSANDER **PA NA**

The goosander is the largest merganser with a body length of 22–26in/56–66cm and a wingspan reaching almost 3.3ft/1m. The male's breeding plumage features a greenish-black head that sports an unremarkable tuft. The breast and flanks are white and pinkish tan. The female is very similar to the female Red-breasted merganser. It is found in one contiguous region in northern Eurasia and North America. There are also isolated populations that breed significantly further south, for example in the Alps. It nests in hollow trees or holes in the ground near lakes and rivers. It winters collectively in non-frozen large bodies of water and rivers. It feeds primarily on fish, diving up to 13ft/4m when feeding.

Oxyura leucocephala

Oxyura leucocephala

WHITE-HEADED DUCK   **PA**

A rusty brown color prevails in the male's courtship plumage. Only its head is white with a black crown and pale blue bill. The female's coloration is generally brownish. The tail is cocked vertically during swimming. It feeds largely on aquatic plants. The most numerous breeding quarters can be found in Central Asia, on salt lakes surrounded by steppe and semi-desert. Residual populations live also in Spain and eastern and south-eastern Europe. The numbers of White-headed ducks have dropped considerably in the last decades down to about 14,000 birds. It is considered an endangered species.

Biziura lobata

MUSK DUCK   **AU**

This slim, dark brown duck lives in shallow freshwater wetlands in southern Australia and in Tasmania. The male is identified by a conspicuous skin pouch below its bill and on the throat. It feeds on invertebrates and fish and is able to dive to considerable depths for them. The nest is built in dense off-shore vegetation. The full clutch has only 2–3 eggs.

Biziura lobata

7. Diurnal birds of prey

Birds belonging to the Falconiformes often range from smaller, blackbird-sized birds to the largest of all flying birds. They inhabit all the continents except Antarctica. Amongst the characteristic features of birds of prey are strong and sharp claws, a hooked and pointed upper part of a powerful bill, and soft, fleshy cere. In addition, they are known for having excellent eyesight and being good fliers. All these adaptations are closely connected with hunting and foraging. They feed primarily on other animals, hunting them actively. The order Falconiformes is less unified than it may seem at first glance. A number of like features of particular groups apparently resulted rather from a similar way of life which gradually called for the creation of similar adaptations. Some taxonomy systems even divide this order into three orders of vultures, raptors and falconids. We use the most frequent classification, under which the 295 species are divided into 5 following families: Cathartidae, Pandionidae, Accipitridae, Sagittariidae, and Falconidae. Cathartids are the representatives of the Old World vultures in the New World. Medium-sized birds can be found among the seven species together with the largest flying bird of all. They feature a bare head and a large wing area which is useful for the main mode of flying – the soaring flight. A number of them evolved an acute sense of smell which is unusal among birds. The osprey is the only member of the Pandionidae family. Specific features are related to its specialization in catching fish, namely a reversible outer toe, the unique spiny foot pads that help to grasp slippery fish in its talons, and the oily plumage maintained by the abundant output of the coccyx gland. Hawks and eagles (Accipitridae) form the richest family of small to large birds of prey who occupy all different kinds of habitats worldwide. The Secretary bird is the only representative of the Sagittariidae family. It is the African species which is fully adapted to the terrestrial way of living. Falconids (Falconidae) include 61 species from almost all over the world. The upper mandible features characteristic projections, tomial teeth. The birds have large heads and eyes, and round nostrils.

Cathartes aura

TURKEY VULTURE   **NA NT**

The Turkey vulture inhabits the entire New World from the south part of Canada to Tierra del Fuego. Northern populations are migratory. The bird's unremarkable brownish black plumage is sparked by a red bare head with a yellow bill. Its body reaches 26–32in/65–80cm in length, with a wingspan of up to 2m. It flies low above the ground, searching for carcasses with the aid of its outstanding sense of smell. It can be often seen along the roadside, consuming animals hit by cars. A female lays two mottled eggs in a ground nest hidden in undergrowth. Incubation lasts less than 6 weeks, and rearing the chicks takes an additional 10–11 weeks.

Cathartes aura

Left: *Haliaeetus leucocephalus*

Coragyps atratus

AMERICAN BLACK VULTURE   **NA NT**

The American Black vulture is all black including the bare head and neck. It resides throughout a breeding region that includes South and Central America, and the southern part of North America. It belongs among the most common raptors of the New World. Hundreds of birds congregate to feed at garbage dumps or on carcasses. It is, however, able to catch live prey, and also consumes fruit.

Coragyps atratus

Sarcoramphus papa

KING VULTURE   **NT**

In comparison with other vultures, the King vulture is clearly the palest and also most colorful. There are yellow and red colors on the black bare head and neck. Its neck ruff is gray, its flight-feathers, rump, and tail are black, while the other parts of its body are grayish white. It inhabits Central America down to northern Argentina. Its habitat includes lowlands overgrown with forest and also savanna-like habitat. Its sense of smell is not well-developed and thus it follows other vultures with better sensory perception to a sought-after carcass.

Vultur gryphus

ANDEAN CONDOR   **NT**

The Andean condor's length of 3.3–4.3in/100–130cm, a weight of 18–33lb/8–15kg and a wingspan of 10.5ft/320cm make it the largest of all flying birds in the world. It is well distinguished by a reddish head and neck and a large peculiar comb on base of its bill and forehead. There is no difference between the male's and female's coloration, but the male is larger.

Sarcoraphus papa

It lives in the South American Andean zone, mostly at altitudes of 9,850–16,500ft/3,000–5,000m, descending to sea-level in the south of the continent. It is the master of exploiting the updraughts and can soar for hours in search for carcasses. If it is successful, it is able to eat an amount of meat equaling half of its body weight. On the other hand, it can survive five or six months without feeding. The incubation of a single egg, laid by a female in a cavity of a rocky cliff, takes over 8 weeks, parental care an additional 6 months. The Andean condor is often bred in zoological gardens and it is common for it to breed in captivity.

Vultur gryphus

Pandion haliaetus

OSPREY   **PA AF OR AU NA NT**

The osprey can be found on all the continents except Antarctica, though only during the winter months in South America, a large part of Africa, and the West and East Indies. The upperparts of the body are dark brown, while the underparts are snow white. It feeds almost exclusively on fish, hunting for them by quartering, circling, or hovering above the water. When a fish is spotted close to surface, the osprey swoops down with its long feet stretched forward, burying its talons in the prey. It is able to dive up to 3.3in/1m deep without problems. It forages mostly for fish about 0.33–0.66lb/150–300g in weight but exceptionally can manage a prey over 2.2lb/1kg. The nest is a large structure of sticks built up on tall trees, rocky cliffs or even power poles. The sexual maturity is reached at three years, and the birds can live for 20–25 years.

Pandion haliaetus

Pernis apivorus

WESTERN HONEY-BUZZARD   **PA**

The Western Honey-buzzard reaches about the size of the Eurasian buzzard. Its upperparts are dark brown, while the coloration of the underparts is quite variable. It can be well distinguished in flight by the small, outstretched head and the tail pattern showing a wide gap between the dark terminal band and another bar at the tail base. It is distributed almost all over Europe and western Siberia. It prefers a mosaic of woodland with open areas. The presence of wasps and their larvae which constitute the fundamental part of its diet is necessary for the Honey-buzzard to live in a particular area. Ground nests are made by the scraping of the legs and bill. It migrates in groups as far as sub-Saharan Africa, using updraughts effectively and gliding along a substantial part of the long journey.

Pernis apivorus

Elanus caeruleus

**COMMON BLACK-SHOULDERED
KITE (BLACK-WINGED KITE)**   **PA AF OR AU**

The adult Black-shouldered kite is pale blue-gray above, white below, and only the shoulders are black. Juveniles are toned browner than the adults. Its size and method of foraging are quite similar to the Kestrel. The largest population of the species is found in Africa and Southeast Asia. It can only be found on the Iberian Peninsula in Europe. It prefers open country offering plenty of small rodents on which it depends for food. When the numbers of rodents increase considerably, the birds can breed twice a year, which is quite an unusual phenomena among raptors. In non-breeding times, up to several hundred birds roost together in tree tops or reeds.

Elanus caeruleus

Elanus scriptus

Elanus scriptus

LETTER-WINGED KITE   **AU**

The Letter-winged kite is mostly gray and white except for the black shoulders. It inhabits the inland areas of Australia, frequenting woods along rivers in dry country. It feeds on small rodents, searching for them untypically at night. Its large eyes appear even bigger due to a black eye ring. It nests in loose colonies in tops of live trees 6.5–36ft/2–11m above ground. The breed-

Harpagus bidentatus

ing success directly depends on the phase of the breeding cycle of prey. It is fairly high in a year of rat plague, for example, and much reduced when the number of prey is low.

Harpagus bidentatus

DOUBLE-TOOTHED KITE   **NT**

The Double-toothed kite resembles more a hawk or a sparrowhawk than a kite. Its coloration surely contributes to that: the bird is uniformly dark gray above while the underparts are a densely vermiculated reddish color. It inhabits different types of woodlands, particularly in the tropical zone of the New World. It soars high above the forest, foraging for arthropods and small reptiles in the upper parts of tree tops. A shallow tree nest of twigs is built mostly at the edge of woods, 23–108ft/7–33m above ground.

Milvus migrans

BLACK KITE   **PA AF OR AU**

The Black kite's size corresponds with the Eurasian Buzzard. The overall dark coloration and the longer, slightly forked tail stand out during its frequent soaring. Its large range includes vast parts of Africa, Eurasia and Australia. Most often it can be found near waters of various kinds where it feeds on dead fish or captures them alive. In Africa and Asia, it communally feeds on garbage at rubbish dumps nearby large cities. It normally builds tree nests, although it can also use buildings, rocky cliffs or poles when necessary. In the suburbs, it lines the nest with paper, plastic and other materials found at the dumps.

Milvus milvus

RED KITE   **PA**

The Red kite's distribution is limited only to Europe, north Africa, the Canary and Cape Verde Islands. Similar to the Black kite, it spends a lot of time soaring high above the ground. There are unmistakable whitish patches on the underside of its narrow wings. A long tail is deeply forked. Normally, it frequents park–like country of low or medium altitudes though it reaches 2,000m in northern Africa. A female lays usually two eggs within three days into a tree nest, and incubates them for about a month. The period of parental care in which both adults are involved lasts two months. Carrion are the basis of the Red kite's diet, though it also preys on small vertebrates. It moves to open country in winter and often communally roosts in tree tops.

Milvus migrans

Haliaeetus leucogaster

Haliaeetus leucogaster

WHITE-BELLIED SEA-EAGLE   **OR AU**

The bird is all white except for gray wings, back and bill. The female is larger, mesuring 2.6–2.8ft/80–85cm, while the male is only 2.5–2.6ft/75–77cm. The wingspan of its broad wings which are suitable for soaring and

hovering ranges from 5.9–7.2ft/180 to 218cm. Its region spans from East and West Indies to Australia and Tasmania. It feeds mostly on carrion and also hunts for mammals and aquatic birds up to the size of a rabbit, gull or cormorant. It nests on rocky cliffs or trees 9.8–131ft/3–40m above the ground.

Milvus milvus

Haliaeetus vocifer

Haliaeetus vocifer

AFRICAN FISH-EAGLE   **AF**

The African Fish-eagle is a well-known African bird, weighing up to 8lb/3.6kg with a wingspan of 6.2ft/190cm. Its white head, neck and the upper part of its breast contrast with the chestnut underparts and black upperparts. It occupies banks of large lakes and rivers while also visiting ocean coasts near estuaries. It has its favorite perches in trees along the shore where it spends most of the time. Fish ranging 0.4–2.2lb/0.2–1kg in weight are among its usual prey. However, it does not reject carrion, the young of colonially breeding waterbirds, small mammals and reptiles, and even insects.

Haliaeetus albicilla

Haliaeetus albicilla

WHITE-TAILED SEA-EAGLE   **PA**

The female White-tailed Sea-eagle is larger than the male, averaging up to 2.9ft/90cm, reaching a weight of almost 13.2lb/6kg and having a wingspan of up to 7.8ft/240cm. The overall grayish brown plumage of the adults is broken only by the white wedged tail, yellow bill, and unfeathered legs. Most of the time it soars majestically through its hunting territory to the slow beat of its broad wings. The bird's territory spans from Central and northern Europe to eastern Asia. As for the habitat, it requires a proximity to fresh waters or ocean. It mostly hunts for fish and other medium-sized vertebrates, and readily feeds on carrion. Depending on the habitat type, a spacious nest is built either on a rocky cliff or a tree, and rarely also on the ground. Twenty-seven years is the oldest recorded age of birds in the wild, which is evidenced by ringing, while in captivity they have lived till the age of 42.

Haliaeetus leucocephalus

Haliaeetus leucocephalus

BALD EAGLE   **NA**

The Bald eagle occupies a considerable part of North America. The northern populations are migratory while the southern ones are sedentary. It requires the proximity of water during its breeding season. During non-breeding periods in the winter, the Bald Eagle can be found in very arid areas. Their nests, placed on the ground, cliff, bush or tree and used repeatedly for several years, can be up to 13ft/4m high and 8.2ft/2.5m wide. A shallow nesting depression is lined with grass, seaweed and other herbage. Bald eagles can live for 47 years in captivity.

Haliaeetus pelagicus

Gyps ruppellii

Haliaeetus pelagicus

STELLER'S SEA-EAGLE   **PA**

The Steller's Sea-eagle is a huge bird. The female, which is the larger of the sexes, can weigh up to 20lb/9kg and measure almost 3.3ft/1m. The plumage is predominantly dark brown, only the scapulars, tails and legs are white. The bird is relatively rare nowadays, inhabiting a limited range in the east of Asia. The total bird population is estimated at 7,500, with most of the pairs breeding in Kamchatka. The main reasons for the population decline are the destruction of old forests and hunting. The bird can be found only in a narrow stripe along a sea coast and along the banks of large rivers. Their main prey is salmon. The eagle looks out for them from an elevated perch and captures the fish by a sudden attack or dive.

Neophron percnopterus

EGYPTIAN VULTURE   **PA OR**

The adult Egyptian vulture features overall whitish plumage with black flight-feathers and bill, and a bare yellow face. The wingspan reaches only 5ft/1.5m. Juveniles are brown. Its breeding region spans from southern Europe eastwards to India and includes Africa, north of the equator. It lives in open, arid country and requires rocky cliffs for nesting. It accepts any type of food, such as carrion, cattle waste and rotting fruits. It also actively captures small vertebrates and insects. In addition, it collects other birds' eggs to eat. Large ostrich eggs are opened by dropping stones carried in its bill from great heights.

Neophron percnopterus

Gyps rueppellii

RÜPPELL'S GRIFFON (R.VULTURE)   **AF**

The light blotches on the Rüppell's griffon's dark wings, breast and belly give the bird a scale-like appearance. It prefers dry grasslands between the Sahara and the equator. It also lives at high altitudes in the mountains. When feeding, muscles and inner organs are picked from larger carcasses. The birds are downright gregarious: resting in groups, searching for food by soaring and also feeding and nesting together. Their rocky colonies are comprised of 10–1,000 of nests. The bird is often captured by local inhabitants who use parts of its body in traditional medicines.

Gyps fulvus

Gyps fulvus
EURASIAN GRIFFON
(GRIFFON VULTURE)   **PA OR**

The Eurasian griffon inhabits the strip of land which stretches from Spain and northern Africa to India. Males and females are the same size. Their most pronounced feature is a long white neck that is sunk back between the wings in flight. In addiction to a wingspan of up to 9.2ft/280cm, it reaches a weight of 17.7–24.2lb/8–11kg. It is an expert in eating carcasses of medium-sized to large mammals, particularly ungulates. Formerly, it ate mainly deer and gazelles, but today it feeds on dead domestic sheep, cows and horses. The vultures make a hole in the abdominal cavity and eat all the entrails first. Afterwards, they devour the muscles and other tissues. They nest in colonies of less than 20 pairs with nests placed in rocky cavities. The clutch has one egg which is incubated for about two months, the parental care of a chick lasts four months.

Aegypius monachus
EURASIAN BLACK VULTURE   **PA OR**

Vultures are scavengers from the warm areas of the Old World. They spend long hours soaring at considerable altitudes while searching for suitable food. Unlike some of the condors that are led by their sense of smell, the vultures use only their excellent vision. The Eurasian Black vulture belongs amongst the largest European birds with the body reaching 3.2–3.5in/98–107cm in length, a wingspan of 8.2–9.7ft/250–295cm and a weight of 15.4–27.5lb/7–12.5kg. It inhabits Spain and areas from the Balkans to India. It occupies mainly mountainous country from the forest zone to alpine meadows, reaching up to 14,800ft/4,500m. It consumes also the skin, tendons, cartilages, and other harder parts of carcasses. It nests mostly in trees.

Aegypius monachus

Trigonoceps occipitalis

WHITE-HEADED VULTURE   **AF**

This African vulture is somewhat smaller than the previous named species, with a wingspan of 7.5ft/230cm. A number of pale patches on greater underwing-coverts stand out on otherwise dark wings. Feathering on legs is white as is the top of its head. The bill is red with blue cere. The typical habitat is formed by dry wooded areas and savanna with trees. The nests of sticks are built in the top fork of tall trees. It feeds on carrion, either alone or in pairs.

Trigonoceps occipitalis

Gypohierax angolensis

PALM-NUT VULTURE   **AF**

The Palm-nut vulture is predominantly black and white with pale yellow legs and bill. It is found in sub-Saharan Africa, frequenting mostly margins of waters and forests. It is an exception among the birds of prey because a substantial part of its diet consists of oil palm fruits and also other fruits and seeds. Small mammals and invertebrates constitute only a supplement to the diet. A large nest of sticks is built in tall tree tops, especially palms and euphorbias.

Gypohierax angolensis

Gypaetus barbatus

BEARDED VULTURE (LAMMERGEIER)   **PA AF**

The Bearded vulture is well distinguished in flight from other large raptors by a long, wedge-shaped tail. The broad black eye patch and a long "beard" of feathers on its creamy head certainly catch the observer's attention. It is distributed randomly in the high mountain ranges of southern Eurasia and Africa. In the Himalayas, it was observed even above the 26,250ft/8,000m line. It prefers large, open areas with fairly sparse or low vegetation. It nests alone in holes in inaccessible rock faces. Bones form a substantial part of its diet. The ones that are too big to eat are carried high above a selected rocky area and dropped in order to be broken. Turtles are killed in a similar way. The breeding starts early in the spring so that the young are reared in the late spring when carcasses from prey that have died during the winter start appearing from underneath the melting snow.

Gypaetus barbatus

Terathopius ecaudatus

Terathopius ecaudatus

BATELEUR   **AF**

The bateleur has, in addition to its bare, bright scarlet face and legs and orange back which stands out from its variegated coloring, a distinctive, extremely short tail. The white underwing excels in flight while the tail seems to be completely missing. It is widespread in Africa on savannas of various kinds. It hunts for small vertebrates and insects during its low, gliding flight. Several dozen Bateleurs may congregate at places of swarming termites. The breeding is preceded by an acrobatic display flight. A large nest of dry sticks is built in tall trees, mostly close by a watercourse.

Circaetus gallicus

SHORT-TOED SNAKE-EAGLE   **PA OR**

The Short-toed Snake-eagle is larger than the Eurasian buzzard and has a conspicuously big head. The nearly white underparts sharply contrast with the gray-brown upper breast. It breeds in varied habitats from semi-deserts to dense forests, and from temperate to tropical zones in Eurasia and northern Africa. It migrates to tropical Africa. This eagle preys predominantly on reptiles, especially on various snakes which form over 80% of its diet. These are swallowed headfirst and their tail sometimes hangs from its bill for a while. Larger prey is divided up into smaller pieces for eating.

Circus aeruginosus

WESTERN MARSH-HARRIER   **PA**

The characteristic feature of all harriers is a medium-sized, slender body, with long wings and tail. Their hunting technique involves a wavering, rather hesitant flight low above the ground, combined with a sudden attack at a small vertebrate. They usually nest on the ground. The breeding region of the Western arsh-harrier is in Eurasia and northwestern Africa; the wintering grounds are in the African tropics and in India. As is typical for all the harrier species, coloration of females and the young distinctively differs from adult males. A female is dark brown with a pale yellowish pattern on its head. Brown is also the prevailing color of the male although its tail and wing areas are gray.

Circaetus gallicus

Circus aeruginosus

Circus cyaneus

HEN HARRIER   **PA NA**

The Hen harrier's body is 17–20in/43–52cm long, with a wingspan that reaches 3.3–4ft/1–1.2m. The male is ash-gray with black wing tips. Females and juveniles are dark brown and the only common feature of both sexes is a white rump. The breeding region involves temperate and cold zones of Eurasia and North America. The Hen harrier enjoys open areas like meadows, moorland, and forest clearings where it also breeds. It readily flies to swamps and fields too, in order to hunt for small vertebrates. In winter, it searches for prey together with buzzards and kestrels in fields abundant with voles.

Circus pygargus

MONTAGU'S HARRIER   **PA**

The species is smaller and slimmer than the Hen harrier, and unlike it, the male Montagu's harrier has a black bar on the upperwing. It nests in scattered areas in Europe and also in Asia as far as central Siberia. It prefers large, wet, lowland meadows, although it also will breed in other open areas such as fields. It breeds alone or in loose groups of as many as 10 pairs. Males usually keep two females. A nest, 7.8–15.7in/20–40cm in width, is built on the ground in tall, green vegetation. A normal clutch consists of

Circus cyaneus

3–5 eggs that are warmed by the female for 4 weeks. The chick rearing period lasts over a month. Wintering grounds can be found in sub-Saharan Africa and in India.

Circus pygargus

Accipiter nisus

EURASIAN SPARROWHAWK   **PA**

The breeding range of the Eurasian sparrowhawk includes all of Europe, most of Asia, and also reaches to northwestern Africa. Similar to other hawks and sparrowhawks, the female is significantly larger than the male. While the female is about 15in/38cm long and can weigh over 0.55lb/250g, the male measures only 11in/28cm and weighs 0.3lb/135g. There are also differences in coloration, the most conspicuous one being the pale gray underparts of females compared to the reddish, barred underparts common to adult males. The Eurasian sparrowhawk frequents mainly park-like landscape where woodland alternates with the open country. It cruises fast just above the crowns of trees or bushes, along edges of woods or shrubberies, and captures small birds by surprise with a sudden pouncing attack. It has recently also been observed in populated areas.

Accipiter gentilis

Accipiter gentilis

NORTHERN GOSHAWK   **PA NA**

The Northern goshawk's body shape and method of foraging very much resembles that of the sparrowhawk. The female is about the size of the Buzzard, while the male is significantly smaller. The young differ from the adults in color as they have brown plumage with longitudinal streaks. The Northern goshawk is a secluded bird which lives in the woods of Eurasia and North America. This excellent hunter is successful even in quite challenging terrain. Short, rounded wings and a long tail provide it with considerable maneuvring ability. It feeds mostly on small and medium-sized birds and mammals though it is capable of capturing a rabbit or capercaillie. Its nests are built in tree branches close to the trunk. The breeding is preceded by display flights accompanied with loud calls.

Buteo magnirostris

ROADSIDE HAWK   **NT**

The Roadside hawk resembles the sparrowhawk with its gray upperparts and reddish, barred underparts. However, the body proportions and lifestyle are typical of a buzzard. It frequents open biotopes and thin forests in tropical and subtropical areas of Central and South America. It avoids unbroken forests. It hunts for insects and small vertebrates, diving at them from an elevated perch. A large nest of dry sticks is built in the treetops. A clutch consists of only 1–2 eggs.

Buteo jamaicensis

RED-TAILED HAWK   **NA NT**

The Red-tailed hawk generally resembles the Eurasian Buzzard. Coloration is variable, with gradations from totally pale to quite dark. The region of the Red-tailed Hawk covers Central America, including the Caribbean islands, and North America excluding its most northern areas. It is the most numbered buzzard in these areas and lives in all kinds of habitat from desert and fields to tropical forests and towns. An elevated

Buteo jamaicensis

perch is required for hunting for small to medium-sized vertebrates in the open country. Large nests, 2.3–2.5in/71–76cm in diameter, may be located on trees, cactuses, rocky cliffs, electric poles, or on buildings in towns.

Buteo buteo

EURASIAN BUZZARD   **PA**

This abundant Eurasian species is 20–22in/50–57cm long, reaches the weight of 1.2–3lb/0.55–1.36kg and has a wingspan of 3.7–4.2in/115–128cm. It is sedentary, except for populations from northern Europe and most of Asia that migrate to southern Asia and eastern Africa. Its wings are similar to those of other buzzards: long and broad; the tail is short and widely fan-shaped. In the air, it mainly soars and circles, using the updraughts to maintain height. Its main prey are abundant small mammals, chiefly voles that are hunted over grasslands or fields. A female lays 2–4 eggs in a tree nest. The whole nesting care, including incubation, lasts for about three months. The oldest recorded bird is 25 years of age.

Buteo magnirostris

Buteo buteo

Buteo rufinus

Buteo regalis

Buteo rufinus

LONG-LEGGED BUZZARD   **PA**

Compared to the Eurasian buzzard, the Long-legged buzzard is slightly smaller, has paler color on all underparts and lacks dark bars on its tail. It inhabits steppes and semi-deserts, but also open woodlands of Eastern Europe, Minor and Central Asia, and northern Africa. It can be found up to 8200ft/2,500m. A nest of dry sticks, 2.6ft/80cm wide and 11.5–20in/30–50cm deep, is built mainly on cliffs or steep slopes, or in trees.

Buteo regalis

FERRUGINOUS HAWK   **NA**

The weight of the Ferruginous hawk is around 4.4lb/2kg with a wingspan is almost 5ft/1.5m which makes it the largest of the buzzards. Coloration is very variable. The bird is partly migratory and can be found in western North America from southern Canada to northern Texas, mostly in dry, open terrains. Terrestrial mammals make up the main prey: primarily hares, prairie dogs and ground squirrels. The availability of prey determines the breeding success and number of breeding pairs each year. The bird's large nest is built on trees or cliffs and is about one meter in diameter and 3.3–6.6ft/1–2m in height.

Buteo lagopus

North America. The nest is often placed on a cliff or a rocky outcrop. The complete clutch usually consists of 3–5 eggs but this strongly depends on the breeding cycle of lemmings that make up the substantial part of the Rough-legged buzzards' diet. Wintering grounds can be found in southern parts of the respective continents.

Harpia harpyja

HARPY EAGLE	NT

The Harpy eagle is considered the strongest of all birds of prey. The body measures about 3.3ft/1m, the weight of the considerably larger female reaches 16.5–20lb/7.5–9kg while the male's weight is only 8.8–10.5lb/4–4.8kg. Its large, gray head and neck, decorated with a dark feather crest, are separated from the whitish underparts by a black neck ruff. Extraordinarily mighty claws and bill, which command the respect of an observer, are used for hunting monkeys, sloths and other larger mammals in the South American forest. A female lays usually two eggs in a broad nest of wide sticks built 20–30in/50–75m above ground in the crowns of the tallest trees. It has become rarer in the last few decades as a result of vast deforestation.

Buteo lagopus

ROUGH-LEGGED BUZZARD	PA NA

The Rough-legged buzzard is somewhat larger and usually paler than the Eurasian buzzard and distinguishable from it by its tarsi which is feathered to the base of its toes, and by a white tail with broad black terminal band. The dark bounded carpal patches on its pale wings can be seen from below. It nests mostly in the unforested northern tundra of Eurasia and

Harpia harpyja

Aquila pomarina

Aquila pomarina

LESSER SPOTTED EAGLE	PA OR

The Lesser Spotted eagle is not much larger than the Eurasian buzzard but still possesses characteristics typical of eagles. Among the most conspicuous are the long, broad wings, endowed with finger-like primaries, that are noticeable during its prevailing activity – circling. The plumage is uniformly brown without any outstanding patterns. The breeding region is limited to the eastern parts of Europe and India where there are extensive woods as well as pastures and meadows. The European populations migrate annually to eastern Africa and many of them are killed in the Near East along the migration route.

Aquila clanga

GREATER SPOTTED EAGLE   **PA**

The bird is very similar to the Lesser Spotted eagle, although it is slightly larger and darker. It very rarely creates a pale morph. It is found from southeastern Europe to eastern Asia and migrates to southern Asia and eastern Africa. It nests in large, damp forests next to marshy meadows, peat-bogs and other wetlands. It inhabits mostly lowlands, though it can sometimes be found at altitudes up to 3,300ft/1,000m. The prey, mostly small mammals, are caught by diving from soaring flight of 330ft/100m above ground.

Aquila heliaca

EASTERN IMPERIAL EAGLE   **PA**

The Eastern Imperial eagle is rather smaller than the Golden eagle, its weight ranging between 5.5–10lb/ 2.5kg and 10lb/4.5kg. An adult is distinguished by white shoulder patches and a pale nape. It nests in a scattered pattern from Central Europe to eastern China. It originally nested in individual old trees in the plains. Later, human activity pushed the birds to the large mountain forests. The huge nest placed high in the tree crown is 5ft/1.5m in diameter. A female lays 2–3 eggs at the beginning of March and the chicks are hatched after 6 weeks. Parental care lasts for 11 weeks. The Eastern Imperial eagles migrate to the Nile Valley and to the south and east of Asia. Today, only about 2,000 pairs are left throughout the whole range.

Aquila heliaca

Aquila chrysaetos

Aquila chrysaetos

GOLDEN EAGLE   **PA NA**

The uniformly dark coloration of the adult Golden eagle is interrupted by yellowish cere and legs, and has golden-tinged feathering on its nape. Originally, it bred in a wide variety of habitats from the desert to the tundra margin in North America, Eurasia and North Africa. Due to human pressure, it disappeared from many places completely and retreated mainly to inaccessible mountain areas. Medium-sized mammals are the main staple of its diet – mostly rodents, rabbits and hares, and marmots found in high mountain areas. Occasionally, it also feeds on carcasses of large animals. Repeatedly used nests can be found on high precipices or in trees.

Sagittarius serpentarius

SECRETARYBIRD   **AF**

This African bird leads the truly terrestrial life to which it is well adapted. The extremely long stork-like legs are most conspicuous, together with a slender body, relatively small head and a tail which is as long as the body. When agitated, it erects its feather crest. It is fairly reluctant to fly and lands immediately after any serious reasons for taking off have passed. It lives in pairs on steppes and savannas. The Secretary birds show quite an unique hunting technique for raptors. They stalk slowly while carefully scanning the surroundings. When

the prey – mostly snakes up to two metres long – is discovered, they charge it, kill it gradually by means of powerful, hard kicks, and then swallow it whole. A large nest is built on solitary trees.

Sagittarius serpentarius

Polyborus plancus

Polyborus plancus

CRESTED CARACARA   **NA NT**

Caracaras can be found in the New World. Even
though they belong to the falconids, they have a rather
different lifestyle than the other members of the family. They spend most of their time on the ground and
have plumper bodies and square wings. They do not
possess the dynamic appearance of most of the other
falconids. The Crested caracara is, by and large, an
elegant looking bird. Its black crown, occipital crest,
wings and body are complemented with whitish
cheeks and transversal stripes on the rest of the body.
The cere is orange-red. It prefers open, drier country,
though it does not avoid marshy terrains bordering
watercourses. It feeds mostly on carrion and whole
groups of these birds attack a carcass at once.

Falco naumanni

Falco naumanni

LESSER KESTREL   **PA**

The Lesser kestrel is the first representative of the true
falconids. It strongly resembles the larger Common
Kestrel, but its cinnamon colored upperparts are
unspotted. Females and young, who are inconspicuous in color, are difficult to distinguish from each other. The breeding range stretches from southern Europe and North Africa to China. The Lesser kestrel
requires places of warm, dry climate, with sparse or
low vegetation. It is a fairly social species and breeds
in colonies in tree-hollows or rocky cavities. It feeds
mostly on flying and terrestrial insects. The winter is
spent on African savannas where thousands of birds
may gather to roost on selected trees.

Falco tinnunculus

Falco tinnunculus

COMMON KESTREL   **PA AF OR**

The Common kestrel is one of the most numerous
birds of prey in Europe and is also widespread
throughout most of Africa and Asia. A number of subspecies can be found throughout such a large geo-
graphical area. The most desired habitat is found in
open country with grass and low level vegetation featuring groves of mature trees. It commonly lives in
urban areas where it nests in alcoves of higher buildings. Its diet consists of voles and other small mammals. The kestrel hunts by persistently flying and hovering above the ground. As soon as the prey is
spotted, the raptor dives down to attack it.

Falco sparverius

Falco vespertinus
RED-FOOTED FALCON   **PA**

Sexual dimorphism is well developed in the Red-footed falcon. The male is dark gray except for the chestnut thighs and undertail-coverts, while the female and young are considerably more colorful, with yellowish heads and underparts, whitish cheeks and a black moustache. The Red-footed falcon is a sociable bird. It creates colonies of tens to hundreds of nests in lowland or wooded steppes of Eastern Europe and Asia. The colonies can be found on trees in windbreaks or groves, and not infrequently in colonies of corvids. It feeds on larger insects, capturing them skilfully with its talons in the air or on the ground.

Falco columbarius

Falco sparverius
AMERICAN KESTREL   **NA NT**

The American kestrel's coloration highly recalls the Common kestrel, but the bird is considerably smaller. There are 17 subspecies recognized and found over the vast range that involves almost the entire New World. A wide variety of habitats suits the American kestrel, from tundra to tropical forest to desert, from sea-level to alpine zone, and from agriculture land to urban zones. Insects and small vertebrates are the main source of food. They nest alone in tree-holes, rock ledges or the old nests of corvids.

Falco vespertinus

Falco columbarius
MERLIN   **PA NA**

The looks and the flight silhouette of the merlin resemble the hobby. It flies very low over the ground while hunting for small birds and relies on a moment of surprise to catch its prey. Its breeding zone covers northern parts of Eurasia and North America. It moves southwards for winter. The breeding habitat consists of tundra and forested tundra, and further south it breeds on high mountains, steppes and wooded steppes. The complete clutch of 3–6 eggs is laid by the female into the old nests of corvids, in tree-holes, on cliffs, or in a ground depression. The chicks hatch after a month, and the parents take care of them for another month.

Falco berigora

BROWN FALCON   **AU**

The coloration of the Brown falcon is very variable, as there are completely dark as well as colorful tawny morphs. It lives in all areas of Australia and New Guinea. It prefers woodland, savanna, grassland and cultivated land, but will live in deserts as well. It ranges up to 9,850ft/3,000m in the mountains of New Guinea. Small vertebrates and arthropods are its prey. They are captured by the Brown falcon mostly during its quiet flight from an elevated perch.

Falco subbuteo

EURASIAN HOBBY   **PA OR**

The Eurasian hobby can be called a miniature of the Peregrine falcon as their coloration and behavior are quite similar. It inhabits a large region covering Europe, Asia as well as northwestern Africa. The male and female are almost identically colored, though the female is notably larger. A suitable habitat is found in open country with wooded steppe, pastures and fields where there are groups of old trees available. It does not breed until June and July, using mostly the vacant tree nests of corvids or other birds of prey. It hunts mostly for larger insects, such as dragonflies, beetles,

Falco berigora

butterflies that are eaten on the wing. To a lesser extent, the Eurasian hobby also feeds on small birds, namely swallows, martins and swifts. It belongs among the fastest of all raptors.

Falco subbuteo

Falco biarmicus

Falco cherrug

Falco biarmicus

LANNER FALCON   **PA AF**

The Lanner falcon is quite similar to the Peregrine falcon, but is generally paler and has a yellowish patch on nape. It is mostly distributed throughout Africa, the Arab Peninsula, and partly in southern and southeastern Europe. It inhabits dry, flat areas, but also wet, wooded places in mountains up to 16,400ft/ 5,000m. It hunts smaller birds, especially quails and columbids, but also rodents, bats, lizards, insects, and, when in deserts, spiders and scorpions. It is active at dusk and at night.

Falco cherrug

SAKER FALCON   **PA**

The Saker falcon's coloration is overall brown with paler, dark spotted underparts. A narrow, black moustache stands out on its pale face. Its size is close to the Peregrine falcon. The breeding region falls mostly within Asia as far as western China and reaches Europe only in the east. It prefers steppes though it can be observed in damp floodplain forests fringing agriculture areas in the western part of its range. The main part of its prey consists of smaller birds and mammals, though it dares to charge at a considerably larger prey too. Perhaps that is why it has become a popular object of falconers. It breeds on cliff ledges, and in tall trees in abandoned nests of other raptors.

Falco peregrinus

PEREGRINE FALCON   **PA AF OR AU NA NT**

The Peregrine falcon among the most common raptors. A female is up to a third larger than a male. The adult bird features a dark cap and a wide black moustache, white underparts with dense transversal bands, and a dark gray back. It is found on all the continents except Antarctica. It belongs among the true flying masters, aided by its stocky body, pointed wings and short tail. During a headlong flight, after closing its wings and assuming a characteristic drop-like shape, it is able to reach the temporary speed of 186mph/ 300kph. It seizes mainly flying birds up to 4.4lb/2kg in weight, plunging its sharp claws into their backs. It never builds its own nests, preferring to use either unoccupied nests of other birds or a cavity in rock or tree. The female lays 2–6 eggs.

Falco peregrinus

8. Gamebirds and Hoatzins

The Hoatzins used to be classified with Galliformes. *Nevertheless, a number of their special features suggest this classification to be rather ambiguous. Today, a number of experts are inclined to recognize them in an independent order, and the DNA analysis even suggests relations with cuckoos.*

Galliformes

GAMEBIRDS: TURKEYS, GROUSE, NEW WORLD QUAILS, PHEASANTS, PARTRIDGES, GUINEAFOWL

Birds classified as *Galliformes* are mostly stocky, medium-sized to large birds with powerful, rounded bills and strong, digging legs that feature flat claws. They generally move on land at an outstandingly fast pace. Their plumage is maintained by means of dust-bathing. In many species, the male is distinctly more colorful than the inconspicuously colored female. When attacked, they are able to drop a great amount of feathers at once, and while the predator's attention is caught, they dash away. The breeding season is often preceded by an elaborate courtship "ceremony." Building the nest, warming the eggs, and looking after chicks are mostly carried out by the female. The chicks hatch chiefly precocial and pick their food themselves. *Galliformes* are absent only from the continent of Antarctica. The 291 living species are divided into 7 families: megapodes *(Megapodiidae)*, cracids *(Cracidae)*, turkeys *(Meleagrididae)*, grouse *(Tetraonidae)*, New World quails *(Odontophoridae)*, pheasants and partridges *(Phasianidae)*, and guineafowl *(Numididae)*.

Nineteen forest species of megapodes inhabit mainly the Australasian zoogeographical region. Instead of actively sitting on nests, a male takes care of the eggs in an artificial incubator where the heat is generated by fermentation of piled up mounds of decaying leaves. Cracids include 50 Central and South American long-tailed forest species. They live and also breed in trees. There are two large terrestrial turkey species that inhabit North and Central America. The males have various appendages on their colorful heads. Grouse are preliminary forest birds with short legs. All 17 members of the species are distributed in the northern parts and mountains of Eurasia and North America. Thirty-two species of quails inhabit warmer parts of the New World. Most of them are small terrestrial birds with strong legs and short wings. Pheasants represent the largest family of the gamebirds. The 155 species occupy Eurasia, Africa, and Australia. The stout body of these birds is complemented by a strong bill and short wings. Six terrestrial species of guineafowl live in sub-Saharan Africa. They feature a stocky body and a small head.

Alectura lathami

AUSTRALIAN BRUSH-TURKEY   **AU**

The Australian Brush-turkey is the largest of megapodes. The body is 23–27.5in/60–70cm long and reaches a weight of almost 5.5lb/2.5kg. The overall dark plumage is complemented by its bare red head and neck, while the neck pouch at the base of the neck is yellow. It lives in the rain forest along the coast of eastern Australia. The nesting mound can contain as much as four tons of plant material, reaching 3.3ft/1m in height and 13.1ft/4m in diameter. As soon as the decomposition raises the temperature to 33 C, the female begins to lay eggs in holes at the top of the mound. For successful development the eggs have to be placed with their tips down. Eggs are large – each one is more than 10 % of the female's body weight. She lays over 20 of them in the course of the breeding season. For eight weeks the male watches the temperature to ensure it is accurate for incubation. Chicks are independent after hatching and do not require parental care.

Left: *Dendragapus canadensis*
Alectura lathami

Ortalis cinereiceps

Ortalis cinereiceps

GRAY-HEADED CHACHALACA   **NT**

All the chachalaca species live in the New World, specifically in Central America. They are known for their singing, performed by a majority of their species. Usually at dawn, one bird begins a loud call and is gradually joined by others. This results in a singing chorus that can last for several dozen minutes. The Gray-headed chachalaca's coloration is quite inconspicuous. The bird occupies various woodlands, preferring shrub thickets with individual taller trees. It moves in groups of 6–12 birds in the tree tops and only rarely descends to the ground. The main part of the chachalaca's diet consists of various fruits consumed in the tree tops. By the end of the rainy season a female typically lays three eggs in a platform nest of sticks, leaves and stems. The chocolate brown chicks hatch after three weeks of incubation. They are fed with fruit juice from the parent's crop.

Crax daubentoni

Crax rubra

GREAT CURASSOW   **NT**

The Great curassow male is all black with a white belly and a yellow knob at the base of the bill. The head sports a conspicuous feather crest. The female is pale brown and its white head and neck are darkly vermiculated. The body can measure almost 3.3ft/1m and the weight ranges from 6.6–11lb/3–5kg. It occupies tropical rain forests in Central America and the northwestern part of South America. It spends equal time on the ground as in trees. It feeds on fruits that have fallen to the ground, occasionally pecking a small creature along the way. The female lays two eggs in a small nest built of sticks sometimes lined with fresh leaves 9.8–19.4ft/3–6m above the ground. The Great curassow is the cracid most frequently bred in captivity. It is long-lived with an age of 24 years recorded while in captivity.

Crax rubra

Crax daubentoni

YELLOW-KNOBBED CURASSOW   **NT**

The Yellow-knobbed curassow male is very similar to the Great curassow except for the white tip of its tail. The female does not differ much from the male, but lacks the yellow knob and wattle at the base of the bill. It most frequently inhabits gallery forests near rivers in Venezuela and neighbouring parts of Colombia. It forages in tree tops in small family groups; during the dry season, the flocks consist of up to 15 birds.

Crax alector

BLACK CURASSOW   **NT**

The Black curassow is another species similar to the previous ones, but it has a shorter and thinner feather crest than is seen in other curassows. The bird can be found in areas ranging from eastern Venezuela to northern Brazil and prefers thickets along river banks and forest edges. It feeds mostly on what it finds on the ground, namely various fruits and, to a lesser extent, leaves, flowers, mushrooms and invertebrates. The Black curassow is often reared in captivity where it readily breeds.

Meleagris gallopavo

WILD TURKEY   **NA NT**

The male of this typical North American bird measures up to 3.6ft/110cm and reaches a weight of 22lb/10kg. The female is smaller and slenderer, about half of the male's weight. The usual habitat for turkeys is found in a combination of open country and numerous groves. The breeding season, which takes place in March and April, is preceded by the spectacular courtship display of excited cocks. They gobble and attack each other vigorously. The winner becomes the mate for 2–4 watching hens, but their interest, however, wanes immediately after mating. Each female then finds a suitable place for nesting alone. She lays up to 13 eggs in a simple shallow depression and warms them for four weeks before the precocial chicks hatch. The poults are fairly sensitive to the rainy weather and a female, therefore, covers them carefully with its wings while roosting. In its homeland, the Wild turkey is a sought–after gamebird. After its population dropped to 300,000 in the 1940s, effective measures were taken to prevent further decline, resulting in the present satisfactory population of about 3.5 million birds. There were a number of varyingly successful attempts to introduce the Wild turkey into Europe, Australia and New Zealand.

Crax alector

Lagopus lagopus

WILLOW GROUSE   **PA NA**

The first representative of grouse, the Willow grouse, inhabits extensive northern areas of Eurasia and North America. It now also lives in Great Britain. Its feathers are shaded brown in the spring, but change to pure white plumage in the winter. Only the bill and tail remain black. The body is 14–17in/36–43cm in length, and the weight ranges from 1.1–1.5lb/0.5 to 0.7kg. Arctic tundra with lodged trees is their typical environment and the presence of berry-bearing shrubs is of great importance. In the winter particularly, the birds are heavily dependent on the willow and birch trees whose buds and twigs constitute the main part of their diet during that season. Their diet is more varied during the rest of the year. Their nest is a simple scrape on the ground, lined with dry grass. While the female incubates the clutch, the male guards it. Both parents look after the hatched chicks.

Meleagris gallopavo

Lagopus lagopus

Lagopus mutus

Lagopus mutus

ROCK PTARMIGAN   **PA NA**

The Rock ptarmigan is similar in many ways to the Willow grouse, but its summer plumage is more gray toned and the male always has a black eye stripe. It lives in the rocky Arctic tundra and Alpine zone. Besides the boreal zones, it can also be found in more southern mountains, like the Alps and Pyrenees, as well as in Scotland. It usually breeds in June. Most of the Rock ptarmigan do not migrate unless forced to by severe weather conditions.

Tetrao tetrix

Tetrao tetrix

EURASIAN BLACK GROUSE   **PA**

The Eurasian Black grouse male's coloration is mostly black with a blue gloss. Typical are the lyre-shaped, curved tail-feathers and, during courtship, the bright red combs over its eyes. The female is uniformly a dark mottled brown. The male's weight is about 3.3lb/1.5kg, while the female is smaller. Its habitation range includes the boreal coniferous forest zone in Eurasia. A suitable habitat is formed by coniferous or mixed forests with large clearings, adjoining open areas like pastures, meadows, heaths, and peat-bogs. Birch trees are also of great importance because their catkins, buds and twigs form the core of the bird's winter diet. In the spring, showy vocal and visual courtship displays take place at dawn, performed by one bird alone or in groups. The mother hens look after the family without any assistance from the male. Since the begining of the 20th century, the decline of the Black grouse populations have been observed all over Europe and the bird has disappeared completely from large areas.

Tetrao urogallus

WESTERN CAPERCAILLIE   **PA**

While the mostly dark male Western Capercaillie reaches the weight of up to 14.3lb/6.5kg, the rusty brown female weighs at the most only 4.9/2.2kg. It is found in Eurasia in the boreal and mountain coniferous forest zone. For its solitary lifestyle, it requires extensive areas of woodlands mixed with overgrown clearings, and peat-bogs with berry-bearing shrubs. Early in the spring, a very interesting courtship display starts, featuring a song with distinctive phases. In the phase called "whetting," the external ear is blocked and for a while, a courting male can hear nothing at all. Nidifugous chicks, raised only by the female, eat exclusively ants. They grow fairly quickly and they are able to make flight attemps only 10 days after hatching. Throughout the 20th century, its Eurasian populations have been steadily decreasing and the range diminishing.

Bonasa bonasia
(formerly Tetrastes bonasia)

HAZEL GROUSE   **PA**

The range of this inconspicuously colored and shy forest bird covers considerable parts of Asia and Europe. The most suitable habitat is formed by large, old forests with heavy undergrowth. The Hazel grouse spends most of its life on the ground running fast. Unlike the previous species, the male helps the female rear the chicks.

Tetrao urogallus

Colinus virginianus

NORTHERN BOBWHITE   **NA NT**

This representative of the New World quails reaches a weight of only 0.3–0.4/130–170g. The more conspicuous male is reddish with a black and white head. It inhabits various habitats from open agricultural land to forest edges in Mexico, Cuba, and in the southeastern parts of North America. Various seeds are the main food source, supplemented with insects during the summer. It forms family coveys for most of the year, except for spring when it splits into pairs. It is one of the most popular gamebirds, with over 20 million shot annually in the United States alone.

Tetrastes bonasia

Colinus virginianus

Francolinus sephaena

Francolinus sephaena

CRESTED FRANCOLIN   **AF OR**

The large majority of 40 species of francolins live in Africa; only five of them are found in southern Asia. The Crested francolin is distributed in tropical and subtropical eastern Africa. It features a dark cap and white supercilium. It prefers to live in thorny shrub-woods and forest edges. It appears to stoop when picking food consisting of termites, other insects and a variety of seeds. When threatened, it quickly runs to a vegetation cover with raised head and cocked tail. The nest is bowl–shaped, lined with grass and dry leaves, and rests on the ground. A clutch is comprised of 4–9 eggs and incubation lasts 19 days.

Ammoperdix heyi

SAND PARTRIDGE   **PA**

The Sand partridge is found in the Arabian Peninsula and in Egypt. Of all the phasianids, it is the best adapted to an arid environment, including hot semi-desert and desert. Its habitat consists of steep, rocky slopes with scattered vegetation and the sandy bottoms of dried riverbeds. Unlike the female, the male features a white eyestripe and longitudinal dark stripes on its flanks.

Perdix perdix

GRAY PARTRIDGE   **PA**

The Gray partridge is found throughout Eurasia. While its original habitat were the steppes, it later migrated to agricultural areas that resemble, to some extent, the steppes. The male is distinguished from the female by a notable, dark, horseshoe-shaped patch on its breast. Pairs are formed during the spring months. Eggs are incubated only by the female but the male participates in tending to the hatched chicks. Family coveys break up prior to the next breeding season. The adult partridges feed on seeds, grass leaves, and small invertebrates. The poults are insectivorous only in the first two weeks of their life. The Gray partridge used to be a plentiful species in Central Europe. But, by the beginning of the 1940s, a sharp reduction was caused by harsh winter conditions. Today, they are still few in number.

Ammoperdix heyi

Perdix perdix

Coturnix coturnix

Coturnix coturnix

COMMON QUAIL   **PA AF OR**

This minor bird is 6.3–7.1in/16–18cm long; its weight is approximately 0.15–0.33lb/70–150g. The breeding area includes Eurasia and eastern Africa. The Common quail migrates, an extremely unusual phenomena among gamebirds. The species shows a notable preference for the steppes and wooded steppes, and willingly accepts cultivated areas of the same topography. Their arrival from the African wintering grounds falls within the first half of May, and is announced by a characteristic *whic, whic-ic* call. The male mates with several females during the breeding season, but does not help with incubating and chick rearing.

Rollulus rouloul

CRESTED WOOD PARTRIDGE   **OR**

The Crested Wood partridge male is black with a blue gloss. Its head sports a conspicuous orange crest, while the area around the eye and part of its bill are bright red. The female's plumage has a greenish sheen and lacks all the male's adornments. The weight ranges from 0.44–0.50lb/200 to 230g and its length reaches about 10in/25cm. The bird lives permanently on the ground in the semi-darkness of the Indonesian tropical rain forests. It feeds on seeds, large fall-en fruit, insects, and mollusks. It tends to frequent places populated by wild boars.

Rollulus rouloul

Tragopan temminckii

Tragopan temminckii

TEMMINCK'S TRAGOPAN   PA OR

The Temminck's tragopan is one of the five tragopan species that inhabit the Himalayas and adjacent mountain ranges. The male reaches the weight of up to 3.3lb/1.5kg. Its plumage is red with whitish spots and a blue-black face pattern. The female, about a third smaller than the male, is uniformly dark brown with files of whitish patches. The nesting habitat is provided by dense evergreen or mixed forests as well as bamboo and rhododendron growths. Its diet includes flowers, leaves, bamboo sprouts, moss, berries, seeds and insects. The nests of sticks and leaves are built as high as 26ft/8m above the ground.

Pucrasia macrolopha

KOKLASS PHEASANT   PA OR

The Koklass pheasant lives in Alpine forests and thick bamboo on steep slopes from eastern Afghanistan to eastern China. Due to the isolation of individual populations in the mountain ranges, 10 subspecies of variable coloration evolved. All have an erectable crest and white patches on the sides of their neck.

Lophophorus impejanus

HIMALAYAN MONAL   PA OR

The Himalayan monal is 24–28in/63 to 72cm long and its weight can reach up to 5.3lb/2.4kg. The male is generally dark with a long crest, and features very prominent glossy plumage in the whole palette of colors. The female is uniformly dark brown with a white throat. It lives in the Himalayas above the tree-line at altitudes of 8,200–14,800ft/2,500–4,500m. Its habitat requires dense bamboo and rhododendron forests covering steep slopes. It is truly omnivorous and its diet consists of whatever food is available. It is often reared in zoological gardens where it breeds readily.

Pucrasia macrolopha

Lophophorus impejanus

Gallus gallus

Lophura erythrophthalma

Gallus gallus

RED JUNGLEFOWL   **OR**

All four jungle fowl species live in southeastern Asia. The males are colorful with red bare combs on their heads and long tails which curve down. Females of all species are considerably less distinctive. The Red junglefowl occupies most of the habitat types found in the tropics and subtropics from sea-level up to 6,500ft/ 2,000m. It is polygamous. A female sits on a nest of 4–9 eggs laid on the ground. Precocial chicks hatch after 18–20 day incubation.

Lophura swinhoii

SWINHOE'S PHEASANT   **OR**

The Swinhoe's pheasant lives only in original or mature secondary forests in Taiwan, at altitudes of 1,000–6,600ft/300 to 2,000m. A reduction in suitable habitats has caused a decline in its numbers and it is now considered an endangered species. Most of the male's plumage is blackish-blue, its crown, upperback and upper tail are pure white. The bare facial skin is bright red. The female is brownish with paler spotting and features a red patch around the eye.

Lophura erythrophthalma

CRESTLESS FIREBACK   **OR**

Another interestingly colored pheasant, the Crestless fireback, inhabits forests on the Malay Peninsula, in Sumatra and northern Borneo. The male is about 2.2lb/1kg in weight, dark with pale marbling and an ochre-colored tail. A slightly smaller female is all black.

Lophura swinhoii

Syrmaticus reevesii

Syrmaticus reevesii

REEVES'S PHEASANT   **PA OR**

The Reeves's pheasant inhabits wooded country and areas with tall grass in northern and central China. The brown male, with the white head and a black band across the eye, catches attention primarily by its long tail, which can measure up to 5.3ft/160cm. The tail of the smaller, brownish female is 17.7in/45cm long at the most. Although the Reeves's pheasant is a ground dweller, it roosts in tree crowns. With varied results, it was introduced in different parts of the world. There are no more than 5,000 birds living in the wild today, and thus it belongs among the endangered species.

Phasianus colchicus

RING-NECKED PHEASANT   **PA OR**

The original range of the Ring-necked pheasant spanned from the Caucasus to the Pacific. There are a great number of different subspecies, varying considerably in color. Since the Middle Ages, it has been successfully introduced in Europe, North America, Tasmania and New Zealand. A typical breeding habitat is situ-

Phasianus colchicus

Chrysolophus pictus

Chrysolophus amherstiae

ated by overgrown banks of rivers and open areas, like fields and meadows, interspersed with patches of groves and bushes. It became an important gamebird in Central Europe, but its numbers have dropped considerably during the last few decades.

Chrysolophus pictus

GOLDEN PHEASANT   **PA OR**

The Golden pheasant is a smaller species originating in central China, and weighing under 2lb/0.9kg. The exquisitely colored male, with a golden crest and red underparts, measures up to 3.7ft/115cm, though as much as 2.6ft/80cm of this length are in the tail. The female is inconspicuously brown with dark blotches. In its homeland, it occupies mountain valleys with dense growths of bamboo and shrubs. During the courtship, the male attracts several females to him, abandoning them immediately afterwards. Introduction to the wild in Great Britain was successful.

Chrysolophus amherstiae

LADY AMHERST'S PHEASANT   **PA OR**

The Lady Amherst's pheasant is clearly among the most attractive pheasants. All sorts of colors are present in the cock's plumage, from pure white to yellow, red and deep green. Its white tail with black transversal bands can grow up to 3.7ft/115cm in length. The species is distributed from northern Burma to Tibet and southwestern China. It occupies wooded hills and bamboo thickets or shrubs at altitudes of 6,900–8,000ft/2,100 to 3,600m. Its population is estimated at tens of thousands of birds and, at present, it is not an endangered species.

Argusianus argus

GREAT ARGUS   **OR**

The Great argus lives in the forests of the Malay Peninsula, Sumatra and Borneo. The male, weighing up to 6lb/2.7kg, is undoubtedly striking. The body is 6.6ft/2m long including the 4.6ft/1.4m long tail. The ocelli of the fairly elongated secondaries are prominently exposed during the courtship when the passionate male performs a wedding dance for the female at a prepared dancing ground. The whole tail is raised and the wings are fully spread during this display. The female builds a simple ground nest in which it lays 2 eggs. Dark brown chicks hatch after 24 days of warming.

Argusianus argus

Pavo cristatus

Pavo muticus

Guttera pucherani

Pavo cristatus

INDIAN PEAFOWL   **OR**

Owing to semi-captive breeding in parks and gardens, the Indian peafowl is a well-known species. It originally lived in forests, especially along rivers in the West Indies and Sri Lanka. During the courtship display, a male lifts up and fans its charming train bearing large ocelli which can be up to 5.3ft/1.6m long. In fact, the train is not constituted of the tail feathers, but of the elongated uppertail-coverts, which appears quite clear when looking from behind. The less conspicuous female lays 3–6 eggs in a ground nest usually placed in scrub, which she herself incubates for about 4 weeks.

Pavo muticus

GREEN PEAFOWL   **OR**

The Green peafowl is slightly smaller than the Indian peafowl; the male has a shorter tail and its neck is not deep blue, but speckled yellow-green. It occupies limited areas of the East Indies and Java in open forests and along the edges of deep woods, from lowlands to attitudes of up to 9,850ft/3,000m, but it does not enter rain forests. It feeds mostly on termites, but it also eats seeds and berries. Its wild population apparently does not exceed 1,000 birds.

Guttera pucherani

CRESTED GUINEAFOWL   **AF**

A considerable part of the Crested Guinea fowl's oval body, which is 17.5–22in/45–56cm long, is black with fine, white spots. The black crest is conspicuous. Cheeks are bare with blue and red patches. It is found along the edges of the secondary and gallery forests in sub-Saharan Africa. It forages on the ground for food of both plant and animal origin, moving mostly in groups. It nests on the ground. The total population is estimated at 100,000 birds.

Acryllium vulturinum

VULTURINE GUINEAFOWL   **AF**

The largest of guinea fowls, the Vulturine Guinea fowl, reaches a weight of over 3.5lb/1.6kg. Except for its gray, bare head, the bird is blue and black with white spotting. The conspicuously elongated neck hackles create a kind of overcoat. It lives in flocks on dry grasslands with scattered trees in the eastern part of tropical Africa. It is very vigilant, and some birds, standing upright, are always on guard, while the others graze. Unlike other guinea fowl, it almost never requires liquid. It is an abundant species whose total number exceeds a million birds.

Acryllium vulturinum

Opisthocomiformes

HOATZIN

This order includes only one family, genus and species: the hoatzin.

Opisthocomus hoazin

HOATZIN   **NT**

The body length of the hoatzin ranges 23.5–27.5in/ 60–70cm and its weight 1.5–2lb/0.7–0.9kg. Its small head, decorated with a long crest, supports a stout bill. The hoatzin inhabits the tropics of South America where it lives in flocks in bushes and trees. It is quite distinctive in many ways. It eats young leaves and buds that gather in its foregut. Here takes place the breaking down of the cellulose by means of symbiotic microbes and bacteria by means of a similar principle as in the ungulates. The fermentation processes are probably the source of an unpleasant odour that rises around hoatzins. The nest is built in branches above the water. Besides the breeding couple, several non-breeding helpers join to help in the nest's construction. Incubation of 2–4 eggs lasts over four weeks and involves all the social group. The chicks of reddish down are able to see and after a few days, they skillfully climb in the tree's branches. They are helped by their bill and the two free claws that grow out of a bend in the wing. If they fall in water, they are able to swim and dive very well, using the wings to help them. As they mature, the claws on the wings eventually recede.

Opisthocomus hoazin

9. Cranes and Allies

This chapter brings together two related groups of mostly aquatic or wetland birds. Due to their common habitat, their body shape and behavior are similar.

Gruiformes

CRANES AND ALLIES

Birds who belong to the Gruiformes order are often of very different shapes. All of them have walking legs with an elevated hallux, or hind toe, which can be dwarfed. Those of the species requiring an aquatic habitat have feet with webs that are formed somewhat like wattles. The great majority of the members of this order, excluding cranes, feature short wings. The chicks are fully agile immediately after hatching. The order is divided into seven suborders, of which four are presented. Probably the most prominent is the suborder *Grues* (cranes) which includes three families: cranes *(Gruidae)*, trumpeters *(Psophiidae)*, and rails *(Rallidae)*. Cranes are large birds with long legs, neck and bill. They inhabit the whole world except Greenland, South America and Antarctica. Seven of the 15 existing species are threatened with extinction. Trumpeters are medium-sized, terrestrial birds with longish legs and neck, and a short and strong bill. Three species are known. One hundred and thirty-three species of rails, gallinules and coots *(Rallidae)* form the most numerous family of small to medium-sized birds and inhabit all types of habitats. They have strong legs, longish neck, short wings and tail, and a weak bill. They are present in all the continents, except Antarctica, and a number of species also live on oceanic islands. Thirty-three rallid species have been listed among the endangered. The following suborder of *Eurypygae* has just one family with one species: the Sunbittern. The Seriemas *(Cariamidae)* include only two long-legged, terrestrial species. Finally, bustards *(Otididae)* form the suborder of 25 large to medium sized terrestrial birds.

Balearica pavonina

BLACK CROWNED CRANE   AF

The Black Crowned crane lives in sub-Saharan African tropics north of the equator. A suitable habitat provides still, shallow waters with adjacent grassland. The most distinctive feature of this bird is the thick yellow crest and a cheek patch. Its body is up to 3.6ft/1.1m long and it has a wingspan which reaches up to 6.6ft/2m. Its breeding is dependent on the advent of the rainy season (normally between July and October). The nest is a platform of grass and sedges in the shore growth of marshy plants.

Anthropoides virgo

DEMOISELLE CRANE   PA

The Demoiselle crane's coloring is overall gray with a darker head and foreneck. It inhabits steppe, usually near water streams and shallow lakes in Eurasia from the Black Sea to China. It winters in India and tropical Africa. It feeds mainly on grass seeds and other plant matter, and in summer, on insects and small vertebrates. The present population is stable, reaching 200–240 thousand birds.

Left: *Calidris ferruginea*
Balearica pavonina

Anthropoides virgo

Anthropoides paradisea

Grus rubicunda

Grus antigone

Anthropoides paradisea

BLUE CRANE   **AF**

Compared to the very similar *A. virgo*, the Blue crane is paler and features a white crown and an elongated dark tail. It reaches a weight of up to 11.7lb/5.3kg. It can be found in a rather small region in the south-eastern tip of Africa. Its original habitat was a dry natural grassland with growths of grasses and sedges but today it also frequents agricultural land. It congregates and breeds on wetlands.

Grus antigone

SARUS CRANE   **OR AU**

The uniformity of the Sarus crane's gray coloration, which covers a large body, up to 5.8ft/176cm long and 26lb/12kg in weight, is broken only by the red head and neck. Its range is divided into three regions: northern Australia, northern India, and also Cambodia and southern Laos. It became adapted to human presence in India and frequents canals and village ponds. It is omnivorous. When foraging, it walks slowly with its head held down, always prepared to catch insects and small vertebrates or to retrieve desirable seeds.

Grus rubicunda

BROLGA   **AU**

The Brolga resembles the Sarus crane, but it is about a third smaller, with dark legs and a red coloration limited to its nape. It is found exclusively in Australia and New Guinea. It prefers swamps 1.6ft/0.5m deep. The nest is a large heap of grasses and sedges, up to 5ft/1.5m in diameter. The complete clutch consists of two eggs.

Grus grus

Grus grus

Grus grus

EURASIAN CRANE   **PA**

The Eurasian crane is approximately as big as a stork, with a wingspan reaching up to 8ft/240cm. It can be easily identified by the black and white head, neck and a small red patch on its crown. The sexes cannot be distinguished by coloration. Juveniles are grayish brown. Like all cranes, and unlike the herons, it flies with its neck stretched forward. It breeds primarily in marshy areas of northern Eurasia. The breeding itself

Grus grus

is preceded by spectacular courtship dances. The nest is up to 2.6ft/80cm wide and consists of a mound of trampled wetland vegetation in which a female lays two gray-green eggs. Both parents regularly exchange incubation duties. When the pair is preparing to trade positions on the nest they call to each other with trumpet-like calls that can be heard from a far distance. The nestlings are reared also by the pair. Even if the Eurasian crane is omnivorous, vegetables form the core of of its diet, especially in the non-breeding season. The migrating cranes travel in regular V-formations and often draw attention by calling. During the migration, they enjoy resting in fields where food can be obtained. The wintering grounds can be found in the south of Europe and Asia and in Africa.

Grus japonensis

RED-CROWNED CRANE   **PA**

With its weight of up to 26.5lb/12kg the Red-crowned crane is amongst the largest of the cranes. The plumage is overall white, except for the red crown and the black neck, face and tail. With only 1,700–2,000 birds left, it is considered to be the second rarest crane next to the Whooping crane. Animal as well as plant food is picked in fields and grasslands. It migrates in winter to southeastern China and the Korean Peninsula.

Grus japonensis

119

Psophia crepitans

Psophia crepitans

GRAY-WINGED TRUMPETER   NT

Similar to two other species of trumpeters, the Gray-winged trumpeter's hump-backed body shape recalls jungle fowls. It is 17–20in/45–52cm long and weighs 2.2–3.3lb/1–1.5kg. A small head features a stout, pointed bill. It is generally black, only the fine feathering on its back, overlying the wings, is paler – ochre and gray. The habitat suitable for this bird is the tropical rain forest north of the Amazon River. It forms organized social groups with a strict hierarchical order that fiercely guard their resident territory against other groups. The borders are proclaimed principally by calls. All kinds of fruits make the core of its diet. Only the dominant female, who mates with three males, lays a clutch of three eggs in a tree cavity high above the ground. Not long after hatching, the chicks, answering the encouraging calls of the whole group, jump from their nests to join the adults on the ground.

Gallirallus striatus

Gallirallus striatus

SLATY-BREASTED RAIL   OR

The body of the Slaty-breasted rail is grayish with a contrasting black and white barring on flanks and back, while the upper parts of its head and neck are reddish. Its range involves almost the entire Oriental region. It lives on wetlands of various kinds, but also in dry, shrubby areas and forests. It ranges up to 6,100ft/1,850m.

Laterallus leucopyrrhus

RED-AND-WHITE CRAKE   NT

The Red-and-white crake's coloration roughly resembles the Slaty-breasted Rail. The body though, which is 6.3in/16cm in length and under 0.1lb/50g in weight, is about half as big. Its white throat, foreneck and the breast are distinctive. It inhabits open marshes, densely overgrown with wetland plants, in South America between southern Brazil to northern Argentina. It builds an overhead spherical nest of grass with a side entrance.

Laterallus leucopyrrhus

Gallirallus philippensis

BUFF-BANDED RAIL   OR AU

The Buff-banded rail can be found from Indonesia to New Zealand. The isolation of the individual island populations has contributed to the evolution of more than 20 subspecies with varied plumage coloring, one of which is already extinct. Most of them have a chestnut nape, and transversely barred flanks and belly. The body length does not exceed 13in/33cm and its weight is somewhere around 0.45lb/200g. It is fairly tolerant when it comes to the habitat and can be found in all types of environment, from wetlands to dry grasslands and forests. Nor does it avoid parks

Gallirallus philippensis

Porzana porzana

and gardens. The nest of grass is built on the ground or closely above. A clutch consisting of 4–8 eggs is incubated by both parents for almost three weeks. The birds may, in some areas, breed as many as five times a year.

Rallus aquaticus

WATER RAIL   **PA**

The Water rail's range involves almost all of Europe, a considerable part of Asia and North Africa. The gray body, brown back and the long red bill are complemented with black and white barring on flanks which is a typical feature of all the rails of this genus. The slightly larger male reaches a maximum weight of almost 0.45lb/200g. It consumes all kinds of dense wetland vegetation. It is especially active at twilight and night. The essential parts of its diet are various invertebrate animals and small vertebrates. To a lesser ex-

tent, it also consumes seeds and fruits. The nest is usually well-concealed amidst vegetation. The newly hatched chicks are all black and become very active within seconds of birth.

Porzana porzana

SPOTTED CRAKE   **PA**

This migratory Eurasian species lives secretively on freshwater marshes with dense vegetation cover. The wintering grounds are located in eastern Africa and southern Asia. Its plumage is inconspicuously brownish with pale and dark spotting and bluish head. It feeds on animal as well as vegetable food.

Rallus aquaticus

Porphyrio porphyrio

PURPLE SWAMPHEN   **PA AF OR AU**

More than 10 subspecies varying in coloration and size have evolved throughout an extensive area which includes southern Europe, Africa, southern and southeastern Asia, Australia and New Zealand. All members of the species are, however, predominantly or entirely blue, and feature a stout, red bill, red shield on the forehead, and pinkish legs. The undertail-coverts are white and literally flash with every jerk of the tail. The Purple swamphen occupies mainly fresh and brakish waters and swamps richly overgrown by reeds, reed-mace, sedges and *Cyperus*. It feeds mostly on sprouts, leaves, rootstocks, flowers and seeds of aquatic and marshy plants. Animal foods, like mollusks, small crabs, insects and spiders, are included in its diet only in limited amounts. It may also consume small fish and amphibians.

Porphyrio martinica

Porphyrio martinica

AMERICAN PURPLE GALLINULE   **NA NT**

Its coloration resembles the Purple swamphen though it has a uniformly deep green back, yellow legs and the blue frontal shield. It is also considerably smaller. It lives almost all over South and Central America, and in the southern parts of North America. It frequents overgrown swamps from lowlands to mountains, occuring up to 13,100ft/4,000m in Peru.

Gallinula chloropus

COMMON MOORHEN   **PA AF OR NA NT**

It can be found everywhere except Australia and pronouncedly cold areas. The body is up to 15in/38cm long and its weight ranges between 0.45–1.1lb/0.2–0.5kg. The head, neck and underparts are grayish brown, while the back is brown-black. There are white lines along the flanks and white edges on the undertail-coverts. The red bill has a yellow tip. The bird does not have high requirements for its habitat, and small wetlands with thick aquatic and marsh vegetation are completely satisfactory. It often swims off into open water or walks on dry land while foraging. The nest is built in a cluster of sedges or in reeds not far from the bank. After three weeks of warming the relatively large eggs, chicks covered with black down are hatched and soon follow the adult female into the water.

Fulica atra

COMMON COOT   **PA OR AU**

It inhabits an extensive area which includes almost the entire continents of Europe, North Africa, a considerable part of Asia as well as Australia and New Zealand. The plumage of the plump coot which can weigh up to 2.5lb/1.2kg, is generally grayish with a black head and neck which causes the white bill and frontal plate to truly stand out. It inhabits still and slow-flowing waters of various types, fringed with

thick vegetation. Even though it is omnivorous, aquatic plants form the core of its diet. A massive nest of leaves and reed stems is placed on the water surface and anchored to nearby plants. Newly hatched chicks strongly resemble the young of the Common moorhen, but unlike them, they have red heads.

The nidicolous chicks hatch from the usual clutch of two eggs after a month and are looked after by both parents. The sunbittern has a long life span, and has lived for 30 years in captivity.

Eurypyga helias

SUNBITTERN   **NT**

The shape of its body may resemble a small heron. It weighs less than 0.45lb/200g and is about 20in/50cm long. Its long and slender, yellow bill is striking in conjunction with its short legs of the same color. The Sunbittern has a fairly colorful plumage. Especially noticeable are two characteristic white stripes on its dark head. With its open wings, it resembles a beautiful butterfly. It occupies wet tropical forests in Central and South America with open spaces near the ground. Importantly its habitat is associated with water, no matter whether still or flowing. It feeds on aquatic vertebrates and invertebrates, capturing them with a sudden stab forwards or by picking. It breeds at the beginning of the rainy season. The nest of mud, leaves and grass is built on a branch close to the trunk.

Eurypyga helias

Cariama cristata

Cariama cristata
RED-LEGGED SERIEMA   **NT**

It is 2.3–3ft/75–90cm tall and reaches a weight of about 3.3lb/1.5kg. Its head, decorated with a thin crest on the forehead, red bill and a blue arena around the eyes, takes on a strict appearance. The plumage is generally grayish brown with darker upperparts. It can

Chunga burmeisteri

be found in the wild on South American pampas. It has a penetrating call that can be heard at great distance. It feeds mostly on arthropods, and to a lesser extent on small vertebrates, various seeds and fruits. A rather untidy nest is built at the top of low trees.

Chunga burmeisteri
BLACK-LEGGED SERIEMA   **NT**

The Black-legged seriema is somewhat smaller than its closest relative. It lacks any pronounced crest and its bill and legs are black. It frequents open forests and savannas in the lower altitudes of northeastern Argentina.

Otis tarda
GREAT BUSTARD   **PA OR**

The species features a pronounced sexual dimorphism in terms of both the size and coloration. The male is over 3.3ft/1m long and can reach a maximum weight of as much as 40lb/18kg. Its gray head is decorated during courtship with long, whitish whiskers. A female measures only 2.5ft/0.75m and its weight only occasionally exceeds 11lb/5kg. Their inconsistent range reaches to Europe, Asia, and the margins of northwestern Africa. The chief habitat of this bustard is extensive areas of steppe with short grass and usually no trees at all. It is partly able to adapt to large agricultural areas. The main part of its diet consists of various plant matter, though it also consumes small mammals and invertebrates. Incubation of two eggs laid in a simple pit as well as the rearing of the chicks is carried out only by the female. The population dropped rapidly during the 20th century and the species has completely disappeared from many places.

Otis tarda

Ardeotis kori

Tetrax tetrax

Ardeotis kori

KORI BUSTARD   **AF**

The male of this species of African bustard can reach a weight of up to 42lb/19kg and a length of 4ft/120cm. It has a long, gray neck and a flattened head whose black crown projects into a horizontal crest. The bird is brown above and white below. The female is similar in plumage, but much smaller. It frequents arid zones with short herbage cover, like savanna or thin scrubland.

Tetrax tetrax

LITTLE BUSTARD   **PA OR**

Both male and female of this minor bustard measure about 17in/43cm and weigh less than a kilogram. The bird is generally brownish with white undersides. In addition, the male shows a black ruff with white margins, and a bluish gray head. The breeding area stretches to the temperate and warm zones of Europe and Asia. The most suitable habitat is a steppe or a country similar to a steppe. Their diet switches from animal sources in the summer to primarily vegetable in the winter.

Charadriiformes

PLOVERS, SNIPES, GULLS, TERNS, AUKS AND ALLIES

Three former orders were integrated to form the *Charadriiformes* order and they are now recognized as its suborders: *Charadrii, Lari* and *Alcae*. Most of the members live on the water or in its proximity. They have a well developed wax uropygial gland and thick, tight-fitting plumage. The Charadrii suborder currently includes 13 families, eight of which shall be specified. Jacanas *(Jacanidae)* feature extremely long toes that are useful for walking on leaves floating on the water surface. The female is normally larger and the male takes care of the egg incubation and chick rearing. They live on all the continents except Eurasia and Antarctica. Eight species are recognized. Oystercatchers *(Haematopodidae)* are medium-sized birds with black-and-white or black plumage that are primarily tied to sea coasts all over the world. Eleven species have been described so far. Stilts and avocets *(Recurvirostridae)* are slim birds distributed on open wetlands all around the world. They have long legs, neck and bill. Seven species are known. Thick-knees *(Burhinidae)* very much resemble bustards and were formerly classified as such. Their head and eyes are large and suggest a crepuscular or nocturnal lifestyle. A total of nine species live mainly in dry areas of the Old World. Coursers and pratincoles *(Glareolidae)* are gregarious birds occupying arid and warm areas of the Old World where 17 species were described. Plovers *(Charadriidae)* are small to medium-sized birds with large eyes and heads, short necks and long wings. They are distributed in open terrains all over the world with 67 species described altogether. Snipes, sandpipers and phalaropes *(Scolopacidae)* are small to medium-sized birds with long bills and rather cryptic plumage. Eighty-six species of scolopacid waders inhabit all the continents except Antarctica. The last mentioned family is the *Pedionomidae,* once classi-

Actophilornis africana

Jacana jacana

Haematopus ostralegus

fied to Gruiformes, with a single Australian species, the Plains-wanderer. The *Lari* suborder is further divided into four families: skuas, gulls, terns and skimmers. Skuas *(Stercorariidae)* are medium-sized to large birds with elongated rectrices. They are predatory, or perform kleptoparasitism, especially on the ocean coasts or in the tundra. Seven species are known. Gulls *(Laridae)* include 61 aquatic species of small to medium size. They feature extremely long wings, glide very well and the plumage of most of them is either black, white or gray. Terns *(Sternidae)* are small to medium-sized, slender varieties; 44 species occupy waters all around the world. Skimmers *(Rynchopidae)* are highly specialized water birds with elongated lower mandibles; three species inhabit mainly the tropics. Auks *(Alcidae)* form the only family of the *Alcae* suborder. Twenty-two species of strictly marine birds live in cold waters of the Northern Hemisphere and specialize in hunting sea creatures.

Actophilornis africanus

AFRICAN JACANA   AF

It is identified by a chestnut body, black and white neck and head, and a gray-blue bill and bare frontal shield. It inhabits shallow swamps in Africa south of the Sahara. The greatly elongated toes allow the bird to walk on floating vegetation to glean various invertebrates. It flies only reluctantly for short distances.

Jacana jacana

WATTLED JACANA   NT

The bird's head and neck are black, while the rest of its body is chestnut brown. There are yellow wattles at the base of its bill. It lives from Argentina to Central America. It is found on fresh waters with surfaces covered with floating leaves, over which the bird easily moves. The considerably larger female lays eggs in the nests of up to three different males who are instrumental in the incubation and rearing of the chicks after hatching.

Haematopus ostralegus

EURASIAN OYSTERCATCHER   PA

A combination of deep black upperparts and pure white underparts creates an elegant appearance. It breeds on sea coasts and beside large inland water bodies in Europe, Asia and New Zealand. It feeds mostly on lamellibranches, gasteropods, limpets and other mollusks found on rocky shores. In order to get into the shells of its prey, the Oystercatcher uses a variety of techniques including pounding the shell on a rock. The nest is only a simple hollow in mud or sand in which a female lays 2–4 eggs. Even though the young look very mature soon after hatching, the parents often bring them food until fledging. The oldest recorded age for this bird is 40 years.

Cladorhynchus lencocephalus

Himantopus himantopus

BLACK-WINGED STILT   **PA AF OR AU NA NT**

The bird is predominantly white except for the black bill, back and wings, and red legs. Its weight does not usually exceed 0.45lb/200g. It inhabits a very extensive region which involves all the continents to a great extent. The most desirable habitats are shallow waters of tropical and temperate zones, fresh or saline. It feeds on a wide range of invertebrates and small vertebrates in mud or water and only occasionally pecks a seed or other plant matter.

Cladorhynchus leucocephalus

BANDED STILT   **AU**

Its coloration and size resemble those of the Black-winged Stilt, but the bird has a chestnut band on the breast. It breeds in the saline (even extremely saline) shallow waters of southern Australia, primarily feeding on all kinds of small crustaceans. The tight breeding colonies are comprised of tens of thousands of nests containing 3–4 eggs with a density as high as 28 nests per square mile.

Recurvirostra avosetta

PIED AVOCET   **PA AF**

A distinctive feature of this contrasting black and white colored bird is the bill which curves upward at about half of its length. There are very fine lamellae inside the bill which act as a filter for small invertebrates. While foraging, the Pied avocet tirelessly moves its bill from side to side. It frequents mostly shallow salt waters in Eurasia and Africa. It usually breeds in fairly numerous colonies.

Himantopus himantopus

Recurvirostra avosetta

Recurvirostra novaehollandiae

Recurvirostra novaehollandiae

RED-NECKED AVOCET   AU

This Australian avocet features a brown head and its plumage is black and white. The typical breeding habitat is formed by shallow saline lakes. It nests either alone or in colonies of up to 150 nests.

Burhinus oedicnemus

Burhinus oedicnemus

STONE-CURLEW   PA OR

The Stone-curlew has large yellow eyes and is streaked brown with a black and white band on the wings. It requires a dry steppe habitat where it can easily avoid being seen if it crouches to the ground. The range involves a part of Europe, southwestern and southern Asia and northern Africa. It moves about on the ground and often runs quickly in search for invertebrates and small vertebrates. It is active particularly at night when it can be identified only by its unique call. Its nest is just a shallow scrape in the ground, ringed with grass or small stones. The female lays two large, spotted eggs.

Burhinus senegalensis

SENEGAL THICK-KNEE   AF

It inhabits wet and muddy river banks as well as dry, grassy areas distant from water. It closely resembles the Stone-curlew, but is perceivably smaller. Its region spans the equator to the Sahara.

Burhinus capensis

SPOTTED DIKKOP   AF

The Spotted dikkop is a sedentary inhabitant of savanna and open forests or even larger parks in sub-Saharan Africa. It is whitish below and brown above with characteristic dark, heart-shaped spots. Like the Stone-curlew, it is over 16in/40cm long at the most and weighs about 1.1lb/0.5kg. It dwells in the shade of trees or among boulders during the day, becoming

Burhinus senegalensis

Stiltia isabella

fully active when it is overcast and at nightfall. They breed in single pairs at the end of the dry season and at the beginning of the rainy period.

Stiltia isabella

AUSTRALIAN PRATINCOLE	AU

The bird's plumage is inconspicuously brownish, only the distinctive red base of the bill stands out. The pratincole it is 8.3–9.5in/21–24cm long and reaches a weight of 0.15lb/about 65g. The breeding area spreads throughout central and northern Australia. The bird frequents arid, bare areas with scattered clusters of grass and low shrubs as well as barren shorelines of shallow lakes. It needs to drink frequently and therefore it is rarely found far from watering places. The Australian pratincole feeds on various insects that are mostly picked from the ground, but also occasionally captured in flight. It nests in a shallow depression on bare, rocky ground, lined with small stones and dry plant matter.

Glareola pratincola

COLLARED PRATINCOLE	PA AF OR

The uniformly grayish plumage is relieved by a large yellow black bordered patch on its throat. It shows its chestnut underwings in flight and thus differs from the other species of this genus. It inhabits dry open areas with low vegetation in Eurasia from the Iberian Peninsula to Lake Baikal, and seeks a similar environment is in Africa. It cannot live too far from water. It forages in groups for flying insects, mostly at dawn or dusk, and sometimes also in the moonlight. It often follows swarms of grasshoppers.

Burhinus capensis

Glareola pratincola

Vanellus vanellus

Vanellus armatus

Vanellus spinosus

Vanellus vanellus

NORTHERN LAPWING   PA

This generally known species about the size of a pigeon has a palearctic distribution. Its contrast plumage with dark and white panels, complemented with a long crest, is distinctive, and so are the acrobatic aerial stunts and vocal displays performed when it is protecting its breeding territory. A suitable habitat is provided by various open bare areas or places with low vegetation, such as wet meadows or fields. The nest is a small hollow in the ground, thinly lined with dry vegetation. A single clutch most commonly consists of 4 eggs. Outside the breeding season flocks gather on mudflats or in quite dry areas. The essentialy requirement is the availability of food, particularly various invertebrates.

Vanellus armatus

BLACKSMITH LAPWING   AF

The popular habitats of this South African lapwing are sparsely vegetated dry places not far from water bodies and muddy areas in their vicinity. Its coloration is mostly black with white patches on its forehead and hindneck, and gray wings. When foraging, it nervously runs back and forth, picking insects and other invertebrates off the ground. It frequently calls out with a metallic sounding alarm.

Vanellus spinosus

SPUR-WINGED LAPWING   PA AF

Besides the pale brown upperparts, this lapwing is black with white lower cheeks and sides of neck. While it is resident in Africa between the Sahara and the equator and in the Nile valley, there are migratory populations scattered throughout Asia Minor and the Middle East. It does not demand much from its habitat, occupying mostly dry, open areas not too distant from water.

Vanellus indicus

RED-WATTLED LAPWING   PA OR

The bird is slightly smaller than the Northern Lapwing. It again features the black and white plumage, except for the pale brown upperparts, yellowish legs, and a red bill and eye ring. It inhabits mainly open areas close to fresh and brackish waters, but can also be found in fields, large gardens and mown, grassy stretches along roads. Its habitat includes the Near and Middle East, and southern and southeastern Asia.

Vanellus indicus

Vanellus chilensis

Vanellus miles

MASKED LAPWING   **AU**

This large Australian lapwing is grayish brown above, while the rest of its plumage is white except for a black cap. The bill, its curious appendages in the form of wattles, and a patch above the eye are rich yellow. Its requirements for habitat and food are similar to those other lapwings. Its population is estimated at more than a quarter of a million birds.

Vanellus chilensis

SOUTHERN LAPWING   **NT**

This fairly ornamental bird, 12.5–15in/32–38cm long, lives on pastures and other short grass meadows of South America. It is predominantly gray with a white belly and a white vertical facial band in front of the eye which separates a black patch stretching from the forehead down to its breast. An area with a metallic sheen on the scapulars is distinctive and the elongated black feathers on its nape form a crest. It feeds largely on insects, annelidans and other terrestrial invertebrates.

Vanellus miles

Pluvialis apricaria

EURASIAN GOLDEN PLOVER   **PA**

Its body is 0.35–0.7lb/26–29cm long and its weight ranges from 0.35–0.68lb/160–310g. It has a wingspan 2.2–2.5ft/67–76cm. The entire underpart of the bird is black in the breeding plumage, while above it is yellow mottled with black. The two sections are divided by a white band. Its breeding grounds can be found in extensive peatbogs and marshy tundra in the north of Europe and northwestern Asia. It migrates during the winter to southern Europe and northern Africa. Three quarters of its diet are comprised of insects and other invertebrates; the rest consists of seeds, berries and other plant parts.

Charadrius hiaticula

COMMON RINGED PLOVER   **PA NA**

The Common Ringed plover is about the size of a larger lark. The plumage is dominated by pale brown, white and black colors. As is typical for all the *Charadrius* species, it runs quickly on the sand or shingle ocean coasts of northern Eurasia, Greenland and northeastern parts of North America. It migrates over fairly long distances, and winters not only in the south of Europe and Asia, but a part of its population also flies as far as the southern part of Africa. It forages for small crustaceans, mollusks, polychaetes and other invertebrates during both day and night.

Charadrius hiaticula

Charadrius wilsonia

Charadrius vociferus

Charadrius dubius

LITTLE RINGED PLOVER　　　　**PA OR AU**

It inhabits a large range which involves almost all of Europe as well as a considerable part of Asia and North Africa. It is only slightly smaller than the previous species and also its coloration is quite similar. It differs, however, because it lacks a white patch behind the eye. For its habitat, it chooses bare areas near waters, for example, sandy shores of great rivers and lakes, bottoms of drained lakes, sand-pits, exploited peat-bogs, etc. It clearly avoids tall, dense shore vegetation. A slight scrape in the ground makes a nest lined with pieces of plants or tiny pebbles. The clutch usually consists of four mottled eggs. The chicks hatch after 3–4 weeks of incubation and immediately follow their parents as soon as they dry out.

Charadrius wilsonia

WILSON'S PLOVER　　　　**NA NT**

The Wilson's plover features an unusually long and thick bill instrumental for getting into the shells of crabs which provide its favorite diet although it accepts other food too. It is among the birds most closely associated with the ocean coasts of southern North America and the northern coast of South and Central America.

Charadrius vociferus

KILLDEER　　　　**NA NT**

This large plover reaches a weight of almost 0.22lb/ 100g. Besides the dark brown upperparts, the two black bands on its breast are distinctive. It occupies open areas with low vegetation not necessarily located near water. Various agricultural areas are also suitable. Its habitat is to be found mostly in North America. Its diet consists mostly of beetles, flies and grasshoppers. It is active at day as well as night, and never congregates in large flocks.

Charadrius alexandrinus

KENTISH PLOVER　　　　**PA AF OR NA NT**

The Kentish plover can be found on all the continents except Australia and Antarctica. It is distinguished by somewhat unfinished black stripes on its breast and forehead. Seacoasts are the most sought habitat, although it also lives on the open shores of shallow saline and brackish lakes. It prefers sandy or muddy banks while avoiding rocky sites.

Charadrius alexandrinus

Charadrius morinellus

Scolopax rusticola

Charadrius morinellus

EURASIAN DOTTEREL   **PA**

The larger female reaches a weight of 0.22–0.3lb/
100–140g, which is about 20 % more than the male.
Both sexes have a dark crown, white cheeks with
a dark stripe across the eye, blue-gray neck, orange
lower breast and white lower belly. It is a typical example of the Arctic-alpine species. A substantial part
of its habitat reaches as far as the northern tundra,
while small, isolated areas can be found in more
southern mountains high above the tree line. The
Eurasian dotterel's behavior is very inconspicuous
during the breeding season and so the bird can easily
go unnoticed. Its wintering grounds are in North
Africa.

Scolopax rusticola

EURASIAN WOODCOCK   **PA**

The plump body with short legs measures 13–14in/
33–35cm and reaches a weight of 0.5–1lb/230–440g.
Reddish brown plumage is offset by darker and paler
spots, bars and vermiculations. Its regions of habitation lie in Europe and Asia. The Eurasian woodcock
is one of the few truly forest Charadrii. It leads a se-
cret life in damp places where, mainly at twilight, it
picks various invertebrates from the ground by means
of probing in the soil. There is a high density of tactile receptors placed at the tip of its bill that can de-
tect the prey. Due to a unique muscle arrangement, the
bird is able to open the tip of its bill like a pair of
tweezers, enabling it to capture prey hiding below the

Gallinago gallinago

surface. The ground nest normally has 4 eggs. In case of danger, the female carries the young away one at a time by clutching the nestling between its feet and flying away.

Gallinago gallinago

COMMON SNIPE   **PA NA**

The Common snipe reaches about the size of a Blackbird, and its coloration resembles the Eurasian Woodcock. It is distributed throughout Eurasia and North America. It frequents open freshwater or brackish wetlands with dense herbage growths, mixed with muddy areas. It forages, mainly at twilight for various invertebrates. The breeding is preceded by a remarkable courtship display during which the male erratically zigzags above its territory and occasionally drops 33–66ft/10–20m. During such a descent, the outer tail feathers are held wide apart to produce a mysterious bleating sound. There are usually four dark, spotted eggs in the nest that is placed on the ground amid the dense, grassy vegetation.

Limosa limosa

BLACK-TAILED GODWIT   **PA**

Its body, about the size of a turtle-dove, stands atop long legs. The bird's long neck is topped by a small head with a straight bill. The male's breeding plumage is more colorful than the female's. The breeding region in Europe and Asia is rather scattered. The Black-tailed godwit nests in wet meadows, often in loosely organized colonies. It tenaciously protects the areas surrounding its nest by charging towards intruders using stooping motions and loud calls as a warning. The nest is built on the ground in low vegetation.

Numenius phaeopus

WHIMBREL   **PA NA**

The breeding region of the Whimbrel is to be found in the northern parts of Eurasia and North America. It migrates for very long distances, often to the other side of the world. Its body is 15.5–18.5in/40–46cm long and its coloration is fairly inconspicuous. A white patch on its rump shows in flight. The breeding takes place in boreal peat bogs, thin birch forests and tundra.

Numenius arquata

EURASIAN CURLEW   **PA**

The Eurasian curlew's most distinctive feature is the long, downward-curving bill. The brown streaked body is 20–23.5in/50–60cm long. Throughout its Eurasian range, it breeds on peat-bogs, wet meadows, extensively cultivated farmland or coastal marshes. The nest is built on the ground and both partners take part in incubating eggs and rearing the hatched

Limosa limosa

nestlings. The bulk of their diet is made up of annelidans, mollusks, various arthropods, seeds and berries, and occasionally also small vertebrates. The winter is spent primarily on ocean coasts.

Numenius phaeopus

Numenius arquata

Tringa erythropus

Actitis hypoleucos

Tringa totanus

Tringa glareola

Tringa erythropus

SPOTTED REDSHANK   **PA**

The Spotted redshank is a typical representative of scolopacid waders who breed in northern Eurasia and winter far away in central Africa or in southern Europe and Asia. Similar to all other sandpipers, it features a long neck, bill and legs. Its body is about 11.8in/30cm long. Its breeding plumage is all black with fine white speckling on its back. The winter plumage is pale gray. The habitat is formed by open wooded tundra and swampy pine and spruce forests. It feeds mainly on aquatic insects and their larvae though it is able to capture and swallow a fish up 3in/7cm long.

Tringa totanus

COMMON REDSHANK   **PA OR**

This Eurasian species inhabits a broad variety of coastal and inland wetlands. The typical features are the bright red legs and the broad white band on the wings which is clearly shown, together with the white rump, in flight. It breeds on the ground, either in pairs or in loose colonies. The density may reach 160–500 nests per square mile in coastal areas.

Tringa glareola

WOOD SANDPIPER   **PA**

The Wood sandpiper is grayish brown above and whitish below. Its body is about the size of a thrush. It breeds in peat bogs and open marshy areas of the coniferous forest zone in Eurasia. While in distant African, South Asian and Australian wintering grounds, it occupies mainly shores of various inland waters. It forages in shallow water for all different kinds of invertebrates and occasionally even swims while hunting. It has also been observed catching flying insects.

Actitis hypoleucos

COMMON SANDPIPER   **PA OR**

The Common sandpiper is about the same size as a starling and has inconspicuous gray-brown plumage. Shortish legs and bill are typical. It can mostly be observed on the shores of various water bodies right next to the water. When walking, it typically teeters its body and bobs its head. When taking off, the bird emits a moaning sound. It usually flies low over the water using jerky wingbeats. The breeding region covers a great deal of Eurasia. It moves towards the south for winter and sometimes even reaches southern Africa and Australia.

Arenaria interpres

RUDDY TURNSTONE   **PA NA**

Its robust body, about 10in/25cm long stands on rather short legs. The short bill is curved slightly upwards. The breeding plumage is remarkably bright. It inhabits rocky coastal plains and the tundra of the far north of Eurasia and North America. After breeding, it can be found primarily on ocean coasts often half a world away from its starting point. During the breeding season, it feeds mostly on adults and larvae of dipteran insects and butterflies, beetles and spiders. In the non-breeding coastal range, the main part of its diet is made up of crustaceans, polychaete worms, mollusks or small fish deposited by the sea. When foraging, it uses its bill and breast to move or turn over stones that may be heavier than the bird itself.

Arenaria interpres

Calidris alba

SANDERLING   **PA NA**

Calidris sandpipers are small to medium-sized birds with slender, longish bills. Their plumage is usually uniform, darker and mottled above, pale below. They cover tremendous distances during migrations. The sanderling breeds in the Arctic tundra zone in Eurasia and North America. It prefers stony areas, sparsely grown with dwarfed willows and saxifrages. Outside the breeding season, it inhabits mostly sandy beaches of seas and oceans all around the world, including the southernmost ones.

Calidris alba

Calidris minuta

Calidris minuta
LITTLE STINT   **PA**

The breeding male of this tiny species features a brown speckled head, neck, breast and upperparts. In the autumn and winter, these parts become gray. It breeds in the lowland Arctic tundra of Europe and Asia from late June. Immediately after rearing the chicks, it moves to wintering grounds in southern Europe, Asia, and in Africa. It forms flocks of varied sizes during the migratory movements.

Calidris temminckii
TEMMINCK'S STINT   **PA**

In size and coloration, it resembles the Little stint. Its breeding region also covers the northern parts of Europe and Asia but reaches further south than that of the Little stint. The nesting sites can be found in zones of shrub and wooded tundra, at places with low herbal vegetation and scattered shrubs. In non-breeding times, it frequents diverse wetlands, showing a preference for inland waters. The chief wintering grounds are located in Africa between the Sahara and the equator, and in southern Asia.

Calidris ferruginea
CURLEW SANDPIPER   **PA**

The Curlew sandpiper can be easily identified during breeding by reddish plumage, and throughout the rest of the year by its longish, decurved bill. The breeding grounds are in the far thest northern reaches of Asia. It favors open lowland tundra with water filled depressions or marshes. It winters on coasts of the southern seas and oceans, with a part of its population flying as far as southern Africa and Australia.

Calidris maritima
PURPLE SANDPIPER   **PA NA**

This medium-sized sandpiper breeds in the Eurasian and North American Arctic. It strongly prefers rocky islands and wet tundra covered with mosses and lichens. In the breeding season, it feeds mostly on insects and their larvae, springtails, and spiders. It also will eat buds, berries and seeds of plants. It migrates during the winter to more southerly rocky ocean coastlines. However, it does not move nearly as far south as most of the other sandpipers.

Calidris alpina
DUNLIN   **PA NA**

Its short-legged body is 6.5–9in/16–22cm long. The black patch on its belly is the most conspicuous feature of its breeding plumage. The nesting area lies in the northern part of Eurasia and North America. The dunlin exploits a broad range of habitats for breeding, from high moors to various types of tundra to damp coastal grasslands and salt-marshes. The breeding begins in June. The nest may be placed right in a grass tussock. It feeds by both day and night, predominantly on insects and other invertebrates. Outside the breeding season, it congregates in large flocks on mudflats of estuaries or inland waters.

Calidris temminckii

Calidris ferruginea

Calidris maritima

Limicola falcinellus

Limicola falcinellus

BROAD-BILLED SANDPIPER   **PA**

A typical feature of this small wader with a somewhat stooped build is the long, broad bill with a slightly decurved tip. It breeds on peatlands and open wet Arctic tundra in the north of Europe and Asia. It forages by walking slowly, searching for food by probing into the mud and shallow water with its bill. It favors fairly distant wintering grounds that may even reach to the Southern Hemisphere.

Philomachus pugnax

RUFF   **PA**

The breeding grounds are located in the Eurasian zone of the coniferous forest and tundra, mostly on peat bogs or water filled meadows. The male is considerably larger than a female, measuring 10–12in/26–32cm and 8–9.5in/20–24cm respectively. In comparison with the other sandpipers, it has taller legs, a longer neck and a relatively short bill. During courtship, the males are decorated with magnificent feather neck ruffs and tufts on their heads that are elevated during the mating activity. These adornments are exceptionally varied in color, and it is even said that no two males can be found with ruffs of the same color. The males perform a group mating display in special areas for the assembled females. The pregnant females by themselves build the ground nests, incubate the eggs and look after the nestlings.

Calidris alpina

Philomachus pugnax

Phalaropus lobatus

RED-NECKED PHALAROPE **PA NA**

It measures only 7–7.5in/18–19cm. The feet feature longitudinal tough-skinned lobes like those of a coot. It has quite a shallow draught when swimming and spins on the water, somewhat resembling a styrofoam toy. It is easily distinguished in its nuptial plumage by conspicuous orange markings on its neck. The female is normally larger and more brightly colored for practical reasons since it is the male who actually takes on all the family duties, including building the nest, incubating eggs and raising the chicks. The breeding range extends over the tundra and forest tundra zone of Eurasia and North America. Wintering quarters are found at sea off the western coast of South America and in the Arabian Sea where the

Pedinomus torquatus

rising water currents bring up nutriments in abundant quantities.

Pedionomus torquatus

PLAINS-WANDERER **AU**

Scattered populations of the plains-wanderer inhabit the natural grasslands of inland Australia. It measures only 6–7.5in/15–19cm. The female is slightly larger and, unlike the uniformly brown speckled male, features a black and white mottled collar, and an orange breast patch. About half of its diet is made up of insects; the remaining part consists of grass and plant seeds. The bird spends about a third of the day foraging. The male takes on most of the responsibilities during breeding. The Plains-wanderer is among the rare species with a total population probably not exceeding 11 thousand birds.

Stercorarius parasiticus

ARCTIC SKUA **PA NA**

The Arctic skua is 16–18in/41–46cm long. It usually breeds in colonies of seabirds or on tundra in the north of Eurasia and North America. The clutch consists of 2 eggs that are incubated for four weeks. The skua's main prey are lemmings. This diet is supplemented with food stolen from fishermen, and other birds such as Atlantic puffins, Black-legged kittiwakes or guillemots. Wintering grounds are in oceans of the other side of the globe.

Stercorarius longicaudus

LONG-TAILED SKUA **PA NA**

The smallest skua has extremely long central rectrices, a black head-cap and yellowish cheeks. It breeds in

Stercorarius longicaudus

Arctic and sub-Arctic mountain tundra of Eurasia and North America. It frequents dry places in the breeding season and feeds mostly on lemmings. It hovers 32–64ft/10–20m above the ground before swooping on them. If the rodents become scarce, it is able to change its focus to shrews, insects, berries, small bird species and the young of seabirds. It migrates in winter to oceans in the southernmost part of the Earth.

Larus pacificus

PACIFIC GULL   **AU**

This rather large gull with dark gray back and wings is a sedentary resident of the southern shore of Australia and Tasmania. Its wingspan reaches almost 5.2ft/160cm. It forages for various animals by hunting on beaches and the tidal zone. It is not yet considered

an endangered species although its total population numbers under 10,000 pairs.

Larus crassirostris

BLACK-TAILED GULL   **PA**

The Black-tailed gull is distributed in a rather limited area from Japan and Korea to Sakhalin, where it frequents bays and estuaries. It breeds on sandy and rocky coasts, on ocean cliffs and off-shore islands, in colonies that commonly comprise more than 10,000 pairs. Its diet depends on the location and season of the year, although the significant part is formed by small fish, crustaceans and insects. It often follows fishing trawl boats.

Larus pacificus

Larus crassirostris

Larus canus

Larus canus
MEW GULL (COMMON GULL)   PA NA

The Mew gull belongs to the group of medium-sized gulls with gray upperparts. It breeds primarily on ocean coasts but also in the vicinity of large rivers and lakes. Its range includes Europe, Asia and North America. Its nest is usually placed on the ground in a shallow cavity or even on trees in the old nests of corvids. It feeds on any available animal food and also partly on seeds.

Larus schistisagus

Larus schistisagus
SLATY-BACKED GULL   PA

This large gull reaches the weight of 2.2–3.3lb/1–1.5kg and has a wingspan of up to 5 ft/1.5m. The mantle of the adult birds is dark gray with white spots on the tips of its wings. The breeding area includes the ocean coasts from Kamchatka to the northern parts of Japan. The wintering sites reach down south to Taiwan. It nests in colonies of up to 1,500 pairs on low ocean cliffs, rocky islands and low estuarine islands. The clutch usually consists of three eggs that are incubated for about four weeks. Looking after the nestlings consumes about the same time. It feeds mainly on fish and ocean invertebrates.

Larus argentatus

Larus argentatus
HERRING GULL   PA NA

The Herring gull is considerably larger than the Mew gull. It lives in Western and northern Europe, northern Asia and North America. It breeds mainly in coastal areas, but also inland on large water reservoirs. The nests are placed on rocky cliffs, islands, sandy beaches or house roofs. As for food, it has quite wide ranging tastes and accepts whatever is available.

Larus cachinnans
YELLOW-LEGGED GULL   PA

It is very similar to the Herring gull in the size and coloration, but differs by having yellow legs. Its range spans from southern Europe as far east as China. It breeds in colonies of up to 8,000 pairs.

Larus cachinnans

Larus fuscus

LESSER BLACK-BACKED GULL   **PA**

It is among the larger gulls: its body measures 20–24in/50–60cm and its wingspan is about 4ft/125cm. The adult birds are white with dark gray upperparts. It nests on sandy, rocky or grassy seashores, rocky islands, riverine and lake islands or buildings in the northern areas of Europe and Asia. Like the majority of gulls, it feeds on fish and other animal food of various origin.

Larus atricilla

LAUGHING GULL   **NA NT**

This medium-sized gull with a wingspan of slightly over 3.3ft/1m features a black head with a white eye-ring and a dark gray mantle. It only inhabits the ocean coasts of the Caribbean as well as the East and West coasts of North America. Breeding colonies of up to 10,000 pairs settle on sandy beaches or salt-marshes. Its main diet consists of aquatic invertebrates, and also, to a lesser extent, fish.

Larus fuscus

Larus atricilla

Larus cirrocephalus

Larus ridibundus

Larus cirrocephalus

GRAY-HEADED GULL   **AF NT**

Besides a gray mantle, this bird also has a gray head, and a bright red bill and legs. It belongs to the fauna of South America and South Africa. It inhabits tropical and subtropical sea coasts and also larger lakes and rivers. It builds its nests on bare ground, in growths of reeds and papyrus, or on islets of floating vegetation. It feeds mainly on fish and aquatic invertebrates.

Larus novaehollandiae

SILVER GULL   **AF AU**

This rather smaller gull has a wingspan of less than three feet. It is white with a gray back and wings. Its strong bill and legs are bright red. It belongs among the Australian species and its population is increasing. It can be found on both ocean coasts and inland waters. It accepts a wide variety of food ranging from aquatic and terrestrial vertebrates to invertebrates and fruit. It enjoys being fed by people.

Larus novaehollandiae

Larus melanocephalus

Larus ridibundus

COMMON BLACK-HEADED GULL   **PA NA**

It is easily identified during the breeding season by its dark head. It is distributed throughout Eurasia and, to a limited extent, also in the eastern part of North America and southern Greenland. It breeds in colonies, mostly in tideland vegetation and on islands in fresh water bodies. Spacious nests are built from plant matter gathered from the nearest surroundings. The complete clutch ordinarily consists of three dark spotted eggs. The incubation takes 22–24 days, the parental care of the chicks another four weeks. The wintering grounds are situated on the ocean coasts and ice-free rivers. The highest recorded age was 32 years.

Larus melanocephalus

MEDITERRANEAN GULL   **PA**

The bird closely resembles the Black-headed gull. However, its hood is very black and reaches to its nape. In addition, its primaries are pure white. Mainly frequenting the Ukrainian coasts of the Black Sea, it has also spread to the North Caucasian Plains and Azerbaijan. Otherwise, its populations are scattered throughout the whole of Europe. The breeding colonies only rarely consist of more than 1,000 pairs. It feeds mostly on insects, flying to quite arid localities up to 50 miles/80km away to forage.

Larus minutus

LITTLE GULL   **PA NA**

Its 10–12in/25–30cm long body and wingspan of less than 3ft/80cm make this bird the smallest gull. The breeding adults feature a black hood. Its relaxed flight recalls rather a tern than a gull. It is distributed from northern Europe to eastern Asia, occasionally also nesting on the Great Canadian Lakes. It breeds mostly in small colonies on densely overgrown fresh waters. It feeds especially on insects, hunting in flight above the water surface or while walking on the ground or in shallow water. It winters primarily on ocean coasts.

Larus minutus

Pagophila eburnea

Hydroprogne caspia

Pagophila eburnea

IVORY GULL   **PA NA**

The Ivory gull is all white except for dark legs and pale gray-blue bill. It is the northernmost sedentary bird. It inhabits pack-ice and cliffs near the Arctic Circle all year round. Small, loose breeding colonies are often in the neighbourhood of gathering places of seals and walruses. It exploits any food available, including carcasses and droppings of seals and polar bears. In winter, it is even able to swallow large pieces of completely frozen food.

Rissa tridactyla

BLACK-LEGGED KITTIWAKE   **PA NA**

This gray and white gull is undoubtedly the most abundant species of the North Atlantic. Its total population is estimated at 6–7 million pairs. It usually breeds in large colonies of about 10,000 pairs, though sometimes even up to 100,000 pairs, together with guillemots, Atlantic puffins, European shags and other seabirds. It builds a sturdy nest of seaweed and mud. The non-breeding times are spent at open sea. It feeds on small fish and crustaceans scooped from the water surface in flight.

Hydroprogne caspia

CASPIAN TERN   **PA AF OR AU NA**

Most terns feature a similar coloration. A white body is complemented by a gray back and wings and a black cap. The Caspian tern is the largest species, with a body length of 19–22in/48–56cm and a wingspan of 4–4.5ft/127–140cm. Besides its size, it is also easily identifiable by its large red bill. It can be found all around the world except Antarctica and South America. It usually frequents larger inland bodies of water and coastal lagoons, and for the most part it does not venture out on the high seas. A considerable part of its diet is comprised of medium-sized fish, although it also seizes eggs and young of other birds. Nor does it refuse to eat carrion, which is unusual in terns.

Rissa tridactyla

Thalasseus sandvicensis

Thalasseus bergii

Thalasseus sandvicensis

SANDWICH TERN   **PA NA NT**

This medium-sized tern whose wingspan barely reaches 3.3ft/1m is closely tied to the ocean coasts. It lives in Europe, and also on the Caspian Sea and in the New World. It breeds in remarkably dense colonies where the individual nests may be as close as 8in/20cm from each other. The largest known colonies are comprised of 35,000 pairs.

Thalasseus bergii

GREATER CRESTED TERN   **PA AF OR AU**

This large species with a wingspan of up to 4.5ft/130cm is distinguished by a stouter, longer bill, flat occipital feather crest and a white forehead. It frequents the coasts of tropical and subtropical seas and oceanic islands. It breeds on coral, rocky and sandy islands. Its main prey is fish 4–6in/10–15cm long, and also squid, crabs, insects and newly hatched turtles. It roosts on rocks in company with other terns and gulls.

Sterna hirundo

COMMON TERN   **PA AF NA NT**

Its body is 12.5–15.5/32–39cm long and reaches a wingspan of about 3ft/80cm. The bill is red with a black tip. The Common tern hunts by hovering above the water. As soon as a fish is spotted below, the bird dives down and plunges into the water after the prey. However, not every attack is successful. It breeds in pairs or in colonies of up to 1,000 pairs on ocean coasts or inland waters of Eurasia and North America. The clutch of 2–3 eggs is laid in a nest formed by just a simple depression in sandy silt. The incubation lasts 3–4 weeks as does the chick rearing period. Both

parents have an equal share of the family duties. The nest is fiercely defended and fearless attacks on an intruder are accompanied by harsh shrieks. In winter, the birds wander along the ocean coasts and in this fashion often get as far as the Southern Hemisphere.

Sterna hirundo

147

Sterna paradisea

Chlidonias hybridus

Sterna paradisaea

ARCTIC TERN   **PA NA**

It resembles the Common tern, but its beak is entirely red. It inhabits the northern regions of Eurasia and North America. The breeding colonies are situated on rocky islands, sandy expanses or tundra close to the coast. It is noted for making remarkably long migratory trips all the way to the Antarctic Ocean, during which the birds cover about 11,000 miles/18,000km. Its diet is dominated by small fish. While in Antarctic waters, it feeds (similarly to whales) on abundant plankton crustaceans.

Sterna albifrons

LITTLE TERN   **PA AF OR AU**

It is the smallest tern with the body size of a lark and a wingspan of about 20in/50cm. The yellow bill and legs are distinctive, as is its white forehead. Besides the New World and Antarctica, it can be found in temperate to tropical zones on all continents. It breeds on both the sea coasts and inland waters.

Sterna albifrons

Chlidonias leucoptera

Chlidonias niger

Chlidonias hybridus

WHISKERED TERN PA AF OR AU NA

It is the first representative of three specific, darker colored terns that occupy all the world except South America and Antarctica. They indefatigably move low above the water surface in effortless flight. The Whiskered Tern, with a body 10–12in/25–29cm long, is the largest marsh tern. It is all gray except for the white cheeks and lower belly, a black cap, red legs and bill. It inhabits all continents with the exception of North and South America. For breeding, it requires shallow, clean waters densely overgrown with marshy vegetation. It nests in pairs or in small colonies on floating leaves of aquatic plants. It preys mainly on aquatic insects, which are picked in flight off vegetation or the water surface.

Chlidonias leucopterus

WHITE-WINGED TERN PA AF OR AU

The whole body is black except for whitish wings and a contrasting white tail. Most of its life is spent tirelessly flying back and forth. When the bird rests on a branch or other object emerging from water, it holds its body horizontal and slightly retracts its head. The breeding grounds are located on fresh water bodies. The nests are often placed on marshy banks and any rise of the water level causes a great deal of damage to many of them. Insects constitute a major part of their diet. They migrate to the tropic and subtropic zones to winter on the ocean coasts or inland waters.

Chlidonias niger

BLACK TERN PA NA

Its head, neck and breast are deep black, while the rest of its body, except for the white undertail-coverts, is dark gray. It breeds in similar places in Eurasia and North America as the previous two species. The clutch of 2–3 eggs is warmed by both sexes for about three weeks. The young are capable of swimming right after

hatching, yet they stay in their nest, unless they are disturbed, where they are fed by parents.

Phaetusa simplex

LARGE-BILLED TERN NT

It is among the large terns with a body almost 16in/40cm long. It features a long yellow bill and a black, helmet-like cap. During the breeding season, it is to be found near large lakes and rivers in South America. It feeds mostly on fish, diving into the water for them from heights of 20–36ft/6–11m. It nests in pairs or in colonies of up to 100 pairs on sandy shores. It winters on rivers, ocean beaches, estuaries and mangroves.

Phaetusa simplex

Gygis alba

Gygis alba

WHITE TERN   AF OR AU NT

The plumage of this 15in/38cm long tern is pure white and extraordinarily fine. The bill is black and its small legs are gray. It inhabits the tropical zones of the Pacific and Indian Oceans. It breeds in trees and shrubs growing on coral islands, on cliffs, or sometimes even on buildings. Most often the single egg is laid on a platform on a branch fork or on an axil of a palm or banana leaf, which is located in an area from the ground up to 65ft/20m high. A nestling hatches within 30–40 days and features strong claws, which it uses to hold tightly to its bed.

Larosterna inca

Larosterna inca

INCA TERN   NT

Its plumage makes it absolutely unmistakable. Dark gray is predominant, while the white edges stand out on black-tipped wings. There is also a white stripe below the eye, which develops into a long feather beard, decurved at rest and fluttering in flight. The Inca Tern breeds on rocky cliffs of the western shore of South America, on the guano islands or places where large numbers of seabirds are concentrated. A female lays 1–2 eggs in a nest placed in a rock crevice or a ground penguin burrow.

Rynchops niger

BLACK SKIMMER   NA NT

It is one of the three skimmer species: peculiar, long-winged birds that inhabit waters of tropical regions. The Black skimmer is 16–18in/41–46cm long. It lives in the southern part of North America, and in Central and South America. It is strikingly black and white, with a long, laterally flattened black and red bill of which the lower mandible is considerably longer than the upper one. When foraging, the bird flies just above the water with its bill held open and the lower mandible constantly submerged in the water. This way it captures small invertebrates and fish. It breeds in colonies of up to 1,000 pairs on sandy beaches together with terns.

Rynchops niger

Alca torda

Alca torda

RAZORBILL   **PA NA**

The razorbill belongs to the seabirds of the northern oceans. It breeds in great numbers on rocky sea coasts along with other seabird species. It is less than 20in/50cm long and reaches a weight of 1.1–2lb/ 0.5–0.9kg. The very compressed, lateral bill is dark with a white line running along it. The legs are set well back on the body, similar to penguins who, in fact, much resemble auks when walking. The razorbill feeds mostly on fish and crustaceans, normally diving to 50ft/15m, but very occasionally reaching depths of as much as 400ft/120m. The female lays one egg in a rocky crag. The chick hatches within 30–35 days.

Fratercula arctica

ATLANTIC PUFFIN   **PA NA**

It inhabits the coasts of the North Atlantic and the Arctic Ocean, from Greenland to Novaya Zemlya. The bird measures only about 12in/30cm. Its high, flat bill is decorated with red, yellow and gray patterns. It breeds in rocky cavities, or in burrows up to 6.5ft/2m long that individual pairs dig with their beaks and claws. The female lays one egg that is warmed by both parents for about 6 weeks. It forages primarily for fish by diving to depths of up to 65ft/20m. The Atlantic puffin is among the most abundant seabirds. The total population is estimated at 6 million pairs.

Fratercula arctica

151

10. Sandgrouse and Pigeons

Until recently, sandgrouse (Pteroclidae) *were considered to be a part of the Columbiformes order until two separate orders were formed. According to some recent opinions, the sandgrouse may be classified together with the Charadriiformes.*

Pterocliformes

SANDGROUSE

All 16 sandgrouse species typically inhabit deserts and semi-deserts, or steppes. They usually nest in places where there is no available water nearby. Therefore, daily, usually in the evening, they fly in flocks to watering places that are often dozens of miles away from their breeding quarters. They drink in an entirely different way than the majority of other birds: they immerse their bills deeply into the water and suck in the water with the aid of movements of the lower mandible. They are highly gregarious. Outside the breeding season they live together in tight flocks while in breeding times the flocks are fewer in number. They are strictly terrestrial creatures and run very fast despite having short legs. Their deft motions on sandy or dusty, soft substrates are supported by wide toes that are partly webbed at the base and sometimes feathered down to their claws. The hind toe is either small and inconsequential or missing. The bill is short and hard, covered with feathers to the nostrils, and is lacking the cere. The soundgrouse nests in a scraped pit in the ground where 2–4 spotted eggs are laid. Like chickens,

Left: *Zenaida macroura*
Syrrhaptes paradoxus

the young are hatched fairly precocial, covered with down, and soon wander off from the nest. They are, nevertheless, fed by their parents, and therefore called semi-nidifugous. The adults water them in a quite peculiar way: at watering places they let the soft plumage on their belly become soaked and the young suck water from there.

Syrrhaptes paradoxus

PALLAS'S SANDGROUSE   PA

The Pallas's sandgrouses' breeding grounds are located from the Caspian Sea to Mongolia and Manchuria. The wings produce whistling sounds in flight. It inhabits the semi-deserts and steppes, especially where there is wormwood cover. During the courtship display, the calling male runs or flies around the female. The female lays usually 3 (2–4) eggs and incubates them for about 30 days with the occasional help from her partner. For reasons that are not very well known, the sandgrouse, from time to time, leave home grounds and appear as far away as Central and Western Europe or Eastern China. Such erratic migrations are called invasions.

Columbiformes

PIGEONS AND DOVES

Pigeons and doves feed on plant food, mainly seeds and fruits. That is why they have a well developed crop with two side wattles that serve to soften the hard food and as a temporary reservoir. A specific phenomena can be observed during breeding: the mucous membrane of the crop swells, begins to peel off and forms a cottage cheese-like material known as "crop-milk" used to feed the nestlings for the first few days after hatching. The volume is sufficient for feeding only two young. Therefore, pigeons increase their breeding rate by laying two or three, and as an exception, even four clutches a year. The uropygial gland is poorly evolved; for preening, a powder is used which peels off the powder-downs. The bill is horny only at its tip while the base is soft, covered by fleshy cere on the upper mandible. The great majority of columbids live in trees yet they move on the ground quite well. They have walking legs with four toes. They drink by immersing their bill and sucking water without raising their heads. All pigeons are excellent, fast and capable flyers, and many of them migrate to distant wintering grounds. Secondarily, non-flying pigeons used to be members of the Raphidae family. They lived on Mauritius, Rodrigues and Réunion Islands, reached a weight of up to 55lb/25kg and became extinct, as a result of human contact, during the 16th and 17th centuries. The most known is the Dodo (Raphus cu-

Columba livia

culatus). Some world museums keep remains of skeletons or skin of these birds. Pigeons and doves form monogamous pairs, engaging in conspicuous courting displays during flight. The nests are mostly built on branches of trees and bushes; some species, however, also build their nests in rocky crevices and caves, in tree-hollows and on man-made structures. A clutch consists of 1–2 white eggs that are incubated by both partners. The young are nidicolous, they hatch almost bare, blind and are completely dependent on parental care. Two hundred and eighty three species of columbids are distinguished.

Columba palumbus

Columba livia

ROCK DOVE   **PA AF OR AU NA NT**

The Rock dove lives in Scotland and Ireland, in the Hebrides, Iberian Peninsula, north-western Africa, the Mediterranean, Arabia and India. It is the wild ancestor of all species of pigeons. After several generations, the feral pigeons have come to resemble the Rock dove and inhabit towns all around the world. The typical habitat of the Rock dove are rocks and cliffs with ledges, cracks and caves suitable for breeding. In India, however, the Rock dove nests on buildings in a manner similar to the semi-wild feral pigeons and breeds up to four times a year.

Columba palumbus

COMMON WOODPIGEON   **PA**

The Common woodpigeon is the largest European pigeon. It lives in Eurasia, from the Iberian Peninsula to western Siberia and the Himalayas, and also in North Africa. Originally, it lived in woods of all kinds; in the last decades, it also has begun to nest and breed in town parks and gardens. The northern populations are migratory. The males are distinctive in the spring because of their aerial courting display which involves the clapping of wings at the peak of their flight and loud hooting calls. It nests in thinly woven nests in tree crowns; only in the Orkneys, where trees are scarce, does it nest on the ground. It feeds mainly on various seeds including acorns, beech nuts and spruce cone seeds. Mollusks, earthworms and insects are also part of the woodpigeon's diet.

Streptopelia turtur

Streptopelia decaocto

buildings, beams, gutters, poles, etc. Sometimes it uses non-traditional material to build its nest, and is known for building a nest made of wires.

Streptopelia semitorquata

RED-EYED DOVE   AF

The Red-eyed dove is a common species in most of sub-Saharan Africa, except the furthest southwest area. It lives in gallery and mangrove forests, in acacia forests, on plantations, and in town parks and gardens. The conditions that allow it to proliferate seem to be tall trees and the availability of water. It breeds all year round in bushes or trees in nests from 1ft/30cm to 60ft/18m above the ground.

Streptopelia turtur

EUROPEAN TURTLE DOVE   PA

The European Turtle dove lives in Europe, Asia Minor, Central Asia and also in the Saharan oases. It prefers park-like country where groves and other types of greenery are interspersed with open areas. It feeds mainly on the seeds of cultured and wild plants in these areas. On occasion, it nests in gardens and parks at town edges and in the suburbs. The nests are built low in bushes and shrubs or in palm trees in the Saharan oases. It is migratory throughout most of its range, wintering primarily in the sub-Saharan savanna zone.

Streptopelia decaocto

EURASIAN COLLARED-DOVE   PA OR

During the 17th and 18th centuries, the Eurasian collared-dove migrated from India west all the way to the Balkans. From there, the expansion to Europe took place in the 1930s, and by the 1980s, it had already bred at the Faeroe Islands and Iceland. At present, the bird can be found throughout Europe, Asia, northern China, and Japan. Around 1980, it was introduced in Florida, in the United States, and it is expected that the bird will spread quickly throughout the country. In its original homeland, it inhabited open, park-like country in the vicinity of human settlements. In Europe, it became more integrated into the habitat of towns and villages which enabled it to survive winters, even at high latitudes. The bird is very adaptable and has learned how to use other sources of food, such as offal, fodder, and garbage. It nests not only in trees, but also in alcoves of

Streptopelia semitorquata

155

Streptopelia chinensis

Streptopelia chinensis

SPOTTED DOVE   **OR**

The Spotted dove's original homeland is the Oriental region from India and Sri Lanka to China and Malayan Peninsula. It lives in wet, deciduous forests and frequently in villages and towns. It mostly lives in pairs, large flocks dwell in but the places where there is an abundance of food, like ripe rice fields. In 1870, the bird was introduced into Australia, where it has thrived on the eastern and southeastern coasts, inhabiting towns, town parks and gardens. It can breed any time of the year.

Streptopelia senegalensis

LAUGHING DOVE   **PA AF**

The Laughing dove lives in Africa, eastern Mediterranean Afghanistan and Turkmenia, and in certain areas in Asia Minor. It was also brought to Australia where it does well in the southwest, especially around Perth. It used to inhabit dry, shrubby biotopes with grassy areas in the vicinity of water; later, it appeared in towns where it now has a larger population than in its original habitat. It became tamed in town parks and can be fed from hand. It builds its nests in trees, axil of palm leaves, or alcoves of buildings.

Chalcophaps indica

EMERALD DOVE   **AU OR**

The Emerald dove is found on the Indian subcontinent eastwards to the Philippines, and also lives in northern and eastern Australia. It inhabits various types of forests, from rain and mangrove to dry eucalyptus forests, lowlands, mountains, and also plantations and gardens. It often flies to natural saltpans to replenish its minerals. It is migratory within parts of its range, as indicated by repeated sightings of the bird by boats on the open sea or by lighthouse keepers far from land. However, the details of its migratory ways are unknown.

Streptopelia senegalensis

Chalcophaps indica

Phaps chalcoptera

Phaps chalcoptera

COMMON BRONZEWING AU

The Common bronzewing, found across Australia and Tasmania, breeds abundantly in these areas and is sedentary. It inhabits coastal shrubbery and various types of bush-lands and hard-leafed forests. It is also often found in gardens and along the roads. Unlike the other Australian pigeons from the arid zones, its breeding is not influenced by the rainy season. It nests up to 13ft/4m above the ground. The nest may be just a simple platform of twigs as well as a 4in/10cm high structure.

Ocyphaps lophotes

CRESTED PIGEON AU

The Crested pigeon's flight is accompanied by a whistling sound. The bird noticeably lifts its long tail when landing. It lives across Australia in sparse forests near the water, along roads and railroads, and also in towns, especially in the areas where grain is grown. It builds a flat, fragile nest in the forks of tree branches at heights of approximately 10ft/3m above the ground. It is often reared in captivity in bird aviaries.

Ocyphaps lophotes

157

Petrophassa scripta

Geophaps scripta
(Petrophassa scripta)

SQUATTER PIGEON   AU

In its range in northeast Australia, the Squatter pigeon prefers to reside in sparse eucalyptus forests and adjoining savanna. Previously, it used to inhabit the open plains in the south where today it is very rare. It seems that it breeds all year long with a peak in the dry season. The nest, sparsely lined with grass, is just a small pit in the ground under clumps of grasses or bushes. The young leave the nest very soon after hatching, when they are approximately nine days old.

Geopelia striata

Scardafella squamata

Geopelia striata

ZEBRA DOVE   **OR**

The Zebra dove's home-land is the Indo-Malayan region and the Philippines. Since the last century, it has been introduced to several other areas of the world, such as Madagascar, Hawaii, St. Helena Island, Mauritius, and elsewhere. The introductions of the Zebra dove to these areas were all successful and the bird breeds without problems. It prefers open country with scattered vegetation, but does not avoid cultivated landscapes or suburban gardens. It often breeds in the growth bordering waterways. The nest, which is not very firm, is built in tree branches several meters above the ground.

Scardafella squammata

SCALED DOVE   **NT**

The Scaled dove lives in South America: Colombia, Venezuela, and Guiana as well as central and eastern Brazil, northeastern Argentina and Bolivia. It seeks dry, tropical savannas, with scattered trees and shrubbery, and coastal thickets. It visits cultivated areas as well as residential settings. It nests and breeds in bushes and small trees about 7ft/2m above the ground, and sometimes on the ground.

Caloenas nicobarica

NICOBAR PIGEON   **AU OR**

The Nicobar pigeon lives on the islands of the Indo-Australian region between the Nicobars, Philippines, and New Guinea. It inhabits islands that are densely overgrown with primeval forests or mangroves as well as secondary forests. It only roosts and nests in trees; otherwise, it mostly moves on the ground in the deep shade of dense tree cover. The bird is nomadic and flies up to several hundred miles between the islands when its favourite seeds and fruits have ripened. During the courtship display, the male ruffles its mantle of the elongated feathers. It breeds in colonies usually on small islands. Undisturbed colonies may have thousands of pairs. The clutch contains only a single egg.

Otidiphaps nobilis

PHEASANT PIGEON   **AU**

The Pheasant pigeon, which is a pigeon with pheasant-like looks and behavior, is almost all black except for the chestnut brown wings and red bill. The body is 20in/0.5m long at the most and its weight is approximately 1.1lb/0.5kg. It lives alone, or in pairs, on the ground in the forests of New Guinea. The bird strongly prefers to live in the original rain forests. It is a slow walking bird that feeds on seeds and fallen fruits. The nest, made of thin twigs, is built at the base of a tree or bush. The clutch consists of only one creamy white egg that is incubated for 23 to 26 days.

Caloenas nicobarica

Otidiphaps nobilis

159

Goura cristata

Goura cristata

WESTERN CROWNED PIGEON AU

The Crowned pigeons are the largest pigeons, reaching the size of a small turkey. Their most significant characteristic is their magnificent, large crest of fine feathers. The Western Crowned pigeon inhabits the rain forests of New Guinea and other islands, and is also found in swampy and partly flooded areas and mangroves. The large nest of twigs is built 33ft/10m above the ground. The bird lays just one egg that is incubated by both parents for 28 to 29 days.

Goura victoria

Goura victoria

VICTORIA CROWNED PIGEON   **AU**

The Victoria Crowned pigeon lives in the northern part of New Guinea and surrounding islands. Most of its life is spent on the ground in swampy growths of sago-palm and dry forests where it picks its food of fallen fruits, berries and seeds. This activity is usually done in groups. The nest is often made of palm and reed leaves, stems, and twigs. The young do not return to the home nest. Crowned pigeons are among the endangered species.

Ptilinopus superbus

SUPERB FRUIT DOVE   **AU**

With its coloration, the Superb Fruit dove truly earns its name. It lives on Sulawesi, Moluccas, New Guinea, and other islands. It also can be found on the northeastern coastal area of Australia. In these areas, the bird inhabits both untouched rain forests and mangroves as well as secondary forests, and other areas overgrown with shrubbery, as long as fruit is available. On occasion, it will nest near human settlements. The male sits on the single egg during the day and the female incubates at night.

Ptilinopus pulchellus

BEAUTIFUL FRUIT DOVE   **AU**

The Beautiful Fruit dove is found in New Guinea and the islands of western Papua. It inhabits primary as well as secondary forests, preferring the areas with the highest rainfall. It feeds on fruit that it picks using a variety of acrobatic positions. The nest is only a platform of twigs on the side branches near the top of a tree. The clutch consists of a single egg.

Ptilinopus pulchellus

Ducula bicolor

PIED IMPERIAL PIGEON   **AU OR**

The Pied Imperial pigeon really only has two colors: white and black. It is found from the coast of Burma through the Malayan Peninsula, Indonesia, Philippines and New Guinea. In Australia, it only lives in the northern coastal areas. Its habitats are mainly rain forests, mangroves, and plantations of coconut palms. It usually breeds in colonies on islands. From these islands it flies, in flocks at approximately 230ft/70m above the sea, in order to feed on other islands or on the mainlands.

Ptilinopus superbus

Ducula bicolor

11. Parrots and Allies

Parrots (Psittaciformes) *are the most intelligent birds because they have the most evolved brain of all birds. If they are raised among people, they easily become tame and grow to be darling family pets. They are capable of faithfully imitating all different kinds of sounds, including human words. Their longevity is also remarkable; the large species may live to be 50–60 years old. Due to all these qualities, parrots have become popular cage birds, which has created a danger of extinction for many of them. That is why 71 of 344 parrot species are currently protected worldwide. The parrots are undoubtedly a distinctive bird group with a number of characteristic features. They have high, deep hooked bills with upper mandibles which considerably overlap the lower. The upper jaw is not firmly grown together with the skull, as in other birds, but is attached to it by a "joint" of a kind that allows movements up and down. In addition, the lower jaw can move sideways and thus the bill, along with the very agile tongue, is a versatile, ingenious instrument. The upper mandible of many species has transversal "filing-grooves" which enable firm holding and cracking of hard food. The parrots' tongue is fleshy and features sensoring taste cells. It sometimes even has a pit at its tip, as in cockatoos, which serves as a spoon for picking seeds from gnawn at fruits. Other species, such as lorikeets, have brush-like erectile papillae on their tongues that enable them to lick juices and pick nectar and pollen from flowers. Also, the leg is a self-contained instrument. The tarsus is short, fairly revolving, two toes point forward, while the other two backwards, and the leg is thus perfectly built for climbing in branches as well as for holding food and bringing it to the bill, a characteristic exclusive to the bird kingdom. Very colorful plumage is kept in good condition by the powder formed by disintegrating of powderdowns mainly in the rump area. The uropygial gland is only slightly developed and the parrots therefore do not wax their plumage. Their family life is also quite interesting. The pair bonds are often lifelong and partners pronouncedly cling to each other. Demonstrations of affection can be observed all year long. The birds mutually preen their feathers, touch with their bills and feed each other. Almost invariably, all of them nest in hollows and lay white eggs. Only the Monk Parakeets build large spherical nests in trees. Night Parrots nest in tussocks on the ground. Nidicolous chicks are hatched naked and blind and the parents feed them in the nest for a long time. The parrots' diet is mainly of plant origin, although they also eat insects, especially while feeding their nestlings. The vast majority of parrots are very sociable and live in flocks either all year round, or at least after breeding.*

Left: *Ara ararauna*

Trichoglossus haematodus

RAINBOW LORIKEET   **AU**

The Rainbow lorikeet lives in northeastern, eastern and southeastern Australia, Tasmania, the Solomon Islands, New Hebrides, New Caledonia and other islands. It inhabits various types of woodland including rain and open forests, bush-lands and town parks and gardens. Like other lorikeets, it takes nectar and pollen from flowers with its brushy tongue and licks sweet sap from trees and juicy fruits. In many towns, the lorikeets are so tame that they can be hand-fed. The female lays 1–3 eggs in a tree-hollow and sits on them alone, while the male feeds her regularly. After breeding the families group in nomadic or even migratory flocks, often of up to several hundred birds.

Trichoglossus haematodus

Trichoglossus johnstoniae

Glossopsitta concinna

Trichoglossus johnstoniae

MINDANAO LORIKEET   OR

The parrot's home is the Mindanao Island in the Philippines where it frequents montane forests at altitudes of 3,300–8,200ft/1,000–2,500m. It flies down to lower altitudes and returns at sunrise for roosting. It nests in cavities made by woodpeckers where the female lays two eggs and incubates them alone. The young leave the nest when they are about 6 weeks old. The bird is among the endangered species.

Psitteuteles goldiei (Trichoglossus goldiei)

GOLDIE'S LORIKEET   AU

The Goldie's lorikeet inhabits mountain forests in New Guinea at altitudes of 9,200ft/2,800m. It is a nomadic species that migrates towards flowering trees. It nests in tree cavities, in which the female lays 2 eggs.

Trichoglossus goldiei

Eolophus roseicapillus

Glossopsitta concinna

MUSK LORIKEET   **AU**

The Musk lorikeet is found in eastern and southeastern Australia and Tasmania. It inhabits cultivated open forests and suburban areas. Mature, dense forests are avoided. It nests in hollows in branches or trunks, most often high in a eucalyptus, occasionally near water. The clutch usually is two eggs and is incubated for 21–22 days.

Calyptorhynchus banksii
(C. magnificus)

RED-TAILED BLACK COCKATOO   **AU**

The Red-tailed Black cockatoo lives in western, northern and eastern Australia, especially in eucalyptus and open savanna forests. This bird can be compared to the woodpecker, a species not found in Australia. It peels the bark off and hollows large holes in tree trunks from where it picks insect larvae. It also feeds on various fruits, seeds and sprouts. A female sits on one egg in a tree-hollow. The young does not fledge until after 3 months and reaches sexual maturity at 4 years. The birds live in pairs and form noisy, often large flocks outside the breeding season.

Eolophus roseicapillus

GALAH   **AU**

The galah inhabits all of Australia and is the second most numerous parrot in the area after the Budgerigar. Its range has enlarged during the past 50 years. It can be found in all types of habitat including town gardens. It nests in tree cavities and often several pairs

nest in close proximity. The tree hollow is lined with green leaves on which the female lays 2–6 eggs. She takes turns with the male at warming the eggs. The pair guards the nest hole the entire year and roosts nearby. When the chicks leave the nest, they congregate in nearby trees where they form creches of up to hundred young birds. They can recognize their parents by voice and always fly to the same tree in order to feed. Later, the families join to form flocks, sometimes of up to 1,000 birds, which fly around the area and often cause considerable damage to crops.

Calyptorhynchus magnificus

165

Cacatua sulphurea

Cacatua alba

Cacatua sulphurea

YELLOW-CRESTED COCKATOO   AU

The Yellow-crested cockatoo's homeland can be found in the Lesser Sundas, Sulawesi, Flores and other islands. It was also introduced to Hong Kong and Singapore. It occupies wooded as well as cultivated areas, though it does not live inside the forests. It also can be found in town parks and gardens. A female lays 2–3 eggs in a tree-hole and sits on them, taking turns with her partner, for about 27 days. The young leave the nest after about 10 weeks. Outside the breeding season, the birds live in flocks. It is listed among vulnerable species on the list of the world's endangered species.

Cacatua alba

WHITE COCKATOO   AU

The White cockatoo occupies northern and central Moluccas. Populations in Obi and Bisa islands probably developed from birds that escaped from captivity. During the breeding season, it lives in pairs in forests, nesting in tree-hollows. Even after breeding, the birds keep living in pairs or small groups. No large flocks

Cacatua sanguinea

Nymphicus hollandicus

have ever been observed. The White Cockatoo is also a vulnerable species.

Cacatua sanguinea

LITTLE CORELLA   **AU**

The Little corella is found throughout Australia and New Guinea. The origin of the Tasmanian population is unknown. It lives in moonsoon-like forests and also in semi-desert areas with shrubs and trees. It also is found in agriculture country and in vegetation along watercourses and water reservoirs. It breeds in cavities of trunks and in the branches of trees, most commonly eucalyptus. In non-breeding times, the birds congregate in flocks (as many as 32,000 birds have been observed in a single flock) that forage for seeds, fruits, flowers, insects and their larvae. The Little corella is nomadic in arid areas.

Nymphicus hollandicus

COCKATIEL   **AU**

The cockatiel inhabits almost all of Australia except for some coastal areas. It lives on extensive savannas with bushes and trees, often close to rivers and water reservoirs. Large flocks migrate to places abundant in plant seeds and water. They may not visit a certain area for years and then suddenly appear in great numbers. The cockatiel nests in tree hollows where a female lays 3–7 eggs. She sits on them at night, while the male mainly incubates the eggs during day. The birds enter the nest tail first. Under favourable conditions, the pairs may breed several times a year.

Cyclopsitta diophthalma (Opopsitta diophthalma)

DOUBLE-EYED FIG-PARROT   **AU**

The Double-eyed Fig-parrot is the smallest Australian parrot with a body 5–5.5in/13–14cm long. It lives on the eastern coast of Australia in rain, monsoon-like forests and gallery forests, and wooded savanna. It also inhabits New Guinea and neighbouring islands as well as Aru Island. It hollows out cavities in arboreal termitaria, and frequently several pairs occupy one of these. A female lays only two eggs and incubates them alone for about 3 weeks.

Opopsitta diophthalma

Psittinus cyanurus

Prioniturus mada

Psittinus cyanurus

BLUE-RUMPED PARROT   **OR**

The homeland of the Blue-rumped parrot is southern Burma, southwestern Thailand, Malaysia, Sumatra, and Kalimantan (Borneo). It lives on the edges, and in clearings, of rain forests and on plantations of coconut and oil-palms. It feeds on seeds, fruits and shoots. The nest, in which a female lays 3 eggs, is established high above the ground in hollows of healthy trees. At present, it is nearly considered a endangered species.

Prioniturus mada

BURU RACQUET-TAIL   **AU**

This bird has fairly limited distribution and lives only on Buru Island of the Moluccas. It features elongated rectrices that end in oval discs. It frequents rain forests up to the altitudes of 5,800ft/1,750m. It nests in branch or trunk hollows. The Buru Racquet-tail is among the strictly protected parrot species.

Eclectus roratus

ECLECTUS PARROT   **AU**

The Eclectus parrot is distinctive because it has the most pronounced sexual dimorphism found among bird species. The male and female were for a long time even considered to be two separate species. The male is predominantly green, while the female is red. The bird inhabits the islands of Indonesia and Melanesia, while in Australia, it lives only in the north on the York Peninsula. It can be found in rain and adjacent savanna forests, mangroves, palm plantations, park-like country, and gardens. It breeds in tree-holes. Several birds of both sexes (as many as 8) were observed a number of times in a nest cavity with eggs and nestlings. This suggests that some pairs may have helpers during breeding.

Aprosmictus erythropterus

RED-WINGED PARROT   **AU**

The Red-winged parrot is about 13in/32cm long. The male is predominantly pale green with a blackish-green back and a large red patch on its wings. The green of the female's body is duller. She does not have a dark back and the wing patch is considerably smaller in size. The parrot is found in northern and north-eastern Australia and in southern New Guinea. It most often frequents eucapyptus and casuarina forests and also lives in mangroves, dry acacia shrubberies and forest savanna, only rarely dwelling far from water. It is shy and dwells in tree tops where it feeds on fruits, seeds, blossoms, nectar, and insects and their larvae. It also flies to fields with ripening grain. It nests high in hollows in trunks or thick branches. A female lays 3–6 eggs and warms them for about 3 weeks. Usu-

Eclectus roratus

ally in the morning and late afternoon, the male leaves the clutch for a while in order to feed the incubating partner. The young leave the nest at about 5 weeks of age. After breeding, the birds associate in flocks of up to several dozen.

Aprosmictus erythropterus

Aprosmictus erythropterus

Melopsittacus undulatus

Melopsittacus undulatus
BUDGERIGAR   AU

The budgerigar is the most abundant Australian parrot. It lives almost everywhere on the continent except the coastal areas. It nests in semi-desert and steppe areas with tree and bush cover. It is nomadic and migrates to places where there are plenty of grass seeds and bodies of water. It begins to breed just a few days after the advent of the rainy season and in favourable circumstances, the pairs may breed up to three times in a season. It nests in all kinds of cavities, not only in tree trunks and branches, but also in poles, tree stumps, and hollow trunks lodged on the ground. The juveniles are capable of breeding at the age of 3 months. After breeding, the birds congregate in flocks numbering hundreds of thousands. These, however, always become nearly catastrophically thin dur-

Anodorhynchus hyacinthinus

ing the long-lasting dry seasons. The budgerigar is the most popular cage parrot and many breeds showing color and shape varieties have been cultivated. In the natural form it is, however, always green.

Anodorhynchus hyacinthinus
HYACINTH MACAW   NT

The Hyacinth macaw is the largest parrot in the world measuring as much as 3.3ft/1m. It lives in Brazil, Bolivia and Paraguay in both deep primeval woods and palm forests. It nests mainly in cavities or in holes in clay walls by water. Two to three eggs are incubated by the female alone. The young are fed in the nest hollow by both parents for about 3.5 months. Very often, only one nestling fledges. The parrot feeds mainly on palm nuts. This often proves fatal on guarded coconut plantations. It belongs amongst strictly protected species.

Ara ararauna

Owing to the illegal trade, especially between 1970–90, its numbers were reduced to only 3,000 individuals.

Ara ararauna
BLUE-AND-YELLOW MACAW   NT

The Blue-and-yellow macaw lives in Central and South America from Panama to eastern Peru and northeastern Bolivia. It also used to live in northern Argentina, Paraguay and Trinidad. In Ecuador, it was evidently eradicated by human activity. It inhabits all different types of forests, including tall trees along watercourses, and palms. It nests in hollows of the tallest trees, palms included. Its "marriages" are apparently lifelong and the pairs hold together even in flocks. After breeding, the flocks stick to their regular roosting quarters. The birds disperse early every morning to feed as far as 16 miles/25km away and return back after sunset.

Ara glaucogularis
(Ara caninde)

BLUE-THROATED MACAW   **NT**

The Blue-throated macaw can only be found in northern Bolivia near Santa Cruz. It lives in temporarily flooded savannas with palm trees as well as remainders of the tropical forest. Most frequently, it breeds in hollows in palm trees. It strongly resembles the previous species (some zoologists even consider it a subspecies of *Ara ararauna*) but it has a blue throat and blue stripes on whitish cheeks, while the Blue-and-yellow macaw has black stripes on its chin and cheeks. The other Latin name currently used is *Ara caninde*.

Ara militaris

Ara caninde

Ara chloroptera

RED-AND-GREEN MACAW   **NT**

The breeding region of the Red-and-green macaw stretches from Panama to northern Argentina, Paraguay and southeastern Brazil. It lives in deep primeval forests from lowlands to hills, in swamps with mangrove vegetation and savannas. It spends most of the time in nests found in tree hollows high above the ground and in holes dug out of sand-gravel cliffs. Large flocks of both Military and Red-and-green macaws are regularly observed in southeastern Peru in forests on clay salt pans where they use their bills to scrape off and swallow fine particles. These parrots eat seeds and unripe fruits containing toxic alkaloids.

Ara militaris

MILITARY MACAW   **NT**

The Military macaw is found in Mexico and the western parts of South America in a scattered region from Colombia to Argentina. It lives in evergreen and oak-beech forests, usually at altitudes of 2,000–8,500ft/ 600–2,600m, though it has been seen in the Andes as high as 11,500ft/3,500m. The vegetation along watercourses allows it to live in semi-desert areas. It nests high in tree-hollows, and is also known for nesting in holes scraped in sandy walls. The female lays 2–3 eggs and sits on them for 24–26 days, while the male feeds her. The Military macaw is considered to be a vulnerable species.

Ara chloroptera

Ara rubrogenys

Ara rubrogenys
RED-FRONTED MACAW NT

The Red-fronted macaw occupies only a limited area in central Bolivia. It inhabits dry mountain shrublands, deciduous forests, and cactus growths in mountain valleys and gorges at altitudes of 3,600–8,200ft/1,100–2,500m. It nests in crevices of rock faces, often in loose colonies. The clutch of 1–3 eggs is incubated for about 26 days. The bird is among the highly endangered parrot species, with a total feral population of about 1,000 birds.

Propyrrhura maracana

Propyrrhura maracana
BLUE-WINGED MACAW NT

The Blue-winged macaw is predominantly green, with bluish head. Its forehead and rump are orange red, and the central tail feathers are red at their base. The parrot measures about 19in/48cm and frequents edges of the evergreen tropical forests, gallery forests, and palm groves. The clutch is comprised of 3 eggs. The Blue-winged macaw can be found in Brazil, Paraguay, and northeastern Argentina. It is among vulnerable species and, in last few decades, is hardly found at all in locations where it used to be numerous.

Aratinga finschi
CRIMSON-FRONTED PARAKEET NT

The homelands of the Crimson-fronted parakeet are only in eastern Nicaragua, Costa Rica and western Panama. It nests in light forests and forest margins, on coffee plantations, and in farmed areas with scattered greenery. It often roosts in vegetation near or right in towns. It feeds on flowers and fruits, often wild figs, and sometimes causes damage to corn and grain crops. It breeds in tree holes hewn out of partly rotten trunks or layers of epiphytes. Pairs often nest close to each other. There are 2–4 eggs in a clutch.

Aratinga solstitialis
SUN PARAKEET NT

The Sun parakeet inhabits Guiana, Surinam, and northern Brazil. It seeks open savanna with trees, wooded valleys, and occasionally also flooded and secondary forests. It feeds mostly on fruits, seeds, shoots, and other plant matter. The pairs set their nests in cavities in palms, usually of the *Mauritia* genus. A clutch of 4–6 eggs is warmed by female alone for about 28 days. The young leave the nest approximately after 8 weeks. After breeding, the parrots form numerous flocks numbering up to several hundred birds.

Aratinga finschi

Rhynchopsitta pachyrhyncha

THICK-BILLED PARROT   **NT**

The Thick-billed parrot inhabits northwestern and central Mexico, where it is found in the mountains at high altitudes, sometimes even over 11,500ft/3,500m, and in pine forests. It usually nests in cavities in old pine trees and pine seeds make up the bulk of its diet. In winter, it descends to altitudes of about 5,000ft/1,500m. It is the only parrot ever found in the United States. It used to visit Arizona to harvest pine seeds. Occasionally, individual pairs would also nest there. However, the clearing of the forests in the first half of the 20th century interrupted these migrations and attempts to reintroduce the birds to the region have failed. The species is strictly protected.

Pyrrhura rupicola

BLACK-CAPPED PARAKEET   **NT**

The Black-capped parakeet is fairly common in the subtropical zone of central and northeastern Peru, northern Bolivia, and western Brazil. It inhabits damp lowland and seasonally flooded forests. Its area reaches as far as the foothills of the Andes. Not much is known about its life in the wilderness.

Aratinga solstitialis

Pyrrhura rupicola

Rhynchopsitta pachyrhyncha

173

Amazona leucocephala

Amazona leucocephala

CUBAN AMAZON   **NT**

The Cuban amazon lives in Cuba, the Bahamas,
Pinosu, Great Cayman and several smaller islands in
the Caribbean Sea. It inhabits forests and savannas
with groups of pine and palm trees, mangroves, plantations and gardens. It nests in tree-hollows and in
ground burrows in limestone areas. The female lays
2–6 eggs. The parrot is nearly endangered. The Cuban
population has declined rapidly due to the loss of suitable habitat. About 5,000 birds populated the area in
1988.

Amazona pretrei

RED-SPECTACLED AMAZON   **NT**

The Red-spectacled amazon can be found only in
southern Brazil and very rarely in Argentina and
Paraguay. It lives in forests dominated by *Araucaria*
trees and in forest savannas. It nests in tree-holes, usually not very high above the ground, where 2–4 eggs

Amazona pretrei

are laid. It belongs among the endangered species. Its population was estimated at 7,500–8,500 birds by the beginning of the 1990s. The main reasons for the decline are the destruction and fragmentation of the breeding habitat and the illegal bird trade.

Amazona festiva

FESTIVE AMAZON	NT

The Festive amazon is found from eastern Colombia to Venezuela, Guaiana and northern Brazil. It is principally found in damp or invariably flooded forests along large watercourses avoids dry forests. Details of its breeding and feeding habits are unknown.

Amazona aestiva

BLUE-FRONTED AMAZON	NT

The Blue-fronted amazon can be found in eastern Brazil, northern Argentina, Paraguay, and Bolivia, and is the most numerous of all the amazons. Apparently, cultivation of corn, sunflowers, and other plants, where it causes considerable crop damage, suits the bird well. This is also true for citrus crops. It is a popular cage bird that has a good ability for learning how to "speak." Between 1985–90, almost 250,000 birds were exported from Argentina. During breeding season, it lives in pairs in forests and nests in hollows in old trees that are often used for several years. It also nests occasionally in tree termitaries. The female sits on 3–5 eggs alone for 23–25 days. The young leave the nest after two months.

Amazona aestiva

Triclaria malachitacea

BLUE-BELLIED PARROT	NT

The Blue-bellied parrot is very rare and therefore is strictly protected. It lives only in southeastern Brazil, inhabitings wet forests in the valleys of watercourses. Pairs are mostly found in the tops of trees richly overgrown with bromeliads. It nests in natural holes in trees, including palms. It defends its territory so fiercely that the nests may often be up to 1.3 mile/2km apart. The female lays 2–4 eggs and warms them for about 28 days.

Amazona festiva

Triclaria malachitacea

12. Cuckoos and Turacos

The Cuculiformes order is comprised of two quite different families: turacos (Musophagidae) *with 19 species,* and cuckoos (Cuculidae) *with 130 species. Recent studies have proved their relation through similar types of proteins. Cuckoos and turacos are small to medium-sized birds with arboreal living habits. Their legs are adapted to living in trees. The foot is zygodactylous, or climbing, with the two middle toes directed forward, and the two outer toes backwards. The fourth toe is either reversible (cuckoos) or partly reversible (turacos). The groups also differ sharply in their diet. Cuckoos are purely insectivorous and a number of them eat hairy caterpillars that are rejected by other birds. They are able to "shave" a caterpillar with chewing moves of their bill, yet there are many sharp hairs left that stick in the stomach wall and have to be regurgitated from time to time. Turacos are herbivorous and feed on fruits, buds, flowers, and leaves. Cuckoos are outstanding fliers that winter in the tropics while turacos do not fly very well at all. They can move dexterously through the tree tops branches. They mostly have loud and conspicuous voices. Plumage of most of the turaco species contains pigments, which do not occur in other animals, like turacoverdin that tinges the outer feathers green, and turacin that produces purple coloration. Turacos build simple platform nests and carefully look after their nestlings. On the other hand, the most interesting part of the* cuckoos' life is their brood-parasitism in nesting: they do not sit on their eggs nor do they feed their young but lay the eggs in the nests of other species and let the adopted parents take care of their offspring. The nesting parasitism is evolved in about half of the cuckoo species, and a fair number of interstages between parasitic and non-parasitic behavior can be found. For example, some species of the Coccygus genus lay their eggs in the other birds' nests but incubate them there, thus showing the first stage of nesting parasitism. The cuckoo females lay their eggs not only in the nests of small songbirds (Cuculus genus), *but also in those of corvids (Clamator g.) and pigeons (Tapera g.).*

Corythaixoides concolor

GRAY GO-AWAY-BIRD   AF

The Gray Go-away-bird is noisy and often sits on elevated perches. It can be found in southern Africa, south of Angola and Mozambique. It is a frequent species in dry, open areas with shrubs as well as in woodlands, preferring areas with predominant acacias. It also appears in town parks and gardens. It builds a flat, pigeon-type nest and both partners incubate 1–4 eggs for 26–28 days. It feeds mostly on fruits and flowers and often flies down to the ground to drink and forage for termites.

Left: *Cuculus canorus* juv.
Corythaixoides concolor

Musophaga violacea

VIOLET TURACO   **AF**

The Violet turaco has a peculiar bill shape a yellow horny frontal shield reaching high upon the red forehead. It is the inhabitant of forest edges, vegetation along rivers, dry savannas, and occasionally old parks and gardens with tall trees. It mainly lives in pairs; larger numbers, however, may flock together at places with a bountiful fruit crop. They skillfully run along the major branches of the tree tops. The clutch con-sists of 2 eggs. The species is found in Africa, on a narrow stripe of land between Senegal and Cameroon.

Tauraco persa

GREEN TURACO   **AF**

The Green turaco lives in equatorial Africa from Guinea and Liberia through Uganda and Tanzania to Mozambique and the northern part of southern Africa. It inhabits both lowland and montainous rain forests at altitudes of 9,000ft/2,700m, shrubby savannas, and large gardens with tall trees. It lays 2–3 eggs in a platform nest of dry twigs. The parents look after the young in and out of the nest for almost 3 months.

Tauraco porphyreolophus

PURPLE-CRESTED TURACO   **AF**

The Purple-crested turaco is less than 20in/0.5m long. Similarly to other species of this genus, it is brightly colored, and additionally features a deep purple nuchal crest. It lives in southeastern Africa in wet forests, evergreen shrubberies, and rivers skirting forests. Quite often it can be seen in suburban gardens and parks. It feeds on all kinds of fruits. It breeds from October to March in trees 10–30ft/3–9m above the ground. The clutch has 2–3 eggs that are incubated by both parents for about three weeks. The chicks are fed on regurgitated food.

Tauraco porphyreolophus

Tauraco persa

Cuculus canorus

COMMON CUCKOO   **PA OR**

The cuckoos' voice, the familiar *cuc-coo*, is very well known to everyone. Not everyone, however, knows that it is only the male who calls this way, while the female makes unusual bubbling sounds. The male is dark gray with densely barred underparts. Some females have the same coloration as males, while others are reddish-brown. The Common cuckoo inhab-

Misocalius osculans

its almost all of Eurasia and North Africa. It is migratory and winters as far south as equatorial Africa. It does not live in regular conjugal pairs; the males usually outnumber the females and the birds are polyandrous, with one female mating with several males. The very small eggs have a reinforced shell. The female lays her eggs either directly in the host's nest or brings the eggs to the nest in her bill. At the same time, she usually swallows one of the host's eggs. She lays 10 to 25 eggs per season. The females apparently lay eggs of the same color all their lives, notably resembling those of the species that reared them. Cuckoos have an extraordinarily short incubation period of only 11–13 days because the cuckoo young needs to hatch before the host's chicks or together with them. About 10 hours after hatching, the small cuckoo begins to throw away the eggs or nestlings of the foster parents. It pushes itself under them, holds them on its back with half-open wings and rolls them over the edge of nest. The adopted parents then feed the only nestling until it becomes independent after about 4–5 weeks.

Misocalius osculans
(Chrysococcyx osculans)

BLACK-EARED CUCKOO   **AU**

The Black-eared cuckoo is a small, 7.5–8in/19–20cm long bird. It lives in Australia in open areas with shrubs, dry forests and in vegetation along watercourses. It feeds on insects, especially caterpillars and beetles, and also on seeds. It is brood-parasitic; the hosts are small songbirds whose eggs and young are thrown out by the hatched cuckoo. The bird can be migratory or nomadic. Its breeding coincides with the rainy season.

Crotophaga sulcirostris

GROOVE-BILLED ANI   **NA NT**

The Groove-billed ani lives on the American continent, on a strip along the Pacific coast from the southern regions of North America to Guaiana, north of Chile and northwest Argentina. It inhabits tropical evergreen forests and shrubberies, fields, pastures, and swamps. It is a gregarious species. Several females, who mate with only one male, lay eggs in a single, large hemispherical nest. With each female laying 3–4 eggs, there may be up to 18 eggs in one nest. All females and the male incubate, taking turns at intervals of 30–60 minutes.

Geococcyx californianus

GREATER ROADRUNNER   **NA NT**

The Greater roadrunner ranges in North America from the southwestern United States to Mexico. It has strong legs and a long tail and runs over the ground searching for insects, lizards, snakes, small rodents and other birds. Thanks to its quickness and dexterity, it is even able to hunt down rattlesnakes. It is capable of running as fast as 23mph/37kph, during

Crotophaga sulcirostris

which it makes jumps up to 10ft/3m high. If there is danger, it runs away rather than takes off, and therefore it was previously assumed to be flightless. It was, however, later proved that the bird can fly for at least 700ft/200m. It lives in arid, shrubby areas from lowlands up to 8,200ft/2,500m. The nest is built in a tree or cactus. The male sits on 2–6 eggs at night, while during the day, the birds take turns. According to the weather conditions, the pairs may breed up to three times a season. While the male takes over the care of the dependent young, the female lays another clutch.

Geococcyx californianus

13. Owls and Nightjars

Owls and nightjars present close relationship due to the living habits and certain morphological and anatomical features. The birds are crepuscular or nocturnal, they build no nests, have soft plumage, and similar structure and color of feathers.

Strigiformes

OWLS

The owls form a unified group of 146 species of nocturnal birds with soft plumage, large head, and hooked bill. Their plumage is always fluffed out, which gives the impression of bulkiness. Their body, however, is frail and their bones are thin. Soft, comblike edges on their wings make their flight absolutely inaudible. The plumage on their faces is short and tough and is arranged around eyes in wide circles, so called "facial discs." The skull is relatively small, with notably large eye-sockets and sometimes irregularly placed ear holes, which help the accurate acoustic locating of prey. The eyes are large, forward-facing, and immobile. The bird's field of vision is quite broad due to the expanded mobility of its head. An owl is able to

Left: *Strix varia*
Tyto alba

turn its head more than 180 degrees without any difficulties. The owl's eye is considered to be unparalleled in the animal kingdom. It has tremendous amount of rods which are stimulated by the slightest hint of light. It is believed that the owls' vision is hundred times keener than that of a human. The owls can see equally well by both day and night. The owls' legs are usually feathered down to their claws and feature a revolving outer toe. The crop is missing in the digestive tract. The food is digested quickly in the stomach, while the bones, hairs and feathers stay intact and are regurgitated once or twice a day in the form of lumps. The owls hunt small rodents and, less often, birds, bats, large insects and some other invertebrates. Owls of the *Ketupa* genus also fish. They do not build any nests and lay white round eggs in holes in trees or rocks, in open nests of other birds in thick branches, or on the ground. They start to incubate their eggs immediately after laying the first one. The young, therefore, hatch successively and are of different sizes. They are hatched blind and deaf, covered in dense whitish down, and nidicolous.

Tyto alba

BARN OWL   PA AF OR AU NA NT

The Barn owl has the most pronounced heart-shaped "facial disc" of all owls. It is quite widespread and breeds on all continents. It originally nested on rocks, but gradually came to favor mainly nesting in the proximity of humans in house lofts, church towers, barns, and ruins. The course and success of breeding are heavily dependent on the abundance of the most common prey, which in Europe is the fieldmouse. In the years of a rat plague, the owl may breed twice a season, laying clutches of up to 13 eggs. These are incubated only by the female, while the male regularly feeds her.

Otus scops

SCOPS OWL   PA

The Scops owl is to be found in the southern half of Europe, with St. Petersburg as the northernmost point of its range. It is also found in Asia Minor, in eastern and southern Asia, and along the Atlas mountains in Africa. The European populations winter south of the Sahara as far as the equator. The bird is a thermophile species, inhabiting open forests of wooded steppe areas, old fruit orchards, planted tree rows, vineyards, and abandoned buildings on the outskirts of human settlements. It nests in tree-hollows, in holes in walls, occasionally in old nests of larger birds and in provided nest boxes. The clutch consists of 2–8 eggs.

Otus scops

Otus bakkamoena
COLLARED SCOPS OWL   **OR**

The Collared Scops owl is a common sedentary and exclusively nocturnal species that lives in Southeast Asia from India to the Philippines and th Greater Sundas. It frequents evergreen and deciduous forests as well as secondary forests. It is also found in open terrains with scattered trees, gardens and parks. It nests prevalently at lower altitudes, but can be found up to 7,300ft/2,200m.

Pulsatrix perspicillata
SPECTACLED OWL   **NT**

The Spectacled owl lives in Central and South America from southern Mexico to northern Argentina. It is a lowland forest species, though it also inhabits secondary and gallery forests. It appears in agricultural regions, too, and nests frequently in hollows in trees that shade the coffee plantations. It hunts mainly mice, bats, and in wet forests, crabs.

Bubo virginianus
GREAT HORNED OWL   **NA NT**

The Great Horned owl lives in America from the Arctic to southern Chile and Argentina. Its coloration is

Otus bakkamoena

Pulsatrix perspicillata

fairly variable, from almost white feathers on the birds that live in the Arctic, to very dark plumage on the birds on the Pacific coast. It inhabits primary as well as secondary forests and also coastal mangroves. It also appears in suburban parks. In mountains, it can be found up to an altitude of 10,000ft/3,000m. It lays only 1–2 eggs in tropical areas and 6–7 in northern regions.

Bubo bubo

EAGLE OWL   **PA OR**

The Eagle owl is distributed almost all over Eurasia, excluding the tundra areas, and in northern Africa. The optimum habitat is found in forests with rocky crags, though it also lives in wooded steppe, steppe, and rocky and sandy deserts. Here and there it nests in close proximity to towns and in operating stone quarries. The nest is usually built on a rocky ledge or on the ground, less often it appropriates old tree nests of raptors. The courtship takes place at the end of the winter, and 2–4 eggs, incubated by the female, appear in the nest shortly afterwards.

Bubo virginianus

Bubo bubo

Nyctea scandiaca

Nyctea scandiaca

SNOWY OWL   **PA NA**

The Snowy owl is found in the Arctic zone, inhabiting the northern parts of Eurasia and North America. Its main prey in the tundra are the lemmings whose population oscillates in 4–5 year cycles corresponding to the cycles of Snowy owl, affecting the number of laid eggs and the reared young. This strong owl also hunts the Arctic hare and Willow grouse. In years with a shortage of prey the owl may move to the south.

Strix aluco

TAWNY OWL   **PA OR**

The Tawny owl is an inhabitant of Eurasia and northern Africa. It lives in all kinds of forests with altitudes of up to 10,000ft/3,000m, in avenues of hollow trees, and in town parks and cemeteries. It also nests regularly in large artificial nest-boxes. Its diet is, in comparison to the other owls, very varied, from small rodents through birds, reptiles, amphibians to fish and insects. The formed pairs are likely to be permanent. The nests of ordinarily 3–5 eggs are usually in tree-hollows though they can often be found in the attics of buildings in the forest.

Strix uralensis

URAL OWL   **PA**

The Ural owl occupies the northern half of Eurasia, but occasionally can also be found in central Europe and southeastern Asia. It strongly resembles the Tawny owl and can be distinguished by a noticeably longer tail and much paler plumage. Most often it breeds in old nests of birds of prey. Its optimum habitat is made up of mixed and deciduous primaeval forests.

Strix aluco

Strix uralensis

Strix nebulosa

GREAT GRAY OWL   **PA NA**

The Great Gray owl is a typical inhabitant of taiga in the northern part of Europe, Asia, and North America. Its facial discs of concentric black circles and a black chin with white whiskers are noteworthy. Its nests are usually placed on stumps of broken-off trees. Unlike most of the owls, this owl is able to hollow out a hole in a rotten tree trunk.

Strix hylophila

RUSTY-BARRED OWL   **NT**

This forest owl can be found in Brazil, Paraguay, and northern Argentina. The 13–15in/35–39cm long owl is for the most part dark brown with white and, on its breast, yellow-orange barring. Very little is known about its breeding and feeding habits and there are also certain doubts concerning its systematic classification.

Surnia ulula

HAWK OWL   **PA NA**

The Hawk owl's range is in the northern areas of Eurasia and North America. It inhabits taiga and the transition zone from taiga to birch woods and deciduous forests. It can be sedentary or migratory. In years when rodents are scarce in the north, it is seen in the south, even as far as Central and southern Europe. It shows diurnal activity and enjoys perching at tree tops and other prominent places where it watches for prey. The nest is placed in holes in trees, large old nests, or on the ground.

Strix hylophila

Strix nebulosa

Surnia ulula

Glaucidium passerinum

PYGMY OWL   **PA**

In Eurasia, the Pygmy owl inhabits the coniferous forest region as well as the montainous forests of more southerly located ranges. It is as big as the Bullfinch. A unique feature is the frequent jerking of its tail. It hunts prey that may be much larger than the owl itself. In breeding season, it is active all day long and often produces a simple whistling call. It nests in tree-hollows and in nestboxes. The female sits on 3–7 eggs for about 28 days, while the male brings her food at dawn and dusk. Remnants of the prey, regurgitated lumps, and droppings are thrown out of the hollow daily so

that a pile of garbage develops below the nest after a while.

Glaucidium siju

CUBAN PYGMY-OWL   **NT**

Out of all the *Glaucidium* genus species, the Cuban Pygmy owl has the most limited range. It lives only in Cuba, where it is the most numerous owl, and on the neighbouring Pines Island. It measures only 6–7in/15–17cm and has feathered tarsi. Two color morphs can be found, the gray-brown and the red-brown. It is predominantly a diurnal species that occupies wooded regions. A female lays 3–4 eggs in a nesting tree-cavity, often in a woodpecker hole.

Athene cunicularia (Speotyto cunicularia)

BURROWING OWL   **NA NT**

The Burrowing owl is a terrestrial species of open steppe, semi-desert, and desert terrains. It can run very deftly, thanks to its long legs. It nests in abandoned mammal burrows, on occasion up to 13ft/4m long. It hides there during the day, although it often forages by daylight. In most cases, several pairs nest close by. The owl usually flies low above the ground. However, it is not good flier and often prefers to rely on its fast legs. The clutch is comprised of 2–11 eggs. It lives in the Americas from southwestern Canada and the western United States to southern Argentina.

Athene noctua

LITTLE OWL   **PA AF**

The Little owl can be found up to the northern forest boundary and it also lives in northern Africa. In the 1870s, it was successfully introduced into England, and in New Zealand in 1906. It is identified by a broad, flat head, yellow eyes that are set far apart,

Athene noctua

Aegolius funereus

and a wavy flight. When disturbed, it typically squats. It frequents open landscape with groves, orchards, and tree-lined avenues, yet it does not avoid towns and villages either. The pairs live in permanent, life-long marriages. They nest in hollows in trees or rocks, recesses of walls, in towers, and in attics. The adult birds feed mainly on small vertebrates, while the young are initially fed on invertebrates, especially earthworms.

Aegolius funereus

TENGMALM'S OWL   **PA NA**

The Tengmalm's owl is a typical inhabitant of northern coniferous taiga type forests of Eurasia and North America. It can, however, be also found more in the mixed and deciduous woods of southern Europe as well. It shows black fields around eyes that are placed much closer than in the Little owl and form an equilateral triangle with the bill. Its flight line is straight. The pair bonds are not permanent. The nesting takes place in tree-holes or nestboxes, with the female incubating 3–6 eggs for 26–31 days, while the male feeds her.

Ninox strenua

POWERFUL OWL   **AU**

The homelands of the Powerful owl are the coastal areas of northern Australia where it inhabits open forests and tall tree growths along waterways. It forages both by day and night. The prey caught in the morning is often held in the owl's claws until the afternoon when it is eaten. Unlike the great majority of owls, the male is larger than female, which is also true for other species of the *Ninox* genus. It nests in the holes of other birds, though the male sometimes hollows out a nest himself. The clutch consists of only two eggs.

Ninox strenua

Asio otus

Asio otus

LONG-EARED OWL   **PA NA**

The Long-eared owl lives in the temperate part of Eurasia and North America, and in northern Africa. It is sedentary throughout most of its range, although the northern populations make occasional long moves to the south according to the character of the winter and feeding conditions. Its erect feather-tuft "ears" are distinctive. It nests in forests near open areas, coppices and other types of scattered greenery, usually in the old nests of other birds. It hunts strictly at night. During the courtship display, the male makes two-syllable hooting sounds and performs acrobatic flights accompanied by wing-clapping.

Asio flammeus

Podargus strigoides

Asio flammeus

SHORT-EARED OWL   **PA NA NT**

The range of the Short-eared owl is quite wide: Eurasia, North and South America, the Galapagos, West Indies Islands. The bird is mostly migratory and there are years when its occurence in the south resembles an invasion. In the north, it breeds on tundra, but usually inhabits damper places such as wet meadows, swamps, and peatbogs. The male's wedding aerial displays are even more conspicuous than those of the Long-eared owl, and sometimes take place also during the day. The nest is placed on the ground amid grass and the female lines it with dry grasses, roots and leaves before laying 4–7 eggs, and occasionally even up to 12. In years of rodent "plagues," the pairs may breed twice a year.

Caprimulgiformes

NIGHTJARS

Nightjars feature broad and flat heads with large eyes, essential for their nocturnal life. Their legs are weak and short, with three toes directed forward and one backwards. As they are not able to span a branch, they sit lengthwise along it. Their skin is extraordinarily thin, plumage is soft and of inconspicuous coloration. Nightjars feed on aerial insects, captured by their short, extremely wide bills surrounded by stiff bristles at the base. They mostly nest on the ground, except for the Guacharo, or Oilbird, which breeds in caves in colonies. Two eggs, incubated by both partners, are usually laid in a ground pit. The chicks hatch fairly precocial, covered in down. They can see and hear and soon move about in the vicinity of their nest. They are, however, fed by their parents. There are 103 nightjar species living around the world.

Aegotheles cristatus

Nyctidromus albicollis

Podargus strigoides

TAWNY FROGMOUTH   **AU**

The Tawny frogmouth inhabits all of Australia and Tasmania. It is found in woodlands, yet it migrates from the original biotopes to parks at the outskirts of human settlements. The nest is built in the fork of branches, fractures of trees, or in tussocks of lianas as high as 50ft/14m above the ground. It flies relatively little and waits rather patiently until the prey approaches. The clutch consists of 2–4 eggs.

Aegotheles cristatus

AUSTRALIAN OWLET-NIGHTJAR   **AU**

The bird lives in Australia, Tasmania, New Guinea, New Caledonia, and on the Moluccas, occuring in either reddish or gray color morph. It inhabits continuous as well as open forests from marshy mangroves to dry acacia shrubberies to deep eucalyptus forests. It nests in tree-hollows, lined with just a few dry leaves on which the female lays 3–4 eggs. The incubation lasts 25–27 days.

Nyctidromus albicollis

WHITE-NECKED NIGHTJAR
(PAURAQUE)   **NA NT**

The White-necked nightjar is distributed from Texas in the United States, through Central America to northern Argentina. It lives in both shed and evergreen forests and their clearings, in shrubs and agricultural country with scattered green, and at the edges of human settlements. It is migratory in the northern territories, flying to the central part of South America. It nests on the ground and lays 2 eggs.

Caprimulgus europaeus

NIGHTJAR   **PA**

The nightjar can be found in the temperate part of Europe and Asia up to Lake Baikal, and in northwestern Africa. It is migratory, and its wintering grounds are in eastern and southern Africa. The Asian birds probably migrate to this area as well. It frequents margins and clearings of drier forests, peatbogs and heathlands, steppes and wooded steppes. It nests at altitudes of up to 8,200ft/2,500m in the Caucausus, and on the African wintering grounds may be found up to 16,400ft/5,000m. The male's wedding flights are associated with churring song and wing-clapping. The female lays two eggs in a ground pit and takes turns with the male in sitting on them for 18–19 days. The young are ready to fly within 18 days. At that point, the female is getting ready for another clutch and so the male takes over the parental care.

Caprimulgas europaeus

191

14. Swifts, Hummingbirds, Mousebirds, and Trogons

The Apodiformes order consists of two families: swifts (Apodidae) with 86 species and hummingbirds (Trochilidae) with 338 species. While certain features of mousebirds (6 species) show the resemblance of these birds to trogons (37 species), the others to swifts and nightjars. According to the newest systematic opinions, the swifts, hummingbirds, mousebirds, and trogons form separate orders.

Apodiformes

SWIFTS AND HUMMINGBIRDS

The common features of the Apodiformes are the short secondary and long primary parts of the wing, the impressive development of the flight muscles attached to the high keel of the sternum, and short, weak legs.

Swifts have long, scythe-shaped wings and very short, so-called suspensory legs with all toes directed forward. The legs serve only for grasping rocks, walls or trunks, and not for walking. The birds have short, broad-gaped bill. Sizable salivary glands get swollen primarily at the beginning of the breeding season. At that time, the glands' solidifying secretion serves to glue the nests together. Some species build their nests solely from rapidly solidifying saliva, and such "swallow" nests belong among the delicacies of the East Asian cuisines. The swifts are among the fastest flyers and practically all their life is spent on the wing. They forage in the air for the aerial plankton, small insects and spiders, sleep in the air and even mate there. The young of certain swift species are capable of falling into the state of hibernation, with considerably lowered body temperature and reduced metabolism, during long periods of cold and shortage of food. That explains their ability to survive exceptionally long starving spells of up to 21 days.

The hummingbirds belong to the smallest bird species in the world, with the tiniest ones about the size of a bumblebee. They have only weak sitting legs and extraordinarily colorful plumage with metallic sheen. Their flight whirrs with the rapid beat of their primary and secondary wing, while the axilliary part is almost still. They are able to fly forwards and backwards, rise and fall, and hover for a long time. While hovering, they suck nectar from flowers or possibly pick small insects. Their elongated tongue forms a rifted tube at its tip, which serves for sucking the nectar, and thanks to the long rear edges of the tongue bone, it can be extended quite far. The bill is shaped according to the shape of flowers for which a particular species is specialized. While feeding, the hummingbirds also pollinate the flowers. Because of their tremendous energy demands, the hummingbirds require a large quantity of food, which usually amounts to about 50% of their body weight daily. Their heart is comparatively the largest in the whole animal kingdom and they spend the highest amount of oxygen per gram of body weight of all the vertebrates. They are also able to lower their temperature from a regular 41–42 °C to 8–12 °C and considerably reduce their breathing frequency during times of cold and food shortage. The hummingbirds are very intolerant and aggressive birds, and the males and females keep their own territories. It is necessary because each bird needs at least 7,000 flowers on its territory for its sustenance. Such intolerance is bound to fade away during the courtship that takes place twice or three times a year. The males fly over to the territories of the females who, after mating, lay two eggs. In proportion to the female's weight, the egg is the largest in the entire bird world. A female incubates alone for 14 to 21 days, depending on the species size. The young stay in the nest till they are completely fledged, sometimes up to 30 days.

Apus apus

SWIFT   PA

The swift lives in Europe and northern Africa, in Asia Minor and Central Asia as far as Lake Baikal, northern China and the western Himalayas. It originally in-

Apus apus

Left: *Aglaiocercus kingi*

Discosura longicauda

Colibri coruscans

Chlorostilbon ricordii

Lepidopyga coeruleogularis

Aglaiocercus kingi

habited rocks and hollow trees, but during the last century settled mainly in towns where it nests under roofs, on beams and cornices, and in holes in walls. Occasionally, it breeds in provided nest-boxes. Both European and Asian birds return from their wintering grounds in central and southern Africa to their breeding quarters for only a very short period of time. The nest is a small heap of grass, stalks, and feathers glued together by saliva. Both partners sit on 1–4 eggs. If the weather is bad, they reduce the clutch by throwing one or two eggs away.

Discosura longicauda

RACKET-TAILED COQUETTE   NT

The male Racket-tailed coquette features a conspicuous forked tail with bare and elongated outer rectrices that end up in feathered disks. It is an inhabitant of the tropical zone of Guiana and Venezuela, and northern and eastern Brazil. It mainly occupies lowland rain forests, but also shrublands and savannas.

Colibri coruscans

SPARKLING VIOLET-EAR   NT

This particular species is the first hummingbird brought alive to Europe. It lives in the northern part of South America through Bolivia and north-western Argentina, occupying rain and misty forests, secondary woods, plantations, gardens, and open country with scattered greens at altitudes of up to 11,500ft/3,500m. During its courting display, the male soars vertically up to the height of 65ft/20m and then falls down, with a twittering call. It appears to be the only hummingbird whose male participates in rearing the young.

Chlorostilbon ricordii

CUBAN EMERALD   NT

The Cuban emerald measures 4–4.5in/10–11.5cm. It has forked tail and rather short bill. It can be found in Cuba and the neighbouring Isle de Piños, and in the northern Bahamas. It inhabits woodland and shrubs. It breeds in any season of the year, with the nest wedged in the fork of young branches. On occasion, the same nest will be reused for several years, with the bird improving it each season.

Lepidopyga coeruleogularis

SAPPHIRE-THROATED HUMMINGBIRD   NT

The Sapphire-throated hummingbird is found in the Pacific part of Panama and on the northwestern tip of Colombia. It usually stays low above the ground in mangrove woods, light forests, coastal greens and shrubby clearings. It also finds its way into gardens where it often feeds off orange tree flowers.

Aglaiocercus kingi

LONG-TAILED SYLPH   NT

The Long-tailed sylph lives in the mountains from Venezuela to eastern Peru and Bolivia. It is the inhabitant of forests and shrubberies including coffee plantations. It has a forked tail, the outer feathers of which are about 5in/12cm long in males whose total length is 7in/18cm. The bird uses its tail as a steering device for dexterous manouvering in the dense tangle of branches. The female indefatigably weaves a roofed nest construction of moss, long fibrils, and fine grass.

Coliiformes

MOUSEBIRDS

The mousebirds form a single family, members of which are found exclusively in Africa. They have extraordinarily fine, yet exceptionally dense, plumage which protects them, together with a thick skin, when they crawl through dense, often thorny thickets. They are very skillful and move like mice – hence their appelation in many languages. They are able to turn all four toes forward. The toes have strong and sharp claws, which are useful for suspending upside-down on branches. When climbing along vertical branches, they form a prehensile foot with two toes pointing forward and two rearward. They are also aided by their strong bill in a way similar to parrots. They drink by sucking water just like pigeons. They enjoy sunbathing and dusting. They are highly gregarious and remain in small flocks all the time. For roosting, they suspend themselves on branches as close to each other as possible, forming a kind of a cluster of bodies. In proportion to body size, their eggs are the smallest ones of all the non-parasitic birds.

Urocolius macrourus

BLUE-NAPED MOUSEBIRD   AF

The Blue-naped mousebird lives on the edges and in clearings of woods, on shrubby savannas, and in town parks and gardens. Its diet consists mainly of soft fruits, buds, and leaves. The female lays 3–4 eggs in a cup-shaped nest of roots, grass and bast, occasionally lined with green leaves. It inhabits a narrow strip of African land from Senegal and Gambia to Sudan and farther south to Tanzania.

Trogoniformes

TROGONS

Trogons are small to medium-sized birds with markedly colorful plumage. They sit on branches, for a long time remaining motionless while watching for prey. Then they take off slowly, deftly capture the prey, and return to their perch. They differ from all the other birds by the construction of their feet. The first and second toes, i.e. the rear and inner, point backwards, while the third and fourth ones, the middle and outer, point for-

Urocolius macrourus

ward (heterodactylous leg). They hunt mainly insects, some species also capture small lizards. Their diet is varied by fruits that they pick in flight. They nest in tree hollows, ground burrows, and holes in termitaries. Certain species are able to dig out a cavity in a rotten tree trunk or in a tree termitary.

Priotelus temnurus

CUBAN TROGON   NT

The bird is endemic to Cuba, which means it does not live anywhere else. Similarly to other trogons, it is not overly shy and allows people to come fairly close. The constant jerking of its tail is notable. In breeding season, it produces an unmistakable call at regular intervals that sounds like "tocoloro," and that is how local people have named the bird.

Priotelus temnurus

15. Syndactyls and Zygodactyls

The two orders feature certain specialities in the build of the leg: the Coraciiformes have front toes partly grown together, while the Piciformes have two toes pointing forward and two backward. The members of both orders nest in cavities, either in trees or in the ground.

Coraciiformes

SYNDACTYLS

This order involves 10 bird groups of different external appearance. However, they have common features including their plumage and the inner build of their bodies. In many species, the partial concrescence of basic phalanges of the front toes is apparent, namely between all the toes, or between the second and third, or the third and fourth toes. Plumage is relatively thin and made of stiff feathers that have bright, often metallic coloration. The down is usually missing. They build their nests in tree-hollows or dug-out burrows. The chicks are nidicolous and in many species they grow bristle-like feathering, for the individual feathers stay closed in their sheaths for a long time and look like prickles. The development of the chicks is quite slow. The ten families of this order include 195 species in all.

Megaceryle torquata

RINGED KINGFISHER   **NA NT**

The species is distributed in America from Texas to Tierra del Fuego. It occupies watercourses in lowlands, swamps, mangroves, and even paddy fields and decorative pools in towns. It breeds alone or in small colonies of 4–5 pairs, even though a colony of 150 nesting burrows was also found. The clutch of 3–6 eggs is incubated for about 22 days.

Alcedo atthis

KINGFISHER   **PA OR**

The kingfisher is found in most of Europe except for the northern parts, and from central to southeastern Asia as far as the Solomon Islands. Its living environment requires rivers and larger creeks where small fish, tadpoles, and insect larvae can be captured. It hunts from a branch above the water by plunge-diving. When it brings food for the young, the prey is carried with the head to the front, while if the bird intends to swallow it, the prey is gripped facing the other way. Indigested fish bones are regurgitated. Both partners, using their bills and feet, dig out a burrow in sandy or clay walls for breeding. The burrow is up to 3.3ft/1m long and widened at its far end to form a nesting chamber. Here, twice, sometimes even three times a year, 6–8 eggs appear which are incubated by both sexes.

Left: *Dendrocopos major*
Megaceryle torquata

Alcedo atthis

Ceyx picta

Dacelo novaeguineae

Ceyx picta (Ispidina picta)

AFRICAN PYGMY-KINGFISHER AF

This bird is one of the smallest kingfishers. Its homeland is in sub-Saharan Africa and the island of Madagascar, where it lives in various types of woodland, far from the water and on shores of lakes and rivers. It nests in 12–24in/30–60cm long burrows dug-out in vertical clay walls or in termitaries. It is non-migratory throughout most of its region, except for the birds from the northern and southern regions that do migrate. The migration takes place at night and, allegedly, many birds are killed during the flight as a result of flying into the sides of buildings.

Dacelo novaeguineae

LAUGHING KOOKABURRA AU

The Laughing kookaburra is the largest kingfisher, measuring up to 18in/45cm and weighing 1.1lb/0.5kg. It often erects its tail after landing. It used to nest only in eastern Australia, but thanks to repeated introductions, it now also lives in southwestern Australia, Tasmania, New Zealand's North Island, and other places. Its ideal habitat are open forests and forest margins. It nests in tree-hollows, often using the same hole for many consecutive years. It does not fish and instead hunts mainly reptiles and insects from elevated perches. The Australians are fond of it and often rear the bird at home. When upset, it emits a conspicuous laughing sound, hence its nickname of "Laughing Jack."

Dacelo leachii

BLUE-WINGED KOOKABURRA AU

Another large kingfisher measures 15–18in/40–45cm including the 2.5–3in/7–8 cm long bill. The bird can be found from northwestern to northeastern Australia

and in New Guinea. Unlike its closest relative, the "Laughing Jack," it prefers damper forests, especially along streams, and also wet forestless regions and overgrown swamps. The ranges of the two species often overlap, especially in sugar cane fields, where both birds forage, and at transitional places from wet

Dacelo leachii

Halcyon smyrnensis

Halcyon chloris

forests to dry areas. Its call also consists of harsh laughing sounds. The nest is set up in tree hollows, with the clutch consisting of 3–4 eggs.

lizards. The female lays 3–4 eggs, incubated for about 20 days, in a dug-out burrow.

Halcyon smyrnensis

SMYRNA KINGFISHER   **PA OR**

The Smyrna kingfisher occupies a large part of Asia from Turkey to Indonesia and the Philippines. It is flexible as to the habitat and lives in dry shedding forests as well as in mangrove margins and bamboo forests, on paddy fields, coconut plantations, planted tree rows, and gardens. It digs out its nesting burrows on the clay banks of rivers, channels, and artificial cuttings.

Halcyon chloris
(Todirhamphus chloris)

COLLARED KIGFISHER   **AU OR**

The Collared kingfisher lives in peripheral areas of north-western, northern and north-eastern Australia, and can be found in the Oriental region as well. It inhabits mangroves and other coastal habitats. The nest is built in tree territaries.

Momotus momota

Momotus momota

BLUE-CROWNED MOTMOT   **NT**

The Blue-crowned motmot's range includes a part of America between northern Mexico, Peru, northern Argentina and Venezuela. It can be found in dark lowland forests and shrubberies. It features a long tail with two elongated central feathers. Their tennis racket-shaped lower webs are separated by a gap from the main part of the web. This gap is plucked out by the bird itself. The bird habitually swings its downward pointing tail from side to side as a pendulum. From elevated perches, it hunts insects, mollusks and small

Merops bullockoides

Merops nubicus

Merops orientalis

Merops bullockoides

WHITE-FRONTED BEE-EATER   AF

The White-fronted Bee-eater inhabits Africa south of the equator. It lives in woodlands along seasonal or permanent rivers, in eroded gorges, or on hillsides covered with shrubs. The breeding pairs usually have one or two, but occasionally up to 5, helpers. These are either one-year-old birds or experienced nesters, which help with digging the burrows, incubation, and feeding the young. The roles of helpers and breeders are changed several times in their lifetime. In a breeding colony, one to five pairs, together with their helpers, always form a "clan" of a kind whose members freely visit burrows of the other pairs from the clan, but do not allow members of other clans to enter their nests. Most pairs stay together all their life in the same territory.

Merops nubicus

NORTHERN CARMINE BEE-EATER   AF

The Northern Carmine Bee-eater's homeland is sub-Saharan Africa. It favours shrubby savannas as well as swamps with scattered dead trees, and mangrove forests. The birds often sit not only on the backs of grazing cattle and wild ungulata, but also storks and bustards. They capture insects disturbed by their host's movements. It breeds on the banks of large rivers in huge colonies, with the largest ones containing about 10,000 pairs. There may be up to 60 burrows per square meter.

Merops orientalis

LITTLE GREEN BEE-EATER   AF OR

The Little Green Bee-eater inhabits dry woodland far from the water, steppes with shrubby vegetation, overgrown sand dunes, oases and date-palm groves, and cotton plantations. There must be, however, at least some bare sandy places where the nest is dug, either on level ground, on gentle slopes, or on sheer banks. It may breed alone or in loose colonies. It is also found in large, unified colonies. It lives in northern Africa from Senegal to Ethiopia and Egypt, and also from the Arab Peninsula to India and Vietnam.

Merops apiaster

EURASIAN BEE-EATER   PA AF

The Eurasian Bee-eater can be found in southern, Central and Eastern Europe, western Asia, and northern and southern Africa. It frequents open, warm country with suitable clay or sandy slopes, in which it digs burrows up to 7ft/2m in length. Both partners work together, using their bills and legs. They also take turns warming the 4–8 eggs for 20–22 days. They nest communally in colonies that may total up to hun-

Merops apiaster

dreds of pairs. The European birds winter in tropical and southern Africa.

Coracias garrulus

EURASIAN ROLLER   **PA**

The Eurasian roller frequents open country with groves and rows of mature trees, outskirts of light forests, large clearings, and old orchards. It spends time sitting on the elevated perches, from which it flies down to the ground in pursuit of insects and other invertebrates. The male's courtship display is full of headlong plunges and somersaults, accompanied by loud calling. It nests in old hollow trees or in holes in clay banks where the female lays 2–7 eggs. Both parents sit on them for 17–20 days. Its homeland is Central and southern Europe, Asia up to Lake Baikal, and North Africa. In the autumn, the birds migrate to western and southern Africa.

Coracias caudata

LILAC-BREASTED ROLLER   **AF**

The Lilac-breasted roller is found in bushlands and light forests, grassy savannas with scattered trees, and in large gardens. It favors sitting on dry tree tops, or on poles and wires of electric lines, from which it pounces on prey on the ground. The nest is set up in the cavity of a tree or a termitary, or on tops of dead coconut palms. It ranges throughout the southern half of Africa, from Ethiopia to the northern areas of South Africa.

Coracias garrulus

Coracias caudata

Upupa epops

Tockus erythrorhynchus

Upupa epops

HOOPOE   **PA AF OR**

The hoopoe favors open country with pastures and fallows, interspersed with groves or groups of old trees that feature hollows suitable for breeding. It can, however, also nest in piles of rocks, on the ground under the tree roots, or in holes in man-made structures. Only the female sits on 5–7 eggs, while the male feeds her in the hollow. A secretion of the uropygial gland, especially in nestlings, gives out an intensive smell, which turns out to be an effective defense measure. The hoopoe lives in the temperate zone of Eurasia, a large part of Africa and on Madagascar, and is also found in southern Asia.

Tockus nasutus

AFRICAN GRAY HORNBILL   **AF**

The African Gray hornbill lives in pairs or small groups and is not overly shy. It is mainly arboreal bird, inhabiting dry open country with shrubs and trees. It is non-migratory throughout most of its region. While it lives in pairs in the breeding season, it forms flocks

Tockus nasatus

of up to 30 birds in the winter. It can be found in Africa on a strip of land reaching from Senegal and Liberia to Ethiopia, and in the eastern part of the continent down to the northern parts of the Republic of South Africa.

Tockus erythrorhynchus

RED-BILLED HORNBILL   **AF**

The Red-billed hornbill can be found in eastern and southern Africa, and in some places in the west and center of the continent. It inhabits savannas with scrub cover, thin forests, farms and campgrounds, where it may appear quite tame or even intrusive. It nests in a hole, which the female bricks up by mud, excrements and remnants of food. She starts to lay 3–5 eggs at the advent of rains so that the young are born at a time when there is plenty of food such as locusts, grasshoppers, and beetles, which the birds capture mainly on the ground.

Tockus flavirostris

Buceros bicornis

Tockus flavirostris

YELLOW-BILLED HORNBILL   **AF**

The Yellow-billed hornbill is commonly found in scrub-covered country and forests in northeastern Africa between Tanzania and Ethiopia, and also in the southern part of the continent. It forages on the ground and in fruit-bearing trees. The birds fearlessly approach camps set up by people.

Buceros bicornis

GREAT HORNBILL   **OR**

The Great hornbill is distributed through Asia from India to southern China to the Malay Peninsula and Sumatra. It frequents extensive forests with huge trees, from lowlands up to altitudes up to 6,500ft/2,000m. In small groups, it keeps sitting in tree crowns, or hops along the branches in search for fruits, preferably ripe figs. Throughout the breeding season, it lives in pairs. During courtship, the male makes loud calls, recalling a braying donkey. The casque on its bill serves to amplify the sound. The male then walls its mate into the nesting hollow up to 65ft/20m above the ground. There she sits on 1–3 eggs, moults and, after breaking through the "masonry," leaves the nest with the completely fledged offspring.

Bucorvus leadbeateri

AFRICAN GROUND HORNBILL   **AF**

The ground hornbills live in shrubby savannas in groups that defend a territory of about 40 square miles. Only one pair breeds, being helped by as many as six adult and juvenile birds. All adult males perform a courtship display, during which they feed the dominant adult female. She, however, mates only with the dominant male. The nest can be found in a natural tree-hollow, rock crevice or hole in a bank. The ground hornbills hunt all kinds of terrestrial animals, from insects to frogs and snakes. While walking slowly through grasslands, members of the group keep in contact with each other with their deep, rumbling voices and this "talk" goes on even after nightfall. They take off to fly low above the ground only when flushed or when flying to roost in a tree. The species is found south of Kenya, Uganda and the Congo River Basin, except for the southwestern part of the African continent.

Bucorvus leadbeateri

Megalaima haemacephala

Lybius bidentataus

Lybius dubius

Piciformes

CLIMBERS/ZYGODACTYLS

The climbers feature zygodactylous feet with two toes pointing forward (2nd and 3rd), and two backward (1st and 4th). Apparently, this adaptation, aided by strong toes and sharp claws, is for climbing tree trunks with hard bark. There are additional morphological adaptations found in many species. During climbing the body is propped up by remarkably stiff, pointed tail feathers, and thus the body axis is angled away from the tree trunk to enable a better sway of the bird's bill. The bill itself is strong, with a sharp chisel shaped tip. It is set directly on the skull. The skull bones that are the main support of the bill and protect the brain from violent impacts are thicker than in other birds. The long, harpoon-like tongue features a hard tip with little hooks. The tongue is also covered by a sticky secretion of the salivary glands. With this tongue, the bird is able to catch prey either by piercing or by trapping it with the glue-like coating. The tongue's movement is controlled by the long rear edges of the tongue bone that wind round the whole skull all the way back to the forehead, or even as far as the upper mandible cavity. The climbers nest in tree hollows or ground burrows and lay white eggs. The nidiculous young are hatched bare and blind. Bulky calluses grow on their heels when the chicks are still in the eggs to protect them against bruises in the hard nesting depression. Stiff plumage grows from narrow skin patches, the down is missing. The 338 species of climbers inhabit the whole world except Antarctica, the Australian region and Madagascar.

Megalaima haemacephala

COPPERSMITH BARBET   OR

The bird occupies the West and East Indies, Malaysia, Indonesia, and the Philippines. It has a metallic voice that has led to its popular nickname of "coppersmith." Although it usually lives alone, a great number of birds may gather in trees with ripe fruit. Occasionally, it also feeds on insects. It is a non-migratory inhabitant of forests up to an altitude of 2,000 m. It also lives in orchards and parks. The nesting cavity is hollowed out in tree trunks or limbs.

Lybius bidentatus

DOUBLE-TOOTHED BARBET   AF

The Double-toothed barbet is found in a scattered pattern in a strip of the African continent from Guinea to Kenya and Tanzania. It lives outside unbroken forests in altitudes up to 6,500/2,000m. It nests in tree hollows that are occupied communally by several birds. All of them take care of the clutch of 2–4 eggs and later of the hatched chicks. The breeding pair calls out in unison, and the call is gradually joined by other birds from the group.

Lybius dubius

BEARDED BARBET   **AF**

The Bearded barbet can only be found in a narrow zone in Africa from Senegal to the Central African Republic. It lives on the edges and in glades of light forests, on wooded savannas with tall trees (such as figs, acacias and baobabs,) and on old plantations. It frequently excavates hollows for breeding in dead trees, including palms. Pairs or groups roost together in such cavities. The bird's diet consists of fruit and insects.

Aulacorhynchus sulcatus

GROOVE-BILLED TOUCANET   **NT**

The Groove-billed toucanet is an inhabitant of the coastal mountains of Venezuela. It breeds in forests where it feeds on fruit. The diet is further complemented by invertebrates and small vertebrates. It migrates considerable distances in order to find trees with fruit. The birds often sit in silence in tree crowns and, therefore, are frequently owerlooked.

Aulacorhynchus sulcatus

Pteroglossus beauharnaesii

CURL-CRESTED ARACARI   **NT**

The Curl-crested aracari can be found in Brazil, Guiana, Bolivia, Peru, and Equador. It lives in virgin forests from the mouth of the Amazon River to the lower altitudes of the Peruvian Andes. The clutch consists of 2–4 eggs that are incubated for about 15 days. The Latin name *pteroglossus* stands for "feather-tongued," and refers to the typical construction of the bird's tongue which, similar to other toucans, features fringy protuberances on its sides.

Pteroglossus beauharnaesii

Ramphastos vitellinus

CHANNEL-BILLED TOUCAN   **NT**

The Channel-billed toucan is an abundant species inhabiting the lowland forests and savannas of northeastern South America to central Brazil. Rather small flocks often sit in treetops, also near farming areas. It nests in a tree hole where the female lays 2–4 eggs. Fruit is the staple of its diet.

Ramphastos vitellinus

Jynx torquilla

Dendrocopos medius

Jynx torquilla

WRYNECK PA

The wryneck differs from other woodpeckers because of its weak bill, mimetic outer plumage, and soft rectrices. It does not drum nor does it hollow out cavities for nesting. Instead, it uses finished and abandoned holes or nests in man-made boxes. The wryneck will also move into an occupied nesting site and eject the original in-

habitant (sometimes another wryneck) and its eggs. Both the young and adult wrynecks, taken by surprise in their nest, attempt to intimidate the intruder by turning their heads. This habit provides the basis for the bird's common name in many languages. The wryneck can be found in sparse forests, in groves, planted tree rows, parks, and gardens. It lives in temperate zones of Eurasia from the Atlantic to the Pacific, and in Morocco. It winters in equatorial Africa.

Dendrocopos minor

Dendrocopos minor

LESSER SPOTTED WOODPECKER PA

The Lesser Spotted woodpecker has about the same range as the wryneck. It frequents park-like, cultivated countryside, deciduous groves, larger parks and orchards. Unlike other woodpeckers that sit along a branch, this species sits across it. When foraging, it suspends itself on branches or even small twigs upside-down. The nesting cavity is hollowed out by both birds usually in a rotting tree trunk or a thick branch. The clutch of 4–6 eggs is incubated by both parents for 11–14 days. The bird's predominantly animal diet is supplemented by seeds in the winter.

Dendrocopos medius

MIDDLE SPOTTED WOODPECKER PA

The Middle Spotted woodpecker lives in Europe with the exception of the British Isles, most of Scandinavia and the Iberian Peninsula. It is also found in Asia Minor and Central Asia. It favours deciduous and mixed forests from lowlands to hills, and also breeds in large parks. It often chooses either eroded or dry tree trunks for excavating its nest. The clutch of 5–6 eggs is warmed by both partners.

Dendrocopos leucotos

WHITE-BACKED WOODPECKER   **PA**

This species typically lives in forests, preferring continuous, deciduous woodlands from lowland up to an altitude of 6,500ft/2,000m. It is strongly dependent on dead or dying trees, in which it bores its nesting cavities. Modern forestry methods, which recommend removal of these trees, do not favor this bird's nesting habits. This woodpecker lives in a zone that stretches from Central and northern Europe through the temperate part of Asia to the Pacific Ocean.

Dendrocopos major

GREAT SPOTTED WOODPECKER   **PA OR**

The Great Spotted woodpecker is flexible in its choice of habitat. It lives in all types of forests from lowlands to mountains, and is also found in parks, gardens, and tree rows. It has a wide ranging diet that includes all invertebrates, including wood worms and their larvae. Occasionally, it diversifies its diet by invading other birds' nests and eating the eggs. Between the autumn and the spring, the bulk of its diet consists of seeds of coniferous trees. At times when there is a low crop of seeds, members of the northern subspecies make mass invasions to southwestern areas. The bird's range is spread in temperate zones of Eurasia from the Atlantic to the Pacific, also reaching the Canary Islands and northwestern Africa.

Dendrocopos leucotos

Dendrocopos major

Picoides tridactylus

THREE-TOED WOODPECKER   **PA NA**

As the woodpecker's name suggests, its fourth toe is missing. The bird's unbroken range is in northern and central Eurasia and in North America. This range is accompanied by breeding quarters that are found in the mountains of Central Europe and the North American Midwest, and in the Himalayas. It is non-migratory and inhabits old, virgin forests in the mountains. The nest is situated in a dry or partially rotten tree. Its diet is exclusively animal though it occasionally consumes the resin from the bark.

Picoides tridactylus

Colaptes auratus

Dryocopus martius

Colaptes auratus

NORTHERN FLICKER   **NA NT**

The Northern flicker's range lies primarily in North America from the northern forest boundary to the Gulf of Mexico and down to Nicaragua in Central America. The bird is fairly flexible in its habitat. It

Dryocopus lineatus

inhabits woodlands as well as open terrain, town parks and gardens. It is also frequently found in farming areas. It often hops clumsily on the ground in search of ants and digs them out of their ground nests. The birds from Alaska and Canada regularly migrate south, which is unusual in this family. Northern flickers' coloration is very variable. Three groups of subspecies are distinguished mainly by the color of their whiskers and underwings.

Dryocopus lineatus

LINEATED WOODPECKER   **NT**

With its length of about 15in/35cm, the bird belongs to the group of large woodpeckers. It is black and has a red helmet, nape and beard. It is the only South American woodpecker with a black and white striped throat. It is found in Central and South America from Mexico to Paraguay and northern Argentina. It lives in forests, including mangroves, savannas with shrubs and scattered trees, and gardens.

Dryocopus martius

BLACK WOODPECKER   **PA OR**

The Black woodpecker is found in large, older forests ranging from the lowlands up to 6,500ft/2,000m high in the mountains. Occasionally, it also breeds in large town parks with aging trees. It feeds mainly on wood worms and ants, including the larvae and chrysalides. The nest is hollowed out by both the male and female who take between 10 and 28 days to complete the work depending on the quality of the wood. They actually make several such hollows and use one of them for breeding, while the other ones are left for resting and roosting. Some pairs use the same hole for sever-

Dinopium javanense

Picus viridis

al years, while others make a new nest each year. The bird lives in the temperate zone of Eurasia from France to the Pacific Ocean. Isolated populations are also found in the higher altitudes of southern Europe and Asia.

Dinopium javanense

COMMON FLAMEBACK   **OR**

The Common flameback is a common, non-migratory species found in wet, deciduous and evergreen forests. It also lives in coconut plantations, open forests and gardens. It nests in a cavity hollowed out in a tree trunk or a limb, usually up to 15ft/5m above the ground. The clutch has 2–3 eggs. It lives in pairs, though after breeding it socializes in mixed flocks with other insectivorous birds. Its region is situated from eastern Pakistan to Indo-China.

Picus viridis

GREEN WOODPECKER   **PA**

The Green woodpecker is a typical inhabitant of the European deciduous forest. It can also be found in southwestern Asia between the Black and Caspian Seas. It frequently inhabits park-like country with old trees, in which both members of the pair excavate their nest. Both of them also sit on 4–8 eggs, with the male always incubating at night. Parents bring food for the young in their gullet and regurgitate it gradually in 8–10 portions in the nest. The male roosts with nestlings in the hollow. It feeds especially on ants that are dug out from tree or ground nests for which the birds bore holes as deep as 2.5ft/75cm.

Picus canus

GRAY-HEADED WOODPECKER   **PA OR**

The Gray-headed woodpecker is associated with forests, mainly deciduous and mixed types, and also ranges higher in the mountains than the related Green woodpecker. It also occasionally forms mixed pairs with this other woodpecker. During courting, it drums not only on trees, but also on other well resonating items, like tin roofs, lightning-conductors, or telegraph poles. Its nest is almost always placed in a hole in an eroded or dry tree. The region is in temperate parts of Eurasia and reaches to southern China, Malaysia, and Sumatra.

Picus canus

209

16. Songbirds

Songbirds or Passerines (Passeriformes) *include 5,265 species and form by far the most numerous order with more than half of all bird species. Small to, at most, medium-sized birds are found among members of the order. The shape of their bills varies greatly depending on what they feed on. Their legs show the arboreal origin of songbirds. All four toes are on one level, and the first toe is permanently reversed. The tarsus is covered by small tablet-like scales. Their plumage is moderately dense, the down is thin and grows only on brood patches. One of the few exceptions is the Eurasian Dipper featuring dense down as an adaptation to its water habitat. The characteristic voice produced by passerines is a song. Its character depends on the construction of the voice organ (the syrinx), and on the number and position of singing muscles that may number from 1 to 7. The songbirds are mostly monogamous and live with a single partner for the entire breeding season. However, polygamous species are also known, with the male mating with several females. The songbirds probably build the most elaborate nests of all the bird species. Nests are mostly bowl-shaped, and many of them are examples of perfect construction work. Most notable perhaps are the clay nests of swallows and ovenbirds, the deftly woven nests of Penduline tits and weavers, or the labour intensive dug out burrows of martins. Extremely nidicolous, the young are hatched blind and naked and only rarely are they covered with thin down. For a long time they are completely dependent on their parents. From the first hours after hatching, they beg food from parents by stretching their necks and opening their bills. For better orientation for the parents during the feeding process, the chicks' bills feature conspicuously colored mouth corners, patches on tongues or fluorescent points in the gullet. The classification of songbirds is fairly complicated; it is based on the number and position of the song muscles and on the concrescence of the toe flexor muscles in the foot.*

Myiarchus magnirostris

LARGE-BILLED FLYCATCHER NT

This bird lives exclusively on the Galapagos, where it is a common species on all the major islands. The pairs secure and defend their territories. A nest of plant matter is built in cavities in trees or cacti. The clutch of up to 4 eggs may also be found in an old finch nest.

Pitangus sulphuratus

GREAT KISKADEE NA NT

The Great kiskadee ranges from southern Texas and Mexico to central Argentina. It inhabits shrublands and forest clearings, especially near waters and gardens. It is fairly aggressive and very adaptable. When its habitat is in close proximity to humans, its diet becomes almost completely omnivorous. It often sits on fences and telephone lines along roads. The nest is a large sphere of dry

Left: *Fringilla coelebs*
Myiarchus magnirostris

Pitangus sulphuratus

Myiozetetes cayanensis

Tyrannus savana

Tyrannus caudifasciatus

grass with a side entrance. It is built by both partners, usually quite high in a conspicuous place, such as the top of a telegraph pole.

Myiozetetes cayanensis

RUSTY-MARGINED FLYCATCHER   **NT**

The bird lives in Central and South America from Panama to eastern Bolivia and Brazil as far south as Rio de Janeiro. It can be found in forests as well as in open terrain near rivers and ponds, and on plantations. It habitually sits on a branch, quickly turns its head from side to side, and often ruffles up conspicuous yellow feathers on its breast. It measures about 7in/18cm and features a rather small bill like other members of the genus.

Tyrannus savana

FORK-TAILED FLYCATCHER   **NT**

The bird's area spreads from Mexico to central Argentina. It is common in open country as well as in forests near large rivers, from lowlands to medium altitudes. It frequently sits on exposed perches, such as dry branches or fence poles, from which it flies after insects. It also visits fruit trees. Some populations are migratory, and the birds often migrate in flocks of thousands.

Tyrannus caudifasciatus

LOGGERHEAD KINGBIRD   **NT**

The Loggerhead kingbird measures about 9in/23cm. Its tail is not forked and has a white or grayish tip. Its coloration is fairly inconspicuous. The crown and sides of the head are dark, while the back is olive gray to gray-brown. The species lives in forests though it can often be spotted in fairly open country. It lives in Cuba, the Bahamas, the Cayman Islands, Jamaica, Puerto Rico and other islands. The nest is a bowl-shaped, imperfect structure placed in a tree or bush at various elevations above the ground. The clutch consists of 2–3 eggs.

Chiroxiphia caudata

Xipholaema punicea

Rupicola peruviana

Chiroxiphia caudata

SWALLOW-TAILED MANAKIN   NT

The Swallow-tailed manakin lives in forests, where it dwells almost exclusively in the treetops. Occasionally, it may venture lower on the tree, but rarely below the middle vegetation zones. It is found in southeastern Brazil, Paraguay and northeastern Argentina.

Xipholena punicea

POMPADOUR COTINGA   NT

The Pompadour cotinga male is dark purple above, including the tail which has a brownish tinge. Its wings are white and the bill is yellowish. The female is inconspicuously brownish. The species can be found in the tropical zone in the northern part of South America in Guiana, Venezuela, Colombia, Equador, and Brazil north of the Amazon River. It frequents forests of various types up to an altitude of 5,000ft/1,500m. It builds a rather small, bowl-shaped nest in a fork of a branch or between tendrils. It lays only one egg–perhaps because more than one nestling probably would not fit in such a small nest anyway.

Rupicola peruviana

ANDEAN COCK-OF-THE-ROCK   NT

The Andean Cock-of-the-rock is frequently found from lowlands to medium altitudes in the hills of the Andes from Venezuela to Bolivia. It lives in virgin forests, often near rivers and in gorges. The courtship of the males takes place at communal mating areas in trees that are found from the middle of the rain forest's vegetation zones almost up to the treetops. Individual subspecies differ in their plumage, which can be orange-red to bright red. The wings and tail are black, the white axillaries are elongated and flattened. The male displays them during the courtship in a conspicuous manner together with its high crest. The female chooses her partner herself at the arena. Outside the courting area, the bird lives alone. It feeds mainly on fruit.

Pitta guajana

BANDED PITTA   OR

The Banded pitta's homeland is the area from the Malay Peninsula to Java, Sumatra, and Borneo. The species inhabits virgin forests in particular, including swampy forests. However, it also lives in cleared areas where remnants of tall trees have been left along with the undergrowth. To a lesser extent, it can be found in secondary forests. In Java, it ranges as high as 8,000 ft/ 2,450 m. The nest is a sphere of 8–12in/20–30cm in diameter. The outer framework of the nest is formed by curved twigs as long as 15in/40cm interwoven with dry leaves, grass blades and plant fibres. Both partners sit on the clutch of 3–4 eggs.

Pitta guajana

Menura novaehollandiae

Galerida cristata

Menura novaehollandiae

SUPERB LYREBIRD   **AU**

The home of the Superb lyrebird is in the rain forests of southeastern Australia. Its courtship display is exceptionally interesting. Amidst shaded vegetation, the male scrapes a sort of a dancing floor where it begins to sing. Besides producing its own sounds, it imitates other birds' songs and even the barking of a dog or a car horn. At the same time it dances, it drapes its magnificent tail over its head and shakes it, thus producing a fine, ringing sound. It is polygamous and mates with several females. The female later builds a large nest in a branch fork with a side entrance and lays one egg which is incubated for 47–50 days. A chick hatches bare and blind and its mother looks after it for 47 days in the nest and another 8 months out of the nest.

Melanocorypha calandra

CALANDRA LARK   **PA**

The Calandra lark lives in areas around the Mediterranean Sea including Sardinia, Sicily, and Creta. Farther east, it is found in steppes of Central Asia. It frequents grasslands from the natural steppe to grain

Melanocorypha calandra

fields and terrains with not overly dense shrubs. It breeds in single pairs and marks its territory with loud singing. The nest is placed on the ground, usually by a tussock of vegetation. The clutch of commonly 4–5 eggs is warmed mainly by the female.

Galerida cristata

CRESTED LARK   **PA AF OR**

The original homeland of the Crested lark is the steppes of Eastern Europe. As a result of the expansion of cultivated fields in the 13th and 14th centuries, its range was extended into Central Europe. Habitually a semi-desert species, it inhabits warm and dry areas such as steppes, sand dunes, dry pastures and fallow lands. It has also adapted to the urban habitat where it frequents construction sites, rubish dumps, and training grounds. The nest is always on the ground, though it has lately been also found on flat roofs of apartment houses. The young abandon their nest even before fledging. The current range includes most of Europe, a great part of southwestern and Central Asia and the northern half of Africa.

Lullula arborea

WOODLARK   **PA**

The woodlark favours dry terrain with sparse vegetation and scattered trees as well as heathlands, steppe hillsides, old vineyards, and margins of dry forests. Its beautiful singing is particularly outstanding at night. However, it sings during the day too. Often during its characteristic slow wingbeat, nuptial flight is performed in curves and spirals. The nest is placed on the ground in a sunlit place, well concealed in not very dense vegetation. The clutch of 3–5 eggs is incubated only by the female. The bird's region includes most of Europe, the Near East and northern Africa. It winters in the Mediterranean region.

Alauda arvensis

SKYLARK   **PA**

The skylark inhabits all of the Palaearctic region between 35 and 65 degrees of northern latitude. It was also introduced into Australia, Tasmania, and New Zealand. It was originally a bird of the eastern steppes. Its expansion was helped by humans who created cultivated steppes or fields. It can also be found in meadows and pastures, heaths and peat bogs, sand dunes, and in tundra in the northern areas. Its song, produced almost exclusively in flight, is well-known. At the beginning of the breeding season, the average length of the song is about two minutes. The nest is placed on the ground, and the pairs may breed two or three times per season. In the spring and summer, an-

imal sources make up most of its diet. Later in the year, its diet changes to primarily plants.

Calandrella brachydactylla

SHORT-TOED LARK   **PA**

The Short-toed lark can be found in a zone that spreads from Portugal and Morocco through southern Europe all the way to central China. It nests in steppe and semi-desert biotopes, on fields of low grain, fallow lands, dunes, and sandy coasts with low vegetation. Its expansion in Europe was connected with the expansion of extensively cultivated fields and pastures and the degrading of soil on hillsides. It is migratory. The European populations winter in Africa, while the Asian ones migrate to the northern parts of the Indian subcontinent.

Alauda arvensis

Calandrella brachydactylla

215

Riparia riparia

Riparia riparia

SAND MARTIN   **PA NA**

The Sand martin finds vertical, sandy and clay river banks, in which it digs out its nesting burrows, first with its bill and later also with its legs. Occasionally, it may breed in piles of earth, peat, or slag, in ground ditches, walls of flue ash pits, and even in the walls of culverts. Burrows are 12–60in/30–150cm long and widened at the far end to form a nesting chamber lined with grass and feathers. Sand Martins nest in colonies that may comprise from several dozen to several thousand pairs. They inhabit most of Eurasia and North America, and the northeastern tip of Africa. Wintering grounds can be found in equatori-al and southern Africa, southern Asia and South America.

Ptyonoprogne rupestris

CRAG MARTIN   **PA OR**

The Crag martin occupies the mountains of warm regions from the Iberian Peninsula and African Atlas Mountains through the Middle East and Arab Peninsula to the Himalayas, Tian Shan, and Altai. It breeds alone or in small colonies in vertical rock faces, river gorges, and coastal cliffs.
Its nest, which resembles a swallow's nest, is built on these vertical surfaces. In the Alps, it nests up to an altitude of 8,200ft/2,500m. Populations from more northern areas migrate to Mediterranean regions and northern Africa.

Hirundo rustica

SWALLOW   **PA OR NA**

Swallows are very popular birds, especially in the country. They seek the proximity of humans and build their nests mostly inside buildings, sheds, hallways and gateways. The nest is glued together from pieces of clay mixed with saliva and blades of grass. To build a bowl-shaped, open nest, 750–1,400 lumps of clay are required and the construction is completed in 8–9 days. Only the female builds the nest, while the male brings material. Swallows live throughout most of Europe, Asia, and North America, in the northernmost part of Africa, and in Australia. The European birds winter in tropical and southern Africa. Additional wintering grounds are in South America and southern and southeastern Asia.

Ptyonoprogne rupestris

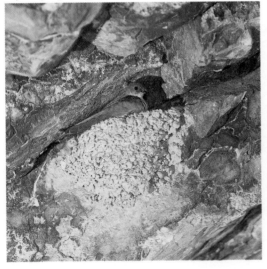

Hirundo rustica

Hirundo daurica

RED-RUMPED SWALLOW   **PA AF OR**

The Red-rumped swallow is distributed from southern Europe through Asia Minor and the Middle East to India, China and Japan. It is also found in central and northwestern Africa. It has maintained its original way of breeding on the rocks, though it sometimes also builds nests on human structures. The nests are usually situated beneath overhanging rocks, in rock holes and crevices, under bridges and balconies or in abandoned buildings. The clay nest has a pronouncedly elongated tunnel entrance.

Delichon urbica

HOUSE MARTIN   **PA**

The House martin also seeks the proximity of humans during its breeding. The nests, however, are not built inside buildings but rather on outside walls beneath roofs and ledges, or on balconies and window alcoves. The original breeding quarters on rocks and cliffs are nowadays used only rarely, although occasionally a nest may be found under a river bridge. The nest is glued together by both partners from pieces of clay mixed with saliva. It is a closed structure that features only a small entrance hole on its upper part. Four to

Delichon urbica

six eggs are incubated by both parents. Their diet consists of aerial insects. The House martin inhabits most of Europe, a good part of Asia all the way to Japan, and northwestern Africa. It winters in sub-Saharan Africa and in India.

Hirundo daurica

217

Motacilla flava

Motacilla alba

Motacilla flava

YELLOW WAGTAIL   **PA NA**

The typical habitats of the Yellow wagtail are wet meadows and wetlands near ponds and rivers, and swamps and bogs up to an elevation of 8,200ft/ 2,500m. The bird favours dense vegetation up to

Motacilla cinerea

17–24in/45–60cm high. Occasionally, it breeds in fields or wastelands. The female builds the nest alone on the ground amidst the vegetation and lays 4–6 eggs in it. The male helps a little with incubating. Its diet consists mainly of insects, and also spiders, worms, and small mollusks. The range, which includes northwestern Africa, all of Europe, and most of Asia, stretches across the Bering Strait to Alaska. Wintering grounds can be found in tropical and southern Africa and southern Asia.

Motacilla cinerea

GRAY WAGTAIL   **PA**

The male Gray wagtail is yellow below and has a black throat and gray back. The female lacks the black throat patch. The bird's long tail is distinctive. Similar to other wagtails, it swings its tail up and down after landing. It inhabits sections of waterways with rapid water. In lowland streams and rivers a weir or rocky floodgates serve quite well as a habitat as do also sluices and races of ponds. The nest is usually placed in a semi-cavity among rocks or roots in the bank of a stream, in holes of bridges and towing paths, and also at times fairly far from water, such as in walls or beams of buildings. It lives in northwestern Africa. In Europe it is found southeast of a line running from Poland to Iran, and in Asia east of the Ural Mountains as far as the Pacific. It winters in southern Europe, Africa and southern Asia as far south as New Guinea.

Motacilla alba

PIED WAGTAIL   **PA OR**

The Pied wagtail's range involves most of Europe, Asia, and Morocco. It can mostly be found near permanent or temporary water bodies. Yet its adaptability allows it to also occupy dry biotopes. Therefore, it breeds not only near wetlands, but also on pastures, fields, gardens and parks, and even in industrial town

Anthus campestris

Anthus pratensis

Anthus trivialis

districts. The nest is a rather massive structure of twigs, roots, blades and leaves that is most often situated in semi-hollows of buildings and rocks, or placed freely on beams and ledges. The bird is non-migratory in southern and western Europe. From elsewhere it migrates to the Mediterranean area and tropical Africa.

Anthus campestris

TAWNY PIPIT **PA**

The Tawny pipit is distributed throughout southern and Central Europe and Central Asia from the Iberian Peninsula and Morocco to Mongolia. As a bird that originally lived in steppes it seeks dry and warm habitats like sandy and rocky areas with sparse vegetation, heathlands, extensive fields, and even places like mine waste piles. The nest of grass and roots is usually sheltered beneath a tussock or a bush and contains 4–5 eggs that are incubated only by the female for 13–14 days. Wintering grounds are found in Africa south of the Sahara, and in Asia as far east as Afghanistan.

Anthus pratensis

MEADOW PIPIT **PA**

The Meadow pipit is almost exclusively a European species that lives in areas ranging from Central and northern Europe to the Ural Mountains. It breeds in the tundra in northern areas, and otherwise in peat bogs and heathlands, wet meadows and pastures. At suitable places, the males congregate in groups and call out to each other. During their singing they fly to great heights, and then, towards the end of the song, descend with open wings and tails down to land on stalks of tall plants and bushes. The nest is well concealed among grasses on the ground. Still unfledged, the young leave the nest after about 12 days and hide themselves in the surrounding vegetation. The autumn migration flies to the Mediterranean area.

Anthus trivialis

TREE PIPIT **PA**

The male Tree pipit sings most often in flight. It takes off from a treetop at an upward angle and then descends in a curve or a spiral, with its wings and tail spread, landing at the same or different perch where the song is completed. It nests mainly at the edges of woods and in forest clearings, in open forests, peat bogs, overgrown hillsides and meadows. The nest is placed on the ground in a grass tussock or below the turf. It lives throughout most of Eurasia, as far as Lake Baikal in the east and the Caspian Sea and the Himalayas in the south. It winters places in areas between the Mediterranean area and tropical and eastern Africa through the Arab Peninsula to India.

Anthus cervinus

RED-THROATED PIPIT **PA NA**

The bird is distributed in the Arctic zone from northern Scandinavia to western Alaska. It breeds in tundra with growths of sedges, willows, and birches. Its nest is usually built on the a side of a tussock or sedge. It is built of moss, grass and other plant matter, and lined with plant fibers and hair. European populations migrate mainly to Africa south of the Sahara. Isolated wintering quarters may also be found in the Mediterranean region and northern Africa.

Anthus cervinus

Anthus spinoletta

Pycnonotus jocosus

Anthus spinoletta

WATER PIPIT   **PA NA**

The bird dwells in broken rock and precipices above the tree line as well as in boulder fields with patches of grass. It is also found on mountain meadows with dwarf vegetation, and pastures up to almost 10,000ft/ 3,000m in Europe. In many locations it lives together with the Meadow pipit. They both choose similar places for breeding but their foraging areas differ. The Meadow pipit prefers dense, tall vegetation, in which the Water pipit rarely forages. The nest is built by the female in a depression below a stone or grass over-hang. The bird's breeding region stretches from Spain through southern and Central Europe, the Caucasus and the mountains south of the Caspian Sea all the way east to the Kamchatka and Tchukotka Peninsu-las. It reaches North America, too. In winter, the birds either descend to lower elevations or fly to the Me-diterranean area and the Arab Peninsula.

Pycnonotus jocosus

RED-WHISKERED BULBUL   **OR**

The bird comes from India, the Andaman and Nico-bar Islands, and southern China. It was introduced into Australia, Mauritius, and the U.S.A. It lives sociably at the edges of forests and also in rural areas, including towns. It breeds low in bushes but also be-neath thatched roofs and in walls. The clutch consists of 2–3 eggs, and their incubation takes 12–14 days.

Pycnonotus xanthopygos

YELLOW-VENTED BULBUL   **PA**

The bird can be found in Saudi Arabia, Egypt, Izrael, Jordan, Lebanon, Syria, and Turkey. It inhabits open country with shrub cover, palm groves, and gardens in towns and villages. It usually breeds in thickets. The

Pycnonotus xanthopygos

Pycnonotus barbatus

220

clutch of 2–4 eggs is incubated by the female (though some authors claim both partners participate in that duty); both parents also bring food for the young. After breeding it sometimes congregates in flocks of up to several hundred to thousands of birds.

Pycnonotus barbatus

COMMON BULBUL   **AF**

The Common bulbul is probably the most numerous and also the most known bird of Africa. It occupies almost the entire continent, from Morocco and Egypt to its southern tip. It is quite similar to the blackbird of Europe. It favors parks and gardens in towns and villages, but also lives in all types of scattered greenery and in forest clearings. In high plateaux it may be found up to an altitude of 8,200ft/2,500m. It is believed that the pairs mate for life. "Helper" birds occasionally give the pair aid in feeding the chicks in the nest. In some locations the bird crossbreeds with the Yellow-vented bulbul and also with the south African Black-fronted bulbul *(Pycnonotus nigricans)*.

Phyllastrephus terrestris

TERRESTRIAL BROWNBUL   **AF**

This 9in/22cm long, dirty-brown bird with paler underparts has its range in southeastern Africa. It mostly forages in groups of six or more birds on the ground in thick coppices of river forests. Its behavior is so secretive that it is rarely observed.

Phyllastrephus terrestris

Hypsipetes madagascariensis

Hypsipetes madagascariensis

MADAGASCAR BULBUL   **AF OR**

The Madagascar bulbul ranges from the island of Madagascar and the Comoros Islands to southern Asia. It is common in mountain forests, and also adapted to secondary forests and sparsely wooded terrains. It is found in parks and gardens, too. It moves agilely, mainly in the tops of trees, where it feeds on flowers and fruit and captures insects. The nest is so loosely constructed that sometimes the eggs may show through the bottom.

Irena puella

ASIAN FAIRY-BLUEBIRD   **OR**

Despite of its conspicuous coloration, the Asian Fairy-bluebird is very difficult to catch sight of it in the shade of evergreen forests. It, however, draws attention to itself by its loud behavior, with ever repeated two-syllable whistling. It often congregates in large flocks on fruiting fig trees. The platform nest of twigs, moss and roots is built by the female who then incubates the clutch of 2 eggs. The bird lives in India, southern China, the Andamans and the Greater Sunda Islands.

Irena puella

Lanius collurio

Lanius excubitor

Lanius collurio

RED-BACKED SHRIKE   **PA**

The Red-backed shrike frequently sits on elevated perches in order to watch for prey, such as insects and small vertebrates. It is the characteristic feature of all shrikes that they store their food by impaling it on thorns on branches. They are further able to regurgitate indigestible parts of food, such as beetle wing-cases, tiny bones, hair, and feathers in the form of small pellets. It is known as an excellent mimic of other birds' singing. It favors dry and warm areas with shrubs. It nests in the thickest tangle of branches, most often up to 7ft/2m above the ground. Its nest is a massive structure with thick walls. 4–6 eggs are incubated by the female. It inhabits most of Europe, western Siberia, and Asia Minor. It winters in eastern and southern Africa.

Lanius minor

LESSER GRAY SHRIKE   **PA**

The bird is like a miniature of the Great Gray shrike and differs from it in a black forehead and rosy underparts. Unlike other shrikes, its flight is not undulating but straight. It is a typical steppe species that has adapted to cultivated areas, too. It lives in open country with field groves and scattered trees, in planted tree rows, orchards, and vineyards. For breeding it definitely prefers deciduous trees. It can be found from the southern half of Europe to the Ural Mountains, and in Central Asia as far as the Altai. It is strictly migratory and the winter is spent in southern Africa. Since the second half of the 20th century, its population has dropped in numbers almost everywhere.

Lanius minor

Lanius senator

Lanius excubitor

GREAT GRAY SHRIKE   **PA AF OR NA**

The Great Gray shrike inhabits Europe as far as Hungary and Romania in the south, the northern part of Asia and most of Canada. It favours open areas with occasional trees or bushes, groves, and forest margins. The firm nest of twigs, stems, root material, and moss is built by both birds in trees and lined with plant wool, hair, and feathers. The clutch of 5–7 eggs is warmed by the female for 15–16 days. The chicks are fed in the nest by both parents for 19–20 days. Birds breeding in northern areas migrate to the southern parts of the range.

Lanius senator

WOODCHAT SHRIKE   **PA**

The Woodchat shrike can be found in Central and southern Europe as far as the Caucausus and Iran, and in northern Africa. It breeds in open country with bushes, in orchards, gardens, at the edges of forests, and in forest clearings. Similarly to most shrikes, three conditions have to be met for their habitat: the existence of bushes, or trees, open terrain with a plentiful

offering of invertebrates, especially large insects, and elevated perches with good views. In principle, it avoids shaded and wet places. The winter is spent on savannas of tropical Africa.

Bombycilla garrulus

WAXWING   **PA NA**

The waxwing lives in northern Eurasia from the Atlantic to the Pacific, and in North America. It is one of the most typical birds of the boreal coniferous and mixed forests, in its case mainly taiga. The nest is placed in trees 10–50ft/3–15m above the ground and is built by both partners. However, the incubation of 4–7 eggs is carried out only by the female. Both parents then feed their offspring with animal food, especially mosquitos that are found in taiga in huge abundance. The considerable fluctuation in the numbers of breeding birds is caused by their occasional invasions southwards and westwards. At that time, waxwings feed mostly on berries. Their digestion is exceptionally rapid. Food passes through their stomachs and intestines and exits the body only half-processed.

Cinclus cinclus

DIPPER   **PA OR**

The dipper has a privileged position among songbirds because it has perfectly adapted to a water environment. Its food, consisting mainly of the larvae of aquatic insects, crustaceans and small mollusks, is found mostly in the water. It also dives during foraging. The thick plumage is always well-oiled by wax from the uropygial gland and therefore does not absorb water. The nest is always found very near water, often under bridges or in roots under a bank. It may also sometimes be placed beneath a weir so that the birds have to fly through the water screen to get to it. The nest is a large, closed oval shape with a side entrance. The dipper is a non-migratory bird that remains in its territory, which can cover 0.3–0.6 miles/0.5–1km along a stream, usually throughout the winter. It lives in the mountains and foothills of Europe and Asia.

Bombycilla garrulus

Cinclus cinclus

Troglodytes troglodytes

Prunella collaris

Prunella modularis

Troglodytes troglodytes

WREN   **PA OR NA**

The wren can be found almost anywhere, from sea level to altitudes above the tree line, and from forests to the treeless tundra. However, it most often frequents areas with dense shrubs, fallen trees, heaps of branches, and boulders. Its large spherical nest with a side entrance is placed in a tangle of roots, in ground holes, or beneath overhangs. The construction is performed solely by the male. He starts building several nests on his territory and tries to attract the female. She picks one of the nests and decorates it with a lining of hair and feathers. Nestlings from the second brood are looked after by parents cooperating with the older siblings. There are some pairs that live together all year round, but often the male mates with several females. The wren is originally an American species which is exceptional in view of its relatively recent successful expansion to Asia, Europe, and northern Africa. The validity of this assumption is supported by the great number of wren species living close to the Bering Strait.

Prunella modularis

DUNNOCK   **PA**

The dunnock lives in Europe, ranging from the Arctic region to the Mediterranean area. It is also found in the Caucasus, Turkey, and Iran. It frequents forests and shrublands, parks, cemeteries and neglected gardens as well as agricultural country that has rows of bushes. It is also typically found at higher elevations in stunted mountain vegetation. The female builds the nest almost exclusively of moss, lines it with hair and moss capsules and lays in it 4–6 beautiful, blue-green colored eggs. The dunnock is partly migratory and moves to southern and western Europe. Many birds, however, remain in their breeding grounds throughout the winter.

Prunella collaris

ALPINE ACCENTOR   **PA**

The Alpine accentor's range includes Europe, southeastern Asia, and the northwestern tip of Africa. It is truly a mountainous bird which breeds above the tree line on stony and grassy hillsides and rocky summits. Its nest is always cleverly concealed in a rocky crag, stony detritus, or below the boulders and bushes. Occasionally, it can be placed in the supporting walls of mountain cottages. Both parents take turns warming the 3–5 eggs for 13–15 days. The advent of cold season makes the birds descend to lower altitudes.

Cercotrichas galactotes

RUFOUS BUSH-CHAT   **PA AF**

The Rufous Bush-chat's European range includes the western and eastern Mediterranean regions. It then extends through the Transcaucasian area to Central Asia as far as the Aral Sea and Lake Balkhash. It also reaches the northern half of Africa and Arabia. The choice of breeding environments includes sunlit bushy hillsides, vineyards, gardens, palm and olive groves, and shrubby edges of semi-deserts and steppes. Its untidy nest is found in thick shrubs or low trees up to 8ft/2.5m above the ground. It often contains pieces of snake skins. The typical posture for the Rufous Bush-chat features a tall, erect tail.

Erithacus rubecula

ROBIN   **PA**

The robin inhabits most of Europe, the Transcaucasian region, Iran, western Siberia, and northwestern Africa. It is partly migratory and winters in southern Europe and northern Africa. It is typically found in a thick coppice of woods, and also in overgrown gardens, parks and cemeteries. It often runs about the ground. When disturbed, it jerks its tail and distinctively "bobs" its head. The male sings on elevated perches often until after dark. The nest is placed low above the ground in a dense spruce, piles of branches or a holllow in a stump. The female lays 4–6 eggs twice a year and incubates them for 13–14 days. The male then comes to help her with rearing the chicks. Their diet consists of various invertebrates, accompanied by small berries in the autumn.

Luscinia megarhynchos

NIGHTINGALE   **PA**

The nightingale favours lowland deciduous forests, dense vegetation along waters, overgrown parks and gardens. The males sing day and night. Not all of them, however, are such brilliant singers as is said, as they learn by listening. Thus, an individual's skill is determined by the teacher. The nest is always well concealed in a layer of fallen leaves, a heap of brushwood, or among bush sprouts close to the ground. It lives in Europe except for Scandinavia, in Asia from the Near and Middle East as far east as Mongolia, and in northwestern Africa. It is mainly migratory and flies to tropical Africa.

Erithacus rubecula

Cercotrichas galactotes

Luscinia megarhynchos

Luscinia calliope

Luscinia calliope

SIBERIAN RUBYTHROAT   PA

The Siberian rubythroat lives in Asia from the Ural Mountains all the way to the Kamchatka Peninsula, Sakhalin Island and Japan, ranging as far as Mongolia to the south. It expands to Europe only on the western slopes of the northern Urals. The wintering grounds are found from India to Thailand and the Philippines. It frequents shrublands with birches, wil-

Luscinia svecica

lows and cherries *(Cerasus avium)*, forest edges and clearings with fallen logs. Its nest is an untidy structure of extremely fine grass blades and plant fibres. The clutch of 4–6 eggs is thought to be warmed solely by the female.

Luscinia svecica

BLUETHROAT   PA NA

The bluethroat lives in most of Europe and Asia (except for the southwestern area). Only recently it has occupied western Alaska. The northern subspecies with a reddish star on its blue breast *(L. s. svecica)* lives in tundra and mountainous areas such as the Alps, Tatras or Carpathians. The Central European subspecies featuring a white star *(L. s. cyanecula)* prefers marshlands with reeds, sedges and shrubs. In some locations, it also lives on arid rocky hillsides (Spain), or in dry ditches of polders and rape fields (Netherlands). The male skillfully mimics all kinds of sounds including other birds' songs. The nest is usually in a ground depression amidst dense vegetation. It migrates to winter in northern Africa, Asia Minor, and southern Asia.

Cossypha natalensis

RED-CAPPED ROBIN-CHAT   AF

This species inhabits a considerable part of Africa where it is among common, non-migratory birds. It often jerks its tail and is able to imitate the voices of other birds. Either individuals or pairs can be observed in coastal thickets, vegetation along the waterways, in woods, parks and larger gardens. It mostly dwells inside of thick shrubberies, though it forages in the surrounding open terrain, most frequently in the early evening.

Cossypha niveicapilla

SNOWY-CROWNED ROBIN-CHAT　　　　**AF**

This bird is found in Africa, from Gambia and Gabun to Uganda and Kenya. It lives in pairs in forests and brush along waterways, and in some places in gardens. It forages mostly on the ground. Its dict consists mainly of large insects. The bird has often been observed near ant swarms where it apparently hunts the disturbed prey. The nest is carefully hidden in a natural semi-cavity or can be found on the stump of a palm tree.

Phoenicurus ochruros

BLACK REDSTART　　　　**PA OR**

Most people recognize the Black redstart as a typical inhabitant of human settlements. However, it originally occupied rock faces, rocky slopes and detritus, and moved into the towns and villages only much later. The mountain redstarts breed in rocky crevices, hollows below stones and in shallow caves, while the town populations nest beneath the roofs of buildings, barns and sheds, or in alcoves and holes in walls. They also readily accept an artificial, half open nest-box. The bird can be found in Europe except for the northern areas, and in a zone stretching from Asia Minor to the Himalayas and western China. It also nests in northwestern Africa. Southern populations are non-migratory, while the northern ones winter in the Mediterranean area, northern Africa and the Middle East.

Cossypha niveicapilla

Phoenicurus ochruros

Cossypha natalensis

227

Phoenicurus phoenicurus

Phoenicurus erythrogaster

Saxicola rubetra

Phoenicurus phoenicurus

REDSTART   **PA**

This fidgety bird, which always squats and swiftly flickers its tail in the same manner as the Black redstart, lives throughout most of Europe, in northwestern Africa, in the Transcaucasian region as far as Iran and farther east to Lake Baikal. Most often it breeds in light forests, groves, parks, gardens, and cultivated tree rows. It favours hollow trees or nest-boxes, and also various hollows in buildings, wall ledges or beams. Twice a year the female lays 5–7 eggs that she alone incubates for 12–14 days. The male helps only with feeding the young. The bird is migratory, with wintering grounds that spread from northern to equatorial Africa.

Phoenicurus erythrogaster

GÜLDENSTÄDT'S REDSTART   **PA OR**

This redstart's breeding range is divided into two parts: the Caucasus including western Iran and the mountains of Central Asia. It frequents even the highest mountainous areas in alpine tundra and rocky terrain just below the permanent snow and ice line, at altitudes of up to 18,000ft/5,500m. It is non-migratory though it descends to river valleys below 15,000ft/500m around the beginning of October. There it finds its prime diet, the buckthorn fruit. In breeding season, however, it feeds mainly on insects. The nest is built in rocky cracks and clefts, in holes under large stones, and in stony moraines.

Saxicola torquata

Oenanthe isabellina

Saxicola rubetra

WHINCHAT   **PA**

The whinchat frequents wet meadows and pastures with occasional bushes, including those in the mountains, and peatbogs. It is also found in dry areas with shrubs. It perches on tops of bushes, protruding plants, poles and wires, among which it flits in a swaggering manner. Upon landing, it jerks its wings and fans the tail. From time to time it swiftly descends to the ground or flies up after insects. The female builds a nest on the ground amid dense vegetation and usually lays 5–6 blue-green eggs that she warms for 12–14 days. The distribution range is mainly Europe, though it extends to Asia as far as the Yenisei River and Altai.

Saxicola torquata

STONECHAT   **PA AF OR**

The stonechat can be found throughout most of Eurasia, and in northwestern and southern Africa. European populations usually winter in Africa, while the Asian ones move to India and southeastern Asia. It breeds on sunlit rocky hillsides, in dry meadows and pastures with isolated bushes located in mountainous elevations, and in wastelands, heathlands and marshes. The nest is built on the ground, often on a slope in a depression beneath overhanging grass or other vegetation. The diet is comprised of insects and their larvae, spiders, small worms, and mollusks.

Oenanthe isabellina

ISABELLINE WHEATEAR   **PA**

The Isabelline wheatear's choice of habitats ranges from steppe to desert. It can, however, be found in wooded steppes from Turkey to the Caspian Sea and farther east to western China and northen Mongolia. It shows preference for terrain with sandy, limestone, or a clay base, featuring isolated bushes and rocks as well as for grassy locations and barrens. It may be found as high as 12,000ft/3,500m on warm, arid plains. It nests in abandoned rodent and bee-eater

burrows, or in natural rock cavities. It is migratory and winters in tropical Africa, Arabia, and in the area from Iraq to northern India.

Oenanthe oenanthe

NORTHERN WHEATEAR   **PA NA**

The Northern wheatear is the most numerous and common species of the *Oenanthe* genus. It has colonized most of Europe and Asia, and also Greenland, western and southern Alaska, the Canadian Yukon and northeastern Canada. It frequents open terrain from sea level to alpine meadows and pastures, and also rocky fields above the tree line (up to an altitude of 10,000ft/3,000m). In the northern regions, it inhabits tundra. It also breeds in stone quarries, dumping grounds, construction sites, and waste grounds. It enjoys perching on stones, and often "bobs" and waves its open tail. The nest is usually disguised inside of a deep hollow – in pile of stones, cracks in walls and rocks, and in various holes including mammal and bird burrows. The winter is spent in tropical Africa and India.

Oenanthe oenanthe

Oenanthe hispanica

Oenanthe hispanica

BLACK-EARED WHEATEAR   PA

The Black-eared wheatear inhabits the southern parts of
Europe and Asia as far as Iran, and north-western Africa.
It winters in Africa in a narrow zone south of the Sahara.
It is found in arid steppes with rocky outcrops, in sandy
and rocky locations of similar character with fields and
vineyards, in limestone hills with scattered bushes (including the edges of the olive groves), and areas with junipers and Mediterranean oaks. It usually lives at medium altitudes, but has been observed at heights of up to
8,200ft/2,500m in Iran. It nests on the ground in shallow holes that are found among stones, amid dense vegetation, or underneath low shrubs.

Oenanthe pleschanka

Oenanthe pleschanka

PIED WHEATEAR   PA

The range of the Pied wheatear stretches from the
western shore of the Black Sea to Mongolia and
northern China, and in the south to Tian Shan and
Pamir (excluding the Himalayas). The breeding habitat is similar to that of the wheatear. In the eastern
regions, it is actually found instead of the wheatear. In
these areas it ranges up to heights of 12,000ft/3,500m.
It nests in holes in rocks or banks, below stones, and
sometimes on buildings. It migrates to winter in eastern Africa and the southeastern part of the Arab
Peninsula. It crossbreeds with the Black-eared
Wheatear.

Oenanthe leucura

BLACK WHEATEAR   PA

In Europe, the Black wheatear nests only in southern
France and the Iberian Peninsula, and further south

Oenanthe leucura

in northwestern Africa. It requires rocks (including
coastal cliffs), bare ground and low, scattered bushes.
It is non-migratory and usually nests in hollows in
rocks and in man-made reinforcement walls. Like the
majority of wheatears it lays 3–5 eggs.

Monticola solitarius

BLUE ROCK THRUSH   PA OR

The Blue Rock thrush ranges from the Mediterranean
area and northwestern Africa through Asia Minor, the
Caucasus, Tibet, and China to Japan and Malaysia.
For breeding, it seeks ocean cliffs, mountain faces and
valleys (in the Atlas Mountains up to 10,000ft/
3,000m), and ruins. In towns and villages, especially
in southern Europe, it also occupies house roofs, towers, castles and churches. The nest is set up in crevices
in rocks, below overhangs, in caves, stone quarries or
in holes in walls. It is partly migratory, the major win-

Monticola solitarius

tering grounds can be found in eastern Africa, the Arab Peninsula, India, and southeastern Asia, including the region's islands.

Turdus torquatus

RING OUZEL   **PA**

The Ring ouzel resembles the blackbird but has a crescent-shaped patch across its breast. It lives only in European mountains from Scandinavia to Spain, and in Iran. However, in the foothills, it may nest as low as 820ft/250m. It particularly favours coniferous woods, including scrub. It also infrequently breeds in mixed forests (especially beech). It forages on the ground in neighbouring meadows, pastures, forest clearings and paths. The nest is built mainly by the female, who conceals it carefully in dense tree branches. The bird is migratory and flies to southern Europe or northern Africa.

Turdus merula

BLACKBIRD   **PA OR**

Besides Europe, the blackbird inhabits northern Africa and a narrow zone stretching from Asia Minor and Central Asia all the way to the Japanese Sea. It was also introduced into Australia. Its appearance and singing enliven even city centers. The process of the bird's urbanization began in the middle of the 19th century and is explained by the better living conditions in towns, especially the availability of food and more temperate climate. Originally, however, the blackbird was a forest bird and a part of its population still remains loyal to this habitat. Blackbirds living in forests are shy and careful, unlike the birds from the towns. They build their nests mainly in bushes and trees, while the town birds build them almost anywhere: on ledges and alcoves of buildings, on a hung ladder, or on a gravestone. They breed twice or three times per a season.

Turdus torquatus

Turdus merula

Turdus pallidus

Turdus pilaris

Turdus pallidus

PALE THRUSH PA

It lives in Siberia as far east as the Kamchatka Peninsula and in Korea and Japan. Its wintering grounds can be found in the area from eastern India and southern China to the Philippines and the Greater Sunda Islands. Its nest is made up of grass and roots held together with mud. A central depression in the nest is lined with dry leaves and pine needles. The nest is placed in small trees 4–16ft/1–5m above the ground. The pairs breed twice a year.

Turdus pilaris

FIELDFARE PA

The fieldfare usually breeds in colonies and occasionally in individual pairs. The bird favors cultivated landscapes. It nests in groves along waterways, in parks and gardens, and at the edges of forests. At higher elevations it can be found up to the tree line. In northern areas it can be found in scrublands above the tree line. Its nest can be located in a tree or bush. The nest is built by the female bird, who then alone incubates 4 to 6 eggs. After 13 to 14 days, both parents begin to feed the

Turdus iliacus

Turdus philomelos

Turdus viscivorus

hatchlings. The young birds remain in the nest for about 2 weeks. The fieldfare lives in Europe in a region ranging on the southen edge from southwestern France to central Romania and northwards. In Asia, it is found in the northern half of the continent up to the Amur River. It migrates in numerous flocks to southern Europe and southern Asia.

Turdus iliacus

REDWING   **PA**

The redwing's distinguishing features are its rusty red flanks and underwing. The main breeding grounds are in northern Europe and eastwards to northern Siberia. Secondary breeding ranges are scattered through southern Europe. It appears now that the main breeding areas are shifting southwards. In the northern areas, it is a common bird of tundra and taiga regions and is also found in rocky areas that have no vegetation. It also nests in parks and gardens. In the south, it breeds in wetlands along the waterways and at the edges of woods near wet meadows. It breeds in solitary pairs within colonies of fieldfares. Its nest is found in bushes and trees and in tundra areas on the ground. It migrates, primarily at night, to the Mediterranean area and southwestern Asia.

Turdus philomelos

SONG THRUSH   **PA**

This bird lives mainly at the edges of forests and in forest clearings. It also lives in bushes along rivers and in parks and gardens. It is much less acclimated to humans than the blackbird for example. In flight, the visible underwing is yellowish in color. It feeds mainly on gasteropods and gains access to them by breaking the shells on rocks and tree stumps. These feeding areas, called "anvils," are littered with piles of broken shells and quite obviously denote the presence of the bird. It also feeds on other invertebrates and various fruit. The nest is characterized by sides painted with a mixture of forest duff and the bird's saliva. It is found mainly in Eu-

rope and in an area that ranges into Asia to Lake Baikal. Part of the bird population is non-migratory. However, most of the birds migrate to the Mediterranean area and Western Europe.

Turdus viscivorus

MISTLE THRUSH   **PA**

The Mistle thrush is mostly found in forested area because it requires tall trees for breeding. However, it favors open areas for foraging. Its appearance in suburban parks is a relatively new phenomena. It is found in most of Europe, in eastern and central Siberia, and southwards to the Himalayas. It is also found in northern Africa. The northern populations migrate to the Mediterranean area. The bird's underwing is whitish.

Turdus leucomelas

PALE-BREASTED THRUSH   **NT**

This bird is found in tropical and sub-tropical zones from Guinea and Venezuela and Colombia to northeastern Peru, Paraguay, northern Bolivia and Argentina. It is found up to an altitude of 8,200ft/2,500m. It prefers

Turdus leucomelas

Garrulax leucolophus

shrubby savannah, light forests near waterways, plantations and gardens.

Garrulax leucolophus
WHITE-CRESTED LAUGHINGTHRUSH   OR

This is one of the noisiest birds to be found. It remains in flocks and colonies year-round. Its range covers an area from Pakistan through Nepal and India to Thailand and Sumatra. It lives in forests with dense ground cover, including second growth forests and bamboo jungles. It particularly favors foothills with ravines and terraces. It forages on the ground and feeds mainly on insects, fruit and seeds. In addition, it feeds on small

Garrulax pectoralis

reptiles and plant nectar. It holds its larger living prey with its legs and tears it with its beak. The female lays 3 to 6 eggs that are incubated by both parents.

Garrulax pectoralis
GREATER NECKLACED LAUGHINGTHRUSH   OR

This bird's range is from eastern Pakistan through India and Bhutan to Vietnam. It lives in dense old-growth and secondary forests and bamboo jungles often in the vicinity of cultivated areas. It hunts primarily for insects on the forest floor, moving by large hopping jumps. It is found in noisy flocks of 10 to 25 birds.

Garrulax formosus
RED-WINGED LAUGHING THRUSH   PA OR

This non-migratory bird lives in southeastern Asia up to the altitudes of 7,000ft/2,000m. It favors the forest undergrowth similar to the other laughing thrushes. It can be found most of the time in flocks of 3 to 30 birds. These flocks have a fairly complicated social structure. The incubation time for the eggs is 13 to 16 days. The young birds remain in the nest for approximately the same length of time.

Yuhina nigrimenta
BLACK-CHINNED YUHINA   PA OR

This bird is found from eastern Pakistan and the foothills of the Himalayas to southern China and Vietnam. It inhabits evergreen forests, secondary jungle and overgrown clearings. It feeds mainly on insects and also on berries, seeds and nectar. It is highly gregarious, restless and noisy. It lives in flocks of 15 to 20 birds, often together with other babblers. The nest is a very compact basket of moss, roots and fine grasses often found hanging within tussocks of moss below the tree branches. The nest can also be interwoven with exposed tree roots on river banks.

Garrulax formosus

Yuhina nigrimenta

Locustella naevia

Panurus biarmicus

BEARDED TIT   **PA**

This bird is found in large reed beds and reed-mace. It nests individually or in groups. The nest can be found in tussocks of sedges, reeds or reed-mace. It is usually up to 30in/75cm above the water or ground and barely visibile from above. The eggs are incubated by both parents and both also feed the young, often with help from neighbouring birds. The birds commonly breed 2 or 3 times a year. The pairs mate for several years. These unions are often formed between very young birds and these new pairs may have their own families started by the end of their first summer. The Bearded tit is non-migratory, but often moves within its range. It can be found in the southern half of Europe and throughout Asia Minor and central Asia to China.

Locustella naevia

GRASSHOPPER WARBLER   **PA**

The Grasshopper warbler inhabits primarily northern and Central Europe and eastward to southeastern Siberia. This migratory bird moves to sub-Saharan Africa for the winter. It may also be found during the winter in the Middle East and India. For breeding it requires dense, low vegetation less than 3ft/1m in height found in meadows, on the edges of ponds and in forest clearings and young forests. It builds its nest in dense tangled plants on or just above the ground. The presence of the Grasshopper warbler is often noted only because of the male's call, which is an uninterrupted single tone ringing warbling that can last for up to 3 minutes.

Panurus biarmicus

235

Locustella fluviatilis

Locustella fluviatilis

RIVER WARBLER   **PA**

The River warbler is unique to Europe and migrates to eastern Africa. It lives secretly as do other warblers. It makes its way through dense vegetation in a deft and unnoticed fashion. The male makes himself visible on the tops of plants and bushes only when singing. It nests in thickets along creeks, rivers and ponds. It is also found in swamps and the thick undergrowth of forests growing in floodplains. In northern Europe, it can be found in fairly dry areas, such as the margins of fields. The nest is masterly hidden in thick undergrowth and access is often gained by means of a bridge of sorts that connects to the side of the nest.

Locustella luscinioides

SAVI'S WARBLER   **PA**

The call of the male Savi's warbler is a deeper, often interrupted warbling that is similar to other warbler species that is heard at night. It nests in swampy groves usually of reeds and reed-mace. It also occasionally can be found in groves of small willow trees. Both parents build the nest from strips of reeds, reed-mace and sedges. The female lays 4 to 5 eggs and the male helps with the incubation. The young birds hatch after about 12 days and leave the nest after about the same length of time. The bird lives mainly in Central and Eastern Europe, southeastern Siberia and northern Africa. It winters in equatorial Africa.

Locustella luscinioides

Acrocephalus schoenobaenus

236

Acrocephalus bistrigiceps

Acrocephalus scirpaceus

Acrocephalus schoenobaenus

SEDGE WARBLER PA

The Sedge warbler prefers groves of reeds, sedges and tall grasses interspersed with single bushes found on the edges of rivers and ponds. It can also be found in swampy meadows and overgrown ditches and drier biotopes, such as shrubberies and grain fields. When singing, the male flies diagonally upwards and then with open wings and tail it descends. The nest is not attached to a strong main plant stem as are the nests of most of the other warblers. It is simply built among the dense layers of old grass, sedge and reeds. It lives in most of Europe and in an extended range across the Ural Mountains to central Siberia and northwestern Africa. It winters in sub-Saharan Africa.

Acrocephalus bistrigiceps

BLACK-BROWED REED WARBLER PA

This Reed warbler is found in wet and damp areas overgrown with dense grasses and bushes. It also inhabits meadows close to bodies of water connected with human settlement. Sometimes it is also found in dry grassy places too. It builds a deep bowl-like nest in dense grass. It lives in the Far East, including Korea and Mongolia. It migrates during the winter to southern China and eastern India.

Acrocephalus scirpaceus

REED WARBLER PA

The Reed warbler inhabits most of Europe up to southern Finland in the north. The range spans into Asia Minor, Iran and Kazakhstan. It also encompasses northwestern Africa. It typically lives in reed and reed-mace beds, either in the water or in marshy areas. It nests in loose colonies. The deep basket-like nest made from reed strips and plant fibers is constructed by both parents and hung on stems and stalks 10–40in/25–100cm above the water or ground.

Acrocephalus palustris

MARSH WARBLER PA

The Marsh warbler does not need as wet a habitat as most other warblers. It can be found not only on the edges of lakes and ponds and along waterways, but also in cultivated grain fields and areas of clover and rape seed. It is also found in the bushy areas used to define field boundaries, in dense weeds, often stinging nettles and nearby village dump areas. The nest is interwoven with plant stems or bush twigs not high above the ground. The bird's diet is similar to most other warblers and consists of insects and their larvae, spiders and small mollusks. In autumn, it also feeds on small berries. Its home is a great part of Europe. In Asia, it can be found only in a small area just beyond the Ural Mountains and also in Iraq and Iran. It migrates to eastern and southern Africa.

Acrocephalus palustris

Acrocephalus arundinaceus

GREAT REED WARBLER   PA

The Great Reed warbler prefers large groves of reeds and reed-mace in places with permanent bodies of water. The female interweaves the nest with several reed or reed-mace stems. The nest is up to 8in/20cm deep with the upper edge curved inward so the eggs will remain in the nest even during bad weather. The clutch of 4–5 eggs is incubated only by the female, while the male flies to the nest to feed her. After 10 or 12 days, the young chicks deftly climb on the stems near the nest, even before they are able to fly. It lives in all of Europe except the extreme northern areas, Asia Minor, and a broad unconnected strip from central to eastern and southeastern Asia. In autumn, it moves to equatorial and southern Africa.

Acrocephalus aedon

Acrocephalus aedon

THICK-BILLED WARBLER   PA

The Thick Billed warbler resembles the Great Reed warbler but posesses a thicker and shorter bill. It nests in eastern Siberia from the River Ob to China, Mongolia and Japan. It winters in an area that ranges from eastern India and southern China to the Andaman and Nicobar Islands. It migrates before the end of summer, during August. It lives in wooded steppes, sparce forests and clearings. The nest is built in birch or sallow trees in forks in the branches 3–5ft/100–150cm. above the ground. The clutch consists of 5-6 eggs.

Hippolais pallida

Hippolais icterina

Phylloscopus trochilus

Hippolais pallida

OLIVACEOUS WARBLER　　　　　　**PA AF**

The range of the the Olivaceous warbler consists of two different areas. One is Spain together with northwestern Africa, while the other is in the Balkans, regions near the Black Sea and Central Asia. The sub-species from these two areas are sometimes considered to be an independent species. The birds winter in the eastern and western parts of equatorial Africa. This bird lives in both a drier habitat of gardens and orchards containing taller trees and in wetter shrubby areas. The nest is built in the branches of bushes or trees. Only the female incubates the eggs for about 13 days.

Hippolais icterina

ICTERINE WARBLER　　　　　　　　**PA**

The Icterine warbler is an accomplished singer and is a master at imitating the songs of other birds. It prefers well-lit, deciduous forests with shrubs, overgrown banks of waters, parks and gardens. The nests, which are placed on deciduous bushes or trees, are among the most beautifully crafted of any of the birds. It is skillfully woven from dry grass, small roots, pieces of moss, cot-

Prinia gracilis

ton-wool and cobwebs. It is often decorated along the upperparts with white strips of birch bark. The species breeds only once a year and the birds soon fly away to central and southern Africa. The breeding grounds are found in Europe from central France eastwards to beyond the Ural Mountains and farther to central Siberia. A separate population lives in Iran.

Prinia gracilis

GRACEFUL WARBLER　　　　　　　**PA OR**

The Graceful warbler is found in dense jungles of tamarisk, in tall grass and other heavy vegetation, in thickets along rivers and water channels. It is found less often in semi-desert areas with shrubs. The nest is placed in bushes or tussocks about 3.3ft/1m above the ground and has the shape of a sphere or pouch with a side entrance in the upper half. The male builds the outer part of the nest, while the female constructs the interior. The bird is non-migratory and is found from Iran to northeastern India and also in northeastern Africa.

Phylloscopus trochilus

WILLOW WARBLER　　　　　　　　**PA**

The Willow warbler lives in the northern half of Europe and Asia reaching all the way east to the Tchukotka Peninsula. It is migratory. Winters are spent in sub-Saharan Africa. It nests anywhere shrubs can be found namely in the undergrowth of deciduous and coniferous forests, in tree nurseries, in overgrown clearings, in subalpine low vegetation, or in birch or willow tundra. The spherical and closed nest with a side entrance is placed near the ground, well hidden in tussocks of grass or blackberry brambles. The female alone builds the nest and incubates the clutch of 5 to 7 eggs. The male assists with raising the young chicks for 12 to 15 days, while they are in the nest and for another week after the chicks leave the nest.

Phylloscopus collybita

Sylvia atricapilla

Phylloscopus collybita

CHIFFCHAFF PA

The chiffchaff is found in all of Europe, the northern half of Asia up to the Kolyma River and northwestern Africa. It sometimes winters in Great Britain, Central Europe and in the Mediterranean area. However, most of the birds migrate to equatorial and eastern Africa and to India. It frequents deciduous and coniferous forests and their edges. In the mountains, it is found in dwarf pines zones. It also inhabits parks and cemeteries. The

Phylloscopus sibilatrix

enclosed nest with a side entrance is woven in a way similar to the nests of other types of warblers and is made up of dry grass, twigs, leaves, moss and strips of bast. The nest's lining is almost always made up of feathers. The nest is placed on, or just above, the ground in blueberry or spruce bushes.

Phylloscopus sibilatrix

WOOD WARBLER PA

The Wood warbler is a European species that ranges also into central Siberia. It is strictly migratory and winters in equatorial Africa. It breeds in deciduous and mixed forests and occasionally in pine forests. The round nest with a side entrance is built by the female under the cover of grass or fallen leaves. It never is lined with feathers. Its diet is similar to other warblers and consists of insects during their various stages of development, and spiders and other arthropods. In autumn, it varies its diet with berries and other soft fruit.

Sylvia atricapilla

BLACKCAP PA AF

The male blackcap has a black cap and the female a brown cap. Of all the *Sylvia* warblers, the blackcap most prefers a woodland habitat particularly deciduous and mixed forests. However, it lives in coniferous forest too. It also favors forested river banks, overgrown parks, cemeteries and gardens. The female builds a loosely woven nest of tiny twigs, stems and grass leaves near the ground in a shaded area. It lives in all of Europe except for the northern most areas, in western Siberia and northwestern Africa. It winters in the Mediterranean regions and even in central Africa.

Sylvia borin

GARDEN WARBLER   PA

The Garden warbler lives in all parts of Europe and the range extends to central Siberia. It can be found in bushy edges and clearings of deciduous and mixed forests and in thickets along the banks of waterways and ponds. Less often it is found in parks and cemeteries with shrub cover. The mating pair construct a bowl shaped, thin walled (sometimes almost transparent) nest of dry grass lined with very fine grass in low shrubs. After a single breeding, the birds fly to tropical and southern Africa.

Sylvia borin

Sylvia communis

WHITETHROAT   PA

The whitethroat's range extends from the Artic Circle in Norway to Morocco and from Portugal to central Siberia. It winters in sub-Sahahran Africa. It frequents open country with rows of shrubs, groves of windbreaks and edges of forests. Sometimes it lives in ditches with dense and high vegetation usually containing nettles. Similar to other *Sylvia* warblers, the male first builds one or more "male's nest" into which it attracts the female. She either accepts and uses this nest or builds a new one with the male's assistance in a dense tangle of branches usually up to 3.3ft/1m above the ground. The diet consists of mainly insects and in the fall, fleshy fruit.

Sylvia communis

Sylvia curruca

LESSER WHITETHROAT   PA

The Lesser whitethroat favors open terrain and avoids deep forests. It nests only on the forest edges and clearings, overgrown slopes, strips of bushes along gravel roadways and in parks and cemeteries. The mating pair builds a poorly constructed nest in bushes 3.3ft/1m above the ground.

They share responsibility for the incubation of 4 to 5 eggs for 10 to 13 days. After raising the second brood of chicks, the birds migrate to eastern Africa and India. The breeding grounds range from Great Britain to Siberia and eastern Mongolia and China.

Sylvia curruca

Sylvia nissoria

Sylvia nissoria
BARRED WARBLER   **PA**

The Barred warbler prefers warm, open terrain with thick shrubberies, in particular areas with thorny bushes, sunlit hillsides, overgrown forest edges and bodies of water. It avoids human settlements. Its nest, built mostly by the female, is often found close to the nest of the Red-backed shrike whom other passerines usually avoid. The mated pairs only raise one brood of chicks and soon leave for eastern Africa. The homeland of this species is Europe, from southern Finland

to Greece and from Denmark and France to the Ural Mountains. Beyond the Urals, the range extends to Central Asia as far as Altai and Tian Shan.

Sylvia melanocephala
SARDINIAN WARBLER   **PA**

In Europe, the Sardinian warbler's range includes primarily the Mediterranean regions and further extends to Syria and Jordan. In Africa, it is restricted to Morocco and the Atlas Mountains (up to 8,000ft/ 2,400m). It breeds in *maquis*, at the edges of oak and pine forests, in olive and citrus orchards, vineyards and suburban gardens. The Sardinian warbler has been expanding its territory since the end of the 19th century, and since then it has occupied Malta, the foothills of the Italian Alps, southern France, Bulgaria and Romania. Except for the northeastern areas, the breeding grounds remain sparsely inhabited throughout the winter, even though most of the birds move southwards to Turkey, northern Africa and Cyprus.

Sylvia cantilans
SUBALPINE WARBLER   **PA**

This warbler species also breeds predominantly in the Mediterranean regions and eastward as far as Turkey. In Africa, it lives from Morocco to northwestern Libya. It is a typical inhabitant of dry and warm areas that feature evergreen shrubs (maquis, garigue) and other vegetation up to 25–30ft/8–10m high with dense undergrowth. It winters mostly in tropical Africa.

Sylvia melanocephala

Sylvia cantilans

Sylvia undata

DARTFORD WARBLER   PA

The Dartford warbler is a minute bird with a long, white-skirted tail that is often diagonally cocked and spread. It inhabits various types of low Mediterranean shrubs with cistus, heather, rosemary, and dwarf oak. It also nests in cork-oak *(Quercus suber)* and pine groves with a thick undergrowth. It is non-migratory and winters mainly in breeding regions, namely from Portugal and southern England to southern Italy and northwestern Africa. The nest is built in dense scrub up to 3.3ft/1m above the ground. The pairs breed two or three times a year.

Regulus ignicapillus

FIRECREST   PA

Together with the goldcrest, these species are the smallest European passerines. It inhabits mainly coniferous, but also mixed forests. The female inter-weaves the nest with the side branches of conifers. Similar to the goldcrest's nest, its upper part is nar-rowed and the walls are highly curved, inside which gives it a sphere shape with an opening at the top. This prevents the eggs or hatchlings from falling out of the nest during heavy movements of the branches

Sylvia undata

in the wind. The centre of its range is in an area from the Iberian Peninsula to Central Europe. It is also found in northern Africa, the Balearic Islands and Madeira. It is mostly migratory and winters in the Mediterranean region.

Regulus ignicapillus

Regulus regulus

Malaeornis pammelaina

Regulus regulus

GOLDCREST PA

The goldcrest's range is considerably larger than that of the firecrest and includes almost all of Europe and Central Asia. Isolated populations live in eastern and

Muscicapa striata

western China. It is fully associated with coniferous, particularly spruce and fir forests. Its globular, thick walled nest is placed high up in the side branches. Both partners participate in the nest construction which takes them about 20 days. While only the female incubates 8–11 eggs, the male helps her with raising the young. The second clutch is comprised of only 5–8 eggs. The goldcrest is non-migratory. In winter, it forms roaming flocks together with tits. It feeds on minute insects, their eggs and larvae, and spiders.

Melaenornis pammelaina

SOUTHERN BLACK-FLYCATCHER AF

This bird bird lives in open forests, bushy areas, forested coastal dunes, riparian vegetation, and in plantations, parks and gardens. The nest is just a simple, rickety structure which is situated at the edge of a semi-hollow in a tree trunk or in a wall, in a branch fork, behind peeled off bark or in the old nests of turtle-doves or thrushes. The clutch consists of 2–4 eggs. The bird is found in Africa from Kenya to Zaire (except for the southwestern tip).

Muscicapa striata

SPOTTED FLYCATCHER PA

In addition to northern Africa, the range of the Spotted flycatcher includes nearly all of Europe and stretches into Asia as far as Lake Baikal. The winter is spent in the southern half of Africa. The bird can breed in the most varied of environments as long as they contain trees. It prefers deciduous forests, old planted tree rows and orchards, parks and gardens. The nest is built mostly by the female in various semicavities and cracks in trees, or in axils and ruptures of branches. In towns and villages, the nest is also found in clefts in walls or in the open on beams. It is a bowl-shaped structure made of roots, stems and moss, and lined with feathers and hair. 4–5 eggs are incubated by the female for 13–14 days with only rare help from the male.

Muscicapa thalassina
(Eumyias thalassina)

VERDITER FLYCATCHER PA OR

The Verditer flycatcher is a common, non-migratory inhabitant of sparse, deciduous and coniferous forests and shrubs along waterways. It can be found in heights from 4,000–10,000ft/1,200 to 3,000m. in the area from Pakistan and India to Vietnam, Sumatra and Borneo. It perches upright on branches before taking off after insects. The nest is built in banks, rock clefts, under bridges, in holes in walls, beneath the building roofs and also in hollows between bracken and moss on tree trunks.

Ficedula hypoleuca

PIED FLYCATCHER   **PA**

The Pied flycatcher mostly frequents mature, deciduous and mixed forests where plenty of hollows suitable for breeding can be found. Occasionally, it breeds in parks and gardens, being attracted by provided nest-boxes. The nest is woven solely of dry grass and strips of bast. The clutch of 5–8 blue and green eggs is warmed by the female for 13–15 days. Hatched chicks are fed with insects by both parents for another 14–16 days in the nest. It ranges from Europe (except for the southern part) to central Siberia, and in northwestern Africa. Its wintering grounds can be found in tropical Africa.

Ficedula albicollis

COLLARED FLYCATCHER   **PA**

The Collared flycatcher is found from Central Europe to the Ukraine and southwestern Russia. Isolated populations live in southern Italy and on the Swedish islands of Gotland and Öland. It migrates to tropical Africa. Its behavior is similar to the Pied flycatcher's: it perches on dry branches from which it hunts and flirts its tail and wings when agitated. For breeding it seeks deciduous and mixed forests with holes in old trees. Polygamy is quite common, the male often mating with several females. Its crossbreeding with the Pied flycatcher has been proved.

Muscicapa thalassina

Ficedula hypoleuca

Ficedula albicollis

Ficedula parva

Ficedula parva
RED-BREASTED FLYCATCHER PA

The Red-breasted flycatcher breeds in boreal taiga and the temperate zone of Eurasia from Central Europe as far east as the Kamchatka Peninsula and northwestern China. It preferably frequents old, deciduous and mixed, mainly beech woods in foothills and in the mountains. In lowlands, it is also found in oak and linden/oak/hornbeam forests. Its nest is placed in semi-cavities (often just cracks), hollows in trees and sometimes in forks of thick branches. Soon after rearing the young, the birds fly away towards their wintering grounds in India.

Ficedula sapphira

Ficedula sapphira
SAPPHIRE FLYCATCHER PA OR

The Sapphire flycatcher can be found in evergreen forests in the mountains at heights of 4,500–8,500ft/ 1,400–2,600m (the knowledge concerning its vertical distribution is still rather vague). It descends to lower altitudes for the winter. The nest is placed in hollows in trees or holes in banks. It ranges from India and Nepal to southern China and Laos.

Aegithalos caudatus

Aegithalos caudatus
LONG-TAILED TIT PA OR

The Long-tailed tit frequents forest margins, waterside vegetation, large parks and old gardens. Its nest is a completely closed elongated sphere with a narrow opening on a side towards the top. The construction takes two builders 9–13 days. The walls are about 0.6–1in/1.5–2.5cm thick and woven almost exclusively of moss, lichens and bast. Both partners take turns in warming the 6–12 eggs. The young from the first brood often help with the rearing of their younger siblings. The species is non-migratory and markedly sociable. The birds remain together in flocks throughout the whole winter. They live in Europe and Asia as far east as central China.

Remiz pendulinus

Remiz pendulinus

PENDULINE TIT   **PA OR**

The Penduline tit is associated with water habitats and lives mainly on shores of ponds, lakes and rivers. It nests in shrubs and trees. Its suspended pouch-like nest is quite unique. It is of a mitten shape with the entrance made through the "thumb." The construction is started by the male who creates a pear-shaped structure consisting of nettle or wild hop fibres. Together with the female, they stuff the basic structure with plant fuzz mixed with saliva. After the female has laid 5–8 eggs, the male adds the tube-like entrance marking the finished nest. Soon afterwards, the male leaves his mate, starts building another nest and tries to woo yet another female. That may work out for him up to three times per season. The Penduline tit inhabits Central and southern Europe and a part of Asia as far as north-eastern China. It is partly migratory and winters as far south as the Mediterranean region.

Parus palustris

Parus palustris

MARSH TIT   **PA OR**

The Marsh tit has a discontinuous range; the European population is separated by 1,250 miles/2,000km from the eastern Asian one that lives between Sakhalin Island and northern China. Another small population can be found in Burma. The bird is associated with deciduous and mixed forests, and wooded areas near rivers and ponds. Occasionally, it nests in large gardens and parks on the outskirts of towns. An abundance of hollows in trees is required because the Marsh tit is low at the pecking order of tits and is ousted by more aggressive species. The pairs are very cohesive and remain together even in the winter when the Marsh tits join flocks of other tits.

Parus montanus

Parus montanus

WILLOW TIT   **PA OR**

The Willow tit inhabits boreal coniferous forests in the northern regions, while in the southern areas, it is found in wet deciduous and mixed forests, especially in alder, willow and birch woods. In the mountains it ranges up to the tree line. The pairs stay together throughout the winter. In spring, they begin to hollow out their dwelling to be in a rotten trunk or a stump. About 90 % of the occupied nesting holes are newly dug out. The nest is woven of moss, lichens and grass and lined with hair and feathers. Only the female sits on the nest of 7–10 eggs for 12–15 days. The male then assists in looking after the nestlings which leave the nest fully fledged after 17–20 days. The bird's extensive range spans from France in Europe all the way to the Pacific coast in the Oriental region.

Parus cinctus

Parus cristatus

gather in roaming flocks. They feed on insects and seeds.

Parus cinctus

SIBERIAN TIT   **PA NA**

The Siberian tit is associated with the boreal coniferous forests in Eurasia, Alaska and the Canadian Yukon. It usually nests in pine, spruce or larch forests, though it can also be found in deciduous and mixed riparian woodlands, and birch groves. The nests are either placed in abandoned woodpecker hollows or the birds excavate the nests themselves in dying trees. They breed only once a season, and then the families

Parus ater

Parus ater

COAL TIT   **PA OR**

The Coal tit is typically found in coniferous forests. In southern Europe, it also lives in beech and oak woods. It is non-migratory, although the northern populations make invasions southwards at intervals of several years. It belongs to the group of hole nesters. However, because hollows cannot be as easily found in coniferous forests as in deciduous ones, the Coal tit more often than other tits, makes do with ground holes, abandoned burrows of small rodents, holes in tree stumps or cracks in walls and rocks. It readily uses nest-boxes, too. The bird ranges throughout most of Europe and in the large part of northern and Central Asia as far as the Pacific. It is also found in Asia Minor and northwestern Africa.

Parus cristatus

CRESTED TIT   **PA**

The Crested tit's homeland is Europe (except for Italy and northern Scandinavia) as far as the Ural Mountains. It breeds in coniferous forests, especially spruce and pine forests. In southern areas, it also breeds in cork-oak and beech woods, and in larch forests in Scotland. The female builds the nest primarily in ready tree-holes. However, she is able to make the hole herself in soft, rotten stumps and tree trunks. It is non-migratory and lives in only small flocks, not socializing much at

Parus major

Parus caeruleus

all with other tits. It feeds on insects. Outside the breeding season, the main bulk of its diet is made up of conifer seeds.

Parus major

GREAT TIT   **PA OR**

The Great tit has the largest region of all the European tits, which includes northern Africa, all of Europe, most of Asia as far as the Kamchatka Peninsula and the Kuril Islands northward, and India, Malaysia and Indonesia southward. Due to its adaptability, it can live almost anywhere trees can be found. Besides natural tree hollows, it often settles in nest-boxes and may occupy even the most odd hollows, such as an unused water pump, metal pipe or a mailbox. The female lays 7–12, and occasionally even more eggs and incubates them continuously for 13–15 days while the male supplies her with food. If she leaves the nest at all, she covers it carefully. It is partly migratory and some of the moves from the northern areas have the character of an invasion.

Parus caeruleus

BLUE TIT   **PA**

The Blue tit can most often be found in deciduous and mixed forests. In the Alps, it also frequents larch woods, while in northern Africa this tit lives in cedar groves. Apart from that, it may nest in planted tree rows, bank vegetation, groves, gardens, parks and orchards, plainly anywhere trees with hollows can be found. However, it also breeds in holes in walls or in artificial nest-boxes. Its prime breeding grounds are in Europe and the range stretches south-eastwards through the Caucasus to Iraq. The bird is partly migratory. Migrations of the northern populations may sometimes be invasive.

Sitta europaea

NUTHATCH   **PA OR**

The nuthatch frequents deciduous and mixed forests, although it can also be found in coniferous forests, mainly in pine woods, and in parks, gardens and cultivated rows of old trees. The construction instinct of the female is admirable. She walls up the entrance of the tree hollow with clay mixed with saliva to such an extent that only she can squeeze through. If nesting in a nest-box, she bricks up not only the entrance but also any openings in the walls and below the roof. The female does all the work; the male helps only while she is incubating the 6–8 eggs. The nest is made almost exclusively of bark scales (usually pine) and dry leaves. Fledged young will pair by the end of the summer. The bird is non-migratory and ranges from Portugal and Morocco to Japan and Kamchatka, India and China.

Sitta europaea

249

Sitta neumayer

Sitta neumayer

ROCK NUTHATCH   **PA**

The Rock nuthatch can be found in the area from Yugoslavia and the Balkans through Asia Minor to Iraq and Iran, and to Israel. Its favorite habitat is constituted by rocky, precipitate cliffs, especially limestone. More rarely it is to be found on coastal hillsides. The nest is set up in holes and cracks of rocks. It may also breed in hollows in buildings, ruins, and old stone bridges. At higher elevations (up to 3,300ft/1,000m), it nests only on sunlit rocks or on hillsides with conifers.

Certhia familiaris

TREE-CREEPER   **PA OR NA NT**

The Tree-Creeper's Eurasian range extends from Spain through the Caucasus, Himalayas, Tian Shan and Siberia to Korea and Japan. In North America, it can be found from southern Alaska and Canada along the

Certhia familiaris

western coast of the United States to Nicaragua. It prefers coniferous and mixed forests, but also inhabits deciduous forests, parks and gardens. A semi-cavity is usually picked as its breeding site. Its nest is built in cracks in tree trunks, behind loose bark, in piled up logs, and in chinks between the boards of forest huts. The nest basis of loose twigs is up to 15in/40cm high. At its top, the tidy nest of grass, moss, lichens, hair and feathers is placed. Five to seven eggs are incubated by the female for about 15 days. The bird's diet consists of various invertebrates.

Climacteris affinis

WHITE-BROWED TREE-CREEPER   **AU**

This birds's home is in the eastern part of Australia. It mainly frequents acacia woods, although it can also be found in forests dominated by trees of the *Callitris* and *Casuarina* genera. According to the newest opinions, tree creepers are related to lyrebirds and bowerbirds. They creep up tree trunks and limbs in search of insects, especially ants. They nest in hollows, obviously cooperatively – the individual birds, mostly males, help with feeding the nestlings.

Nectarinia chalybea

SOUTHERN DOUBLE-COLLARED SUNBIRD   **AF**

The Southern Double-collared sunbird ranges from Angola to the southernmost tip of the African continent. It is a common species in various habitats, from sparse forests and their edges to the town gardens. It uses its thin, decurved bill with tubular tongue to pick insects and nectar from tree flowers. It lives alone or in pairs, although larger groups may gather on flow-

Climacteris affinis

Nectarinia chalybea

Entomyzon cyanotis

ering trees. These birds constantly call, wrangle with each other and fly over and among trees. The nest with two eggs and the entrance in its upper third hangs from the end of a branch. It is built of fine grass stalks and leaves, plant wool, bark and cobwebs.

Entomyzon cyanotis

BLUE-FACED HONEYEATER   **AU**

This species' home is northern, eastern and, to some extent, southern Australia and New Guinea. It frequents the edges of rain and eucalyptus forests and mangrove woods. The northern and southeastern populations are migratory. The birds live in pairs or small groups. They feed on insects, nectar, pollen and soft fruit. The nest of bark strips and grass is usually built in the fork of branches. Occasionally, the birds use abandoned nests of other honey-eaters or babblers after they repair them. The clutch consists of 2–3 eggs.

Manorina melanophrys

BELL MINER   **AU**

The Bell miner is found in the south-eastern part of Australia. It lives in forests and other woodlands as well as in suburban biotopes. Due to its metallic voice, it is called a "bell" by the Australians. It belongs to the short-billed miner species. In order to feed, these species lick sweet secretions produced by certain insects. The extensible tongue with a "brush" at its far end is a fundamental tool for this purpose. When feeding on nectar, the birds often peck out a hole at the base of a flower where nectar can be reached more

easily. They also feed on insects. They breed in colonies where the non-breeding birds assist the breeding ones in feeding the young. The bowl-shaped nest of twigs and bark strips is put in the branch fork and contains 2–3 eggs.

Manorina melanophrys

Miliaria calandra

Emberiza hortulana

Miliaria calandra

CORN BUNTING   **PA**

The Corn bunting's flight is rather heavy, and short fly-overs are made with drooped legs. Primarily, it can be found in lowland locations. This bunting inhabits agricultural country with fields, meadows, scattered trees

Emberiza citrinella

and bushes. In southward areas, it is also found in arid pastures and steppes. The female lays 4–5 eggs in a ground depression and incubates them for 12–14 days. Because the male often mates with several females, the job of feeding the chicks also rests mainly with the female. Their range stretches from Europe (except for the northern parts) to Central Asia, and southwards to Asia Minor, Iraq and Iran. The bird is also found in northern Africa. It is partly migratory: the northern populations move to the southern parts of the range.

Emberiza citrinella

YELLOWHAMMER   **PA**

The yellowhammer frequents open country featuring fields and meadows as well as groups of trees and bushes. It is also found in groves, vegetation along waterways, in forest edges and glades. Nor does it avoid the outskirts of human settlements. The female builds its nest in a ground depression under a turf, beneath or low in a bush, and on field balks. The pairs breed twice, and sometimes three times a year. In autumn, they form roaming flocks with other granivorous birds that move about, often far from their nesting quarters. The bird lives throughout Europe and can also be found in central Siberia and northern Africa. Between 1862 and 1871, it was introduced into New Zealand where its population thrives.

Emberiza hortulana

ORTOLAN   **PA**

Even though *hortulana* means "garden" in Latin, this name does not put a finger on the ortolan's habitat. The

Emberiza cirlus

Emberiza cirlus

bird does not nest in gardens – in the best case it is found in orchards and vineyards. It frequents agricultural country with fields, tree rows along roads, groves and dry warm bushy slopes. It also nests at the edges of light forests. The nest is constructed by the female of dry grass matter, roots, horsehair and hair, and is placed on or just above the ground. The bird's range extends from Europe to Mongolia and southwards through the Caucasus to Afghanistan.

Emberiza cirlus

CIRL BUNTING PA

The Cirl bunting can be found in Western, Central and southern Europe, and also in Turkey and northern Africa. A non-indigenous population lives in New

Zealand. It is non-migratory and breeds on sparsely vegetated shrubby slopes, in warm valleys with bushes and trees, in pastures, orchards and vineyards. The nest is usually built in bushes 7ft/2m above the ground. It nests in pairs, though polygamy is also known to this bird. The diet is similar to that of the other buntings: seeds of various plants including grain, small fruit, insects and other invertebrates.

Emberiza fucata

CHESTNUT-EARED BUNTING PA OR

This bunting lives lives in Afghanistan, the western Himalayas as far as Nepal, in Burma, China and Japan. It is a non-migratory, mountainous species that most often breeds at heights of 5,300–9,000ft/ 1,600–2,700m. It descends to lower altitudes for the winter. It stays on slopes vegetated with cotoneasters, barberries, wild roses and junipers, especially along rivers. Its nest is usually on a steep slope on the ground beneath a grass tussock or a bush. The clutch consists of 3–4 eggs.

Emberiza elegans

YELLOW-THROATED BUNTING PA OR

The Yellow-throated bunting's favourite habitat is young deciduous forests (particularly oak) with individual tall trees. The males sing mostly on side tree branches, though occasionally on the tops of bushes. Its nest is always placed on the ground and shielded by a bush or grass. It is just a shallow depression lined with moss, grass and hair. The bird inhabits the Far East down to the north of the East Indies. It winters in the southern parts of its breeding range and in southern Japan.

Emberiza fucata

Emberiza elegans

Emberiza melanocephala

Emberiza melanocephala

BLACK-HEADED BUNTING PA

The Black-headed bunting ranges from Italy through the Balkan Peninsula, the Ukraine and southeastern Russia to Turkey, the Near East and Iran. It winters in western and central India. It frequents open areas with shrubs, sparse groves, vineyards and orchards. On the coast it is found in warm, karstic valleys. Even though it is predominantly a lowland species, it can be found at heights of up to 7,000ft/2,100m in Turkey. The nest is built in shrubberies, thistles or grass, either on the ground or up to 3.3ft/1m above the ground. The eggs are incubated only by the female who also looks after the nestlings. At the same time, the males continue singing which suggests a polygamous breeding strategy.

Emberiza spodocephala

BLACK-FACED BUNTING PA

This bunting is found from the Ob River valley in western Siberia to Japan, Sakhalin Island and the Kuril Islands. It is migratory and winters in a zone from India to Vietnam. It favors environments with tall grass, bamboo and willow thickets along waterways. It lives in coniferous taiga, occasionally also in deciduous mountain forests, including rhododendron forests. Its nest is placed low, up to 20in/50cm above the ground, and sometimes on the ground amid dense shrubs.

Emberiza schoeniclus

REED BUNTING PA

The Reed bunting favours wet shores of ponds and rivers with sparse willows as well as swamps and marshes overgrown with reed, reed-mace, sedges and other marshy plants. It also lives on tundra in birch, willow and alder clumps. In some locations, it is found in fields of corn, grain and rape. The nest is situated on or just above the ground. It is invariably well concealed in lodged reeds, in sedges or a bush. The

Emberiza spodocephala

Emberiza schoeniclus

Calcarius lapponicus

populations living from Central Europe northwards are migratory and winter near the range's southern boundary. The range encompasses all of Europe and expands through Central and northern Asia all the way to the Sakhalin Island and Japan.

Calcarius lapponicus

LAPLAND BUNTING   PA NA

The Lapland bunting ranges from southern Norway through Arctic Russia to the Kamchatka and Tchukotka Peninsulas and further east from Alaska to the southern half of Greenland. Its habitat is mainly swampy tundra with dwarfed trees (willows, birches). It is decidedly the most numerous Arctic passerine. It breeds in pairs on elevated places in dry grass or other vegetation. It is migratory, its wintering grounds may be found from the Baltics through southern Russia to Central Asia and Manchuria. In North America, it winters in the area from southern Canada to the southern United States.

Plectrophenax nivalis

SNOW BUNTING   PA NA

The Snow bunting has the northernmost distribution range of all the terrestrial birds. It inhabits rocky, sparsely vegetated tundra along the coast of the Arctic Ocean on both the Eurasian and North American continents and in the mountains of Scotland and Scandinavia. The nest is well sheltered in rifts in rock faces, among boulders, in cracks in walls of derelict buildings or in piles of wood. Only the female builds the nest and incubates 4–6 eggs, while the male feeds her. During the short Arctic summer, the pairs breed

just once. For the winter, they migrate mainly to the steppes of Eastern Europe and Asia and to similar habitats in North America.

Paroaria coronata

RED-CRESTED CARDINAL   NT

The Red-crested cardinal is found from southern Brazil and Bolivia to Uruguay and central Argentina. It frequents wetlands with shrubs. The female lays 3–6 eggs in a nest placed in a bush. She incubates them alone for about 15 days, though in some pairs the male assists in that as well. Though the young leave the nest after 17 days, their parents provide them with additional food for another 3 weeks.

Paroaria coronata

Thraupis episcopus

Thraupis episcopus
BLUE-GRAY TANAGER   NT

The Blue-gray tanager is widespread from Mexico to north-western Peru, northern Bolivia and the Amazon regions of Brazil. It lives from the lowlands to medium high altitudes in a variety of environments: it can be found on the edges and clearings of wet forests, in open woodland, plantations and in urban gardens. It usually lives in small groups that forage in tree tops and bushes. That is also where its nest is built.

Tangara arthus
GOLDEN TANAGER   NT

The Golden tanager is small, about 5in/13cm long. Its head and underparts are golden yellow. There is a conspicuous black patch on both cheeks. It can be found in tropical and subtropical zones of South America, from Venezuela through Colombia and Equador to

Tangara arthus

northern Bolivia, up to an elevation of 8,200ft/2,500m. It inhabits various types of woodlands, showing a preference for deep woods with tall trees and sparse undergrowth.

Tangara chilensis
PARADISE TANAGER   NT

The Paradise tanager is among the most colorful of all birds. It lives in the tropical zones of South America from Guiana, Venezuela, Colombia and Equador to Bolivia and the Amazonian part of Brazil. It frequents rain forests and their margins, dwelling in the top parts of trees where it seeks ripe fruit and searches branches with epiphytes.

Tangara chilensis

Piranga olivacea
SCARLET TANAGER   NA

The Scarlet tanager lives in southeastern Canada and the eastern regions of the United States. It is migratory – for the winter, it moves to the northern part of South America, in an area from Colombia to western Amazonia. It favours shaded deciduous forests, especially oak and oak-pine forests. It forages high up in the foliage. During the courtship, the males perform their display on low tree branches. The female builds the nest and warms the eggs alone.

Psarocolius angustifrons
RUSSET-BACKED OROPENDOLA   NT

This bird can be found in the tropical and subtropical regions from Venezuela, Colombia and Equador to Bolivia and the Amazonian Brazil. It lives in various kinds of forests, including both the dense and sparse varieties, with or without undergrowth. It is dark chestnut above,

Piranga olivacea

Psarocolius wagleri

its forehead and bill are more or less yellowish, and the underparts are olive brown. The male averages considerably larger (15–17in/39–43cm) than the female.

Psarocolius wagleri

CHESTNUT-HEADED OROPENDOLA   **NT**

The Chestnut-headed oropendola is mostly black. Its head, with a long narrow crest, and the neck are chestnut brown, while the tail is yellow, with a black center. Its bill is whitish to pale greenish yellow and its eyes are blue. The male measures 12–14in/30–35cm, while the female is smaller. It inhabits tropical areas up to an altitude of 5,000ft/1,500m from Colombia to northwestern Equador. It can be found in various types of forests.

Fringilla coelebs

CHAFFINCH   **PA**

The chaffinch is among the most popular and commonest European birds. Its range includes all of Europe and spans eastwards to central Siberia, and southwards to Iran and northern Africa. It breeds anywhere trees can be found, from forests to centers of large towns. Although it is mostly migratory, a number of birds remain in their breeding grounds throughout the winter. These birds, noted natural scientist Carl Linné, are chiefly males. When he was giving scientific names to the birds, he called the chaffinch "widower" *(coelebs)*. Its nest is closely and firmly woven of moss, fine grass blades and roots, and disguised by lichens, cobwebs and insect cocoons.

Psarocolius angustifrons

Fringilla coelebs

Serinus serinus

SERIN **PA**

The original homeland of the serin is the Mediterranean region. In the 19th century, the bird's range began to expand northwards. Nowadays, it can be found as far

Carduelis chloris

north as Scandinavia, and as far east as Turkey, western Russia and Belorussia. It particularly favors parkland with groves, planted tree rows and bank vegetation, the edges of light woods, parks, cemeteries and gardens. Its small, pretty nest is built by the female in a tree or a bush. Unlike other songbirds, the parents neither swallow nor remove droppings of their nestlings. The droppings accumulate at the edge of the nest and create an easily identifiable sign of the serin's presence. North European populations migrate to Central Europe. In recent years, however, more and more birds are remaining on the breeding grounds throughout the winter.

Carduelis chloris

GREENFINCH **PA**

Originally, the greenfinch was found at forest edges and in shrubberies. Today, it lives anywhere thickets suitable for breeding can be found, even in town parks, gardens and cemeteries. In spring, when deciduous woods are still bare, the female builds its nest in conifers, while for the next breeding, she may also pick a deciduous tree. The bird lives in Europe. In the south, the range reaches to the Sinai Peninsula and to northwestern Africa. An isolated population also inhabits the highlands of Turkestan. The greenfinch was successfully introduced into the Azores, Australia, New Zealand, and

Carduelis spinus

Carduelis carduelis

GOLDFINCH   **PA**

The goldfinch favours park-like country with plenty of trees – cultivated tree rows, groves, bank vegetation, parks, orchards and gardens. It is also found in thin deciduous forests. The nest is built by the female almost exclusively in deciduous, often fruit, trees, usually at the end of a branch towards the edge of the crown. After breeding, the birds wander in small flocks, frequenting dumps and fallow land where they acquire their favourite food from thistles, burdocks and other weeds. They also consume birch and alder seeds. The breeding grounds stretch from Europe to the Himalayas and into northern Africa. The goldfinch also has been introduced into Australia, Tasmania, New Zealand and into the southeastern part of South America.

also into some locations of the southeastern part of South America. It is mostly resident or roaming.

Carduelis spinus

SISKIN   **PA**

The siskin breeds in coniferous forests of the boreal and temperate zones from Spain to Sakhalin. Farther to the south, its populations are scattered in the mountains, from the Pyrenees through the Balkans to the Caucasus. A second part of the world population lives far away in the east, in Mongolia, eastern Russia and China. The female builds the nest usually high up in the densest spruce needles, at the far end of the side branch. Typically, the number of birds on the breeding and wintering grounds fluctuates considerably. Sometimes they make invasions southwards. At that time, the birds seek alder and birch woods because the seeds of these trees constitute their main diet.

Acanthis flammea

Acanthis flammea

REDPOLL   **PA NA**

The redpoll can be found in the northern parts of Eurasia and North America *(A. f. flammea),* while another subspecies *(A. f. cabaret)* lives from Central Europe to Great Britain. The breeding environments of the former subspecies are subarctic and coniferous boreal forests and tundra margins, while the latter one is found in the dwarfed vegetation zone in the mountains. At lower altitudes, it frequents pine and birch woods in peat bogs, clumps of willows and alders near waters, and also park-like country with scattered greenery. It can even be found in parks and gardens of towns and villages. It tends to form colonies on its breeding grounds. It is a non-migratory and roving species. Sometimes the birds make invasion-like migrations as far as the Mediterranean area.

Carduelis carduelis

Acanthis hornemanni

Acanthis hornemanni

ARCTIC REDPOLL   **PA NA**

The bird lives in the wooded tundra zones of Eurasia and North America, north of the redpoll's range. The breeding regions of the two species often overlap. The Arctic redpoll apparently shows preference for willow bushes above the tree line. It also tends to breed in colonies. The nest is located near the tree trunk 3.3–6.6ft/1–2m above the ground. It is made of thin twigs, roots and grass blades and lined with hair, feathers and plant fuzz. There is 4–6 eggs in a clutch. The bird winters farther north than the redpoll and sometimes it can even be found in Central Europe.

Acanthis cannabina

LINNET   **PA**

The linnet favours parkland with bushy slopes, hedges, field groves and areas with low vegetation. It can also be found in parks, gardens and cemeteries. It breeds

Acanthis cannabina

Uragus sibiricus

sociably. Comparing to other finch species, linnets feed to the much higher degree on plant seeds. They eat insects only occasionally and feed insects to their young only for the first few days of their lives. Linnets range from Europe (except for the northern part) to central Siberia and Central Asia and also northwestern Africa. They are partly migratory and winter in the southern part of their range.

Uragus sibiricus

LONG-TAILED ROSEFINCH   **PA**

The Long-tailed rosefinch breeds in valleys and woodlands of southern and eastern Siberia, northern Mongolia, northern and central China, southeastern Tibet and Japan. It winters partially in the southern part of its breeding range, and in south-eastern Russia and in Chinese Turkestan. It inhabits mainly wet forests and thickets along waterways up to an altitude of 6,000ft/1,800m. The bowl-shaped nest is hidden well in shrubs up to 5ft/1.5m above the ground.

Carpodacus erythrinus

COMMON ROSEFINCH   **PA OR**

The expansion of the Common rosefinch from northeastern Europe towards the southwest took place in the second half of the 19th century, with a second wave around 1930. Nowadays, it nests as far west as the Netherlands and Switzerland. The range extends from these areas to the Arctic Circle, eastwards to the Pacific, and to southern China. It is migratory and the

Carpodacus erythrinus

Pinicola enucleator

winter is spent in southern Asia from Iran to south-eastern China. For breeding, it chooses sites near water – overgrown valleys of creeks and rivers, wet meadows with scattered bushes as well as overgrown gardens and parks. In the mountainous areas, it nests as high as the dwarfed vegetation. Its nest, which is not very solid, is built by the female low in a bush or in dense plant vegetation.

Pinicola enucleator

PINE GROSBEAK   **PA NA**

The bird lives in the northern parts of Eurasia and North America. It prefers spruce, fir and pine forests and, in the mountains, birch and juniper woods. It is migratory and roaming. In some years, it undertakes invasive migrations southwards. The female builds its nest low above the ground (2–13ft/0.5–4m). The male feeds her during incubation of 3–5 eggs for 13–14 days. Together they feed the chicks in the nest for about two weeks.

Loxia curvirostra

CROSSBILL   **PA OR NA NT**

The crossbill can be found in the coniferous forest zones all around the northern Hemisphere. However, it also lives in more southerly mountains, for example in southeastern Asia and Nicaragua in Central America. Its life is reliant on crops of spruce (or fir) seeds and it migrates to where seeds are available. Another remarkable feature of this bird is the ability to breed in winter, at the time when the cones ripen. Consequently, the nest of the crossbill is a solid structure with walls as thick as 1.5in/4cm. The female builds the nest high up in a conifer and lays 3–4 eggs in it. She rarely leaves the nest during 14–16 days of incubation. The male supplies her with food during this time.

The young hatch with straight bills and their mandibles cross when they are about 3 weeks old.

Loxia curvirostra

Pyrrhula pyrrhula

BULLFINCH   **PA**

In Eurasia, the bullfinch's range reaches from Spain eastwards all the way to the Kamchatka Peninsula and Japan. The northern edge of its range reaches to the treeline and in the south to the high mountains, from the Pyrenees to Caucasus. The bird frequents mainly coniferous and, in the western areas, also deciduous forests. It will also nest in large parks, cemeteries and gardens. The nest is built by the female with the assistence of her mate and is situated not very high, usually near the trunk of a young thick spruce tree. Outside the breeding season, bullfinches tend to roam through their range. In winter, they are joined by the birds from the northern regions.

Rhodopechys githaginea

TRUMPETER FINCH   **PA OR**

The Trumpeter finch breeds and winters from the Canary Islands and southwestern Spain through northern Africa and the Middle East to western Pakistan and northwestern India. It lives in semi-desert, desert and steppe areas with sparse and very low vegetation, or with low thin bushes.
It can withstand very high temperatures during the day, but requires a daily intake of water. In order to drink, it

Rhodopechys githaginea

Eophona migratoria

Coccothraustes coccothraustes

Coccothraustes affinis

migrates quite considerable distances, especially in the late afternoon. It nests on the ground under stones or grass tussocks, in cracks in rocks or in building walls.

Eophona migratoria

YELLOW-BILLED GROSBEAK   **PA**

The bird dwells in deciduous and mixed forests, orchards and small groves. It is quite tame and allows humans to get close to it. It nests in trees and bushes 3.3–6.6ft/1–2m above the ground and its clutch consists of 4–5 eggs. The parents feed the young with insects. Its region can be found in the Far East as far as the northern part of the East Indies. During the winter, it migrates to China.

Coccothraustes coccothraustes

HAWFINCH   **PA**

The hawfinch has an extraordinarily strong conical bill that serves literally as tools to open the fruit pits that form a part of its diet. It often flies into orchards where it peels off and discards the flesh of cherries, cracks the pits and picks the seed. Even the hardest plum pits cannot resist its bill. It nests in light deciduous and mixed forests, groves, parks, old gardens and fruit orchards. The nest is a fairly large structure whose base is made of rather thick and long twigs that often stick out to the sides. The hawfinch can be found in a strip of land that spans from the Iberian Peninsula to Japan and also in northern Africa. It is partly migratory.

Coccothraustes affinis (*Mycerobas affinis*)

COLLARED GROSBEAK   **PA OR**

The Collared grosbeak inhabits high mountain ranges from Iran to China and Mongolia. It is generally found at elevations over 8,000ft/2,400m above the tree line. In

the Himalayas, it can be found at altitudes of up to 14,000ft/4,200m. It nests in oak, rhododendron and juniper vegetation and in fir woods with a bamboo coppice. In winter, it descends to 5,000ft/1,500m.The basket-shaped nest of twigs and blades is placed in bushes or trees as high as 65ft/20m above the ground. The clutch of 2–3 eggs is incubated by both sexes.

Uraeginthus angolensis

BLUE-BREASTED CORDONBLEU   **AF**

The Blue-breasted cordonbleu is a common, non-migratory species found in southern Africa, except for the southernmost tip. It may occasionally range as high as 5,000ft/1,500m. Pairs or small groups, often with other small, seed-eating birds, tend to gather around a dry, shrubby bush, often near riverbeds or on bare ground under the shrubs. When disturbed, they escape into thickets. Both on the ground and in flight, they always produce a high pitched whistling.

Uraeginthus angolensis

Padda oryzivora

Chloebia gouldiae

Padda oryzivora

JAVA FINCH   **OR AU**

The original homeland of the Java finch is Indonesia, from Sumatra through Java to the Moluccas. Yet in 1870, it was introduced into Sri Lanka, where it can still be found. It was also introduced into Zanzibar and St. Helena Island. Birds that escaped from captivity have created vigorous populations in eastern Africa, southeastern Asia, Japan and Hawaii. In its homeland, it lives in steppes and agricultural areas, where at times, outside the breeding season, it often causes considerable damage to the rice crops. It nests in tree branches, high in palm trees or beneath roofs of houses.

Aegintha temporalis

Aegintha temporalis

SIDNEY WAXBILL   **AU**

The bird can be found in eastern and south-eastern Australia. It favors dense shrubberies interspersed with open grassy areas near streams and small lakes. However, it also lives in agricultural and suburban regions. It feeds on seeds of grasses and weeds as well as on insects. Its bottle-shaped nest with a side entrance is woven of fine grasses low in bushes. The clutch is comprised of 5–8 eggs. After breeding it forms roaming flocks.

Chloebia gouldiae (Poephila gouldiae)

GOULDIAN FINCH   **AU**

The Gouldian finch is one of the most beautiful bird species. It was described in 1844 by an English ornithologist, J. Gould, and named in honour of his wife. Several color morphs can be found: there are three times more black-headed than the red-headed birds and just one yellow-headed bird to 5,000 other birds. It lives in northern Australia on arid savannas and open forests. It nests in hollows in trees and termitaria. Infrequently, it will build a crude nest with a suggested vaulting in thick shrubs or in tall grass. The female deposits 4–8 eggs that are incubated by both sexes by turns.

Dinemellia dinemelli

WHITE-HEADED BUFFALO-WEAVER   **AF**

The bird can be found in northeastern and eastern Africa from Sudan and Ethiopia to Tanzania. It does not migrate. It dwells in arid open, shrubby areas and also in woodlands. It lives in pairs or small groups. It forages on the ground.

Passer domesticus

HOUSE SPARROW   **PA AF OR**

The House sparrow inhabits all of Europe. It also lives in northwestern Africa and in the Nile valley. It was introduced into many countries of the world: Africa, Australia and South America. For several centuries it has been a loyal companion of man and often nests in human settlements. Afghanistan and Turkestan are perhaps the only places where it breeds in open country in larger numbers. In the Himalayas it nests up to 15,000ft/4,600m. The nest, a large, untidy globe with a side entrance, is usually built in hollows and semi-hollows of buildings. Only rarely is the nest found in a tree top. Both partners incubate 4–6 eggs. The House Sparrow breeds up to seven times a year in India.

Dinemellia dinemelli

Passer domesticus

265

Passer hispaniolensis

SPANISH SPARROW   **PA**

The Spanish sparrow is also a highly sociable species that lives in countries around the Mediterranean Sea. It ranges to Kazakhstan and Afghanistan farther east, and also can be found in northwestern Africa. Occasionally, it may crossbreed with the House and Italian sparrows *(P. italiae)*. It usually breeds away from human settlements, in light forests and agricultural country. Typically, colonies are found on river banks in growths of Mediterranean oaks, pines, poplars and eucalyptus, or in shrubberies. Some colonies may be huge: 180 nests have been observed on a single tree, and 7,740 nests in 19 colonies have been counted in Spanish Extramadura. In locations where no House sparrows can be found (such as Italy, Sicily, Creta, or Madeira), it also occupies urban environments.

Passer montanus

TREE SPARROW   **PA OR**

The Tree sparrow commonly breeds in light forests and park-like country where open spaces intersperse with cultivated rows of old trees, groves and vegetation along rivers. It is also found in old parks and orchards. In the far north, it nests solely in villages. Eastwards, it is also increasingly found in the urban habitats, especially in places where the House sparrow is not found. The nests are most frequently placed in tree holes and nest-boxes, occasionally in cracks in buildings and rock holes. They can also be found in the walls of nests of storks and large raptors. However, the Tree sparrow is also able to build a globular nest in tree tops. It lives in almost all of Eurasia except for the northern areas.

Passer montanus

Petronia petronia

Montifringilla nivalis

Amblyospiza albifrons

Petronia petronia

ROCK SPARROW   **PA**

The distribution area of the Rock sparrow spans from southern Europe and northern Africa to the Middle East, Central Asia and Manchuria. Its habitat is found in open, sunlit regions with rocky slopes, in arid, stony steppe with scattered trees and bushes as well as in pastures and near grain fields. The nest is set up in deep holes and crevices in rocks, in ruins or on buildings. It is also found in tree hollows and deserted burrows of bee-eaters, from sea level up to 7,000ft/2,040m.

Montifringilla nivalis

SNOWFINCH   **PA**

The snowfinch inhabits quite an unusual region which consists of a chain of high mountain ranges found in southern Europe, Asia Minor, the Caucasus, southwestern Iran, Pamir, Altai and north-eastern China. It nests in an alpine zone below the snow line. The nests are built in grassy areas between cliffs and rocky outcrops, in boulder slopes and moraine fields, in rocky crevices and also in holes in structures (mountain huts, old fortifications, pylons of ski lifts). It lives in small colonies of 2–6 pairs.

Amblyospiza albifrons

GROSBEAK WEAVER   **AF**

For breeding, the Grosbeak weaver seeks reedbeds or shrubs near rivers and stagnant waters (even in town parks), marshes and other types of wetlands. A beautiful, skilfully woven nest shaped somewhat like a hut with a broad entrance in its upper part is usually fixed to the stems of reed or papyrus, or to branches of a bush, so that the twigs grow right through the nest.

Such a nest, serves only for resting. If the female chooses it for breeding, an additional, slightly down-pointed entrance tube will be built. The bird lives in eastern and central Africa, and sometimes also in western Africa.

Ploceus ocularis

SPECTACLED WEAVER   **AF**

This 6–6.5in/15–16cm long bird can be found in southeastern Africa. Both sexes are yellowish with a brown-toned head. The slightly larger male can easily be distinguished from the female by a black throat patch. It lives mainly in forests on river banks, in lowlands near the sea coast and in suburban gardens and parks. Its suspended nest features a long entrance pipe pointed vertically towards the ground.

Ploceus ocularis

267

Ploceus cuculatus

Ploceus cucullatus

VILLAGE WEAVER   **AF**

The Village weaver is a common and non-migratory species found in eastern and central Africa. It nests in large colonies on branches of trees and bushes hanging over the water, or in reeds. It can, however, be also found far from water in trees and palms near farming areas, or even right on the streets of big towns. Globular nests with a down pointing entrance attachment are suspended at the end of branches. During the courtship display, the males suspend themselves underneath the nest, call, flap their wings and swing from side to side so that they alternately reveal and hide their yellow and black plumage. All this activity is to try and attract a female who will stay if she takes a fancy to the nest.

Lamprotornis superbus

Lamprotornis chalybaeus

Lamprotornis australis

Cinnyricinclus leucogaster

Lamprotornis superbus

SUPERB STARLING   AF

The Superb starling inhabits eastern Africa where it can be found in open, often cultivated country. It is a highly sociable species that lives in small flocks all year round. It roosts on tall trees in large flocks that are quite raucous at dawn and dusk. It feeds on small animals that are snatched from the ground, often close to herds of wild ungulata or domestic cattle. The nest is built on branches of thorny bushes. It features a side entrance and is shielded by thorny twigs.

Lamprotornis chalybaeus

GREATER BLUE-EARED GLOSSY-STARLING   AF

The species can be found in eastern and central Africa. It lives in pairs in a shrubby bush or in woodland, also close to farming areas. In the Kruger National Park, it spends the winter in camps together with humans and is clearly the most abundant bird there. The flocks often look for food in convenient trash heaps and sometimes can be quite annoying in their search. In early spring, the birds disperse to breed in the surrounding area.

Lamprotornis australis

BURCHELL'S GLOSSY STARLING   AF

The largest Glossy starling measures 12 to 14in/30 to 34cm. The species is commonly found in sparce forests of central Africa. Outside the breeding season, it lives in pairs, small groups or large flocks. It forages on the ground, particularly preferring completely grazed areas.

Cinnyricinclus leucogaster

AMETHYST STARLING   AF

The Amethyst starling occupies a considerable part of sub-Saharan Africa minus the southernmost tip of the continent. It is an arboreal, fruit-eating species that is found in riverine forests and other types of woodlands. It breeds in pairs or it forms nomadic flocks that are usually single sex.

Spreo fischeri

FISCHER'S STARLING   AF

The bird can mostly be seen in small flocks in dry acacia forests. It spends much of its time on the forest floor foraging for caterpillars, beetles and other insects. Its nest is a large, round or pear-shaped structure of grasses with a side entrance. Almost invariably, the nest is placed in a thorny tree up to the height of 20in/6m. The bird lives in eastern Africa, Ethiopia, Somalia and Kenya.

Spreo fischeri

Onychognathus morio

Cosmopsarus regius

Onychognathus morio

RED-WINGED STARLING   AF

The Red-winged starling can mainly be found in eastern Africa from Ethiopia down to the Cape. Secondary breeding ranges are scattered north through the tropics. It lives in forested country, near cliffs or right in towns. It breeds in pairs in holes in rocks, in caves and on buildings. It is a common, non-migratory species that forages in tree branches and on the ground, feeding in particular on fruit and various berries. In the non-breeding times, it forms flocks of up to several hundred birds, especially on their common roosting sites.

Sturnus vulgaris

Cosmopsarus regius

GOLDEN-BREASTED STARLING   AF

The species is distributed in northeastern Africa in the area from southeastern Ethiopia to northern and eastern Tanzania. In some locations, such as in open, shrubby areas, it is fairly abundant. It is shy and forages high in the tree tops. It lives in pairs or in small groups. It is resident or moves in connection with the rainy season.

Sturnus vulgaris

STARLING   PA

The starling originally lived in deciduous forests, while today it particularly prefers agricultural country with meadows and pastures suitable for foraging. However, the foraging areas must not be too far away from its nesting quarters. The nests are set up in hollow trees, nest-boxes, in rocky crevices or in holes in buildings. To maintain strength for breeding, the bird limits itself to a flying range of only half a mile from the nest. It is partly migratory. In autumn, huge flocks congregate mostly in reeds and later fly to western and southern Europe and to northern Africa. The starling ranges throughout most of Europe and its region reaches to Iran and Central Asia. Introduced birds have successfully occupied North America, southernmost Africa, southern Australia, Tasmania and New Zealand.

Sturnus unicolor

SPOTLESS STARLING   PA

The Spotless starling replaces the starling in southwestern Europe and in northern Africa. In places where their ranges overlap, the two species may crossbreed. The Spotless starling inhabits Mediterranean forests, olive and citrus groves and parks, the sea coast and agricultural country. It can commonly be found in towns where it nests beneath roof coverings. In locations where the nest-boxes are provided, it also occupies steppe and semi-desert areas and maquis.

Sturnus nigricollis

BLACK-COLLARED STARLING   PA OR

The Black-collared starling is a non-migratory species commonly found in both arid and wet open country with trees and shrubs up to an altitude of about 5,000ft/1,500m. It is also found in towns and villages. The bird's range encompasses southeastern Asia. In some locations (e.g. on the Malay Peninsula), it has expanded its territory to unforested areas.

Sturnus unicolor

Sturnus nigricollis

Leucopsar rothschildi

Acridotheres tristis

Leucopsar rothschildi

BALI MYNA   **OR**

The Bali myna is one of the rarest birds of the world. Its territory is limited exclusively to Bali where only about 35 feral birds can be found on the western tip. They inhabit mangrove swamps, acacia forests and shrubs, and less often savannas with the tree cover. Fortunately, it is easy to rear and readily breeds in captivity so there is a good chance that it will not be added to the extinct races. It is distinguished from the related myna species by its white plumage and a crest. During the courting display, the bird alternately erects its crest, flickers its wings and spreads its tail.

Acridotheres tristis

COMMON MYNA   **OR**

The Common myna is probably the most popular bird in southern Asia. It ranges from India to Java, seeking open, cultivated country. However, it thrives best in towns where it nests most frequently on buildings or in holes in walls. It forages on the ground along the town streets or in the country among the grazing ungulata. It eats insects and their larvae as well as also various plants and garbage. It is cheeky careful and very noisy which is especially noticeable on common roosting grounds. It was successfully introduced into eastern Australia, south Africa (around Durban) and Arabia.

Gracula religiosa

HILL MYNA   **OR**

Being a bird that is very quick to learn and has a rich vocal repertoire, the Hill myna is often reared in captivity. Its homeland is the Indo-Malyan region from India and Sri Lanka to the Philippines, Sumatra and Java. It dwells in mountain forests where it builds its nest in tree hollows. The female lays 2–3 eggs that are incubated for 12–14 days. It feeds on insects and other small animals, fruit and berries. It forages individually or in groups in tree tops.

Scissirostrum dubium

FINCH-BILLED MYNA   **AU**

The homeland of this species is the Sulawesi Island in Indonesia. A massive bill allows it to peck holes into dead trees in order to pick larvae or build its nest. Because it hews at the wood, it has enforced forehead bones like climbers. It breeds in colonies, with up to 50 nests found in a single tree.

Gracula religiosa

Oriolus oriolus

GOLDEN ORIOLE
PA OR

The Golden oriole's range stretches from Europe (except for the northern areas) to Altai and India. It is the only oriole that has moved from the tropical areas northwards. It arrives very late from its wintering grounds in tropical Africa and settles in deciduous forests, vegetation along the waterways and ponds, in cultivated tree rows, field groves and old parks. The nest is woven of stems and leaves of grass, plant fibres and strips of bark and hung on a horizontal fork of the peripheral branches high up in a tree. The clutch of 3–5 eggs is incubated by the female for about two weeks. The main bulk of its diet is made up of insects that are captured on the ground and in the air, and also of spiders and small gasteropods. Towards the end of the summer, it feeds in trees and bushes on pulpy fruit.

Oriolus chinensis

BLACK-NAPED ORIOLE
OR

The Black-naped oriole can be found in the area between India and the Philippines. The population was probably created partially by birds escaped from captivity and partially by the migration of birds from southeastern Asia. It winters on the Sunda Islands and in Malaysia. It is an arboreal species that inhabits the margins of mangrove forests, open landscapes with trees, and old parks and gardens found even in town centers. The diet consists mainly of various kinds of fruit.

Oriolus oriolus

Scissirostrum dubium

Oriolus chinensis

273

Oriolus xanthornus

Oriolus xanthornus

BLACK-HOODED ORIOLE OR

The Black-hooded oriole is an inhabitant of deciduous forests in lowlands and foothills from eastern Pakistan and India to the Greater Sunda Islands. It can be also found in open forests, orchards and gardens where it can be recognized due to its flute-like whistling. The bird also places its nest to the horizontal fork of side branches. It feeds mainly on fruit, though insects constitute an important part of its diet as well. On fruit-bearing trees, it often groups with other fruit-eating species.

Grallina cyanoleuca

MAGPIE-LARK AU

The bird lives in almost all of Australia, in Tasmania, southern New Guinea and on some of the neighbouring islands. It frequents open terrain in the vicinity of waters, especially pastures. It has a closely connected social lifestyle whose nucleus is formed by a group of about ten birds. The company consists of a "breeding unit" formed by the dominant male and several adult females, and of several immature birds. The construction of the nest and feeding the young is a duty shared by all, while the clutch is apparently incubated by adults only. The nest is built of plant fibres connected by mud and is stuck on a more or less horizontal branch. The birds mostly dwell on the ground and favor wading in shallow water with a motion that rather resembles plovers. They feed mostly on insects and molluscs.

Gymnorhina tibicen

AUSTRALIAN MAGPIE AU

The species ranges throughout Australia and has been introduced into New Zealand. It lives sociably in groups of 3–10 birds consisting of one leading male that lives in polygamy with several females. Although the one year old birds are already capable of breeding, the older birds prevent them from doing so. Therefore, they usually do not breed until they are four or five years old. The bowl-shaped nest is built by the female and is situated on the edge of eucalyptus branches. The bird's habitat is light forest and also agricultural country and suburban areas.

Grallina cyanoleuca

Gymnorhina tibicen

Ailuroedus buccoides

WHITE-EARED CATBIRD   **AU**

The White-eared catbird can be found in New Guinea and on several neighbouring islands. It is a rare species that lives inside lowland and highland forests up to 2,700ft/800m. It feeds mainly on fruit, though it has been observed killing and eating small birds caught in nets. It is monogamous and lives in pairs.

Ailuroedus crassirostris

GREEN CATBIRD   **AU**

The Green catbird is to be found exclusively in rain forests on a narrow coastal strip of eastern Australia. Its voice recalls a cat's miaowing and is one of the most typical bird voices that can be heard on the eastern coast, especially during the breeding season. The male, unlike other bowerbirds, does not build the so-called "bower" and mates with only one female. Together with her, he builds the nest, protects it along with a small surrounding territory and helps with raising the chicks. It spends a lot of time foraging in low and middle forest vegetation. It feeds mainly on fruit and leaves.

Sericulus chrysocephalus

REGENT BOWERBIRD   **AU**

The Regent bowerbird inhabits primarily rain forests, but also other woodlands, shrubs and gardens in a narrow zone in eastern Australia. The male builds only a small, tunnel-like bower that is not as perfect and adorned with so many items as that of the Satin bowerbird. It decorates the bower mostly with shells and black-colored berries. The male then performs its displays in front of the bower and tries to woo as many females as possible. After the male finishes his mating and family duties, the female takes control of the family.

Sericulus chrysocephalus

Ptilonorhynchus violaceus

Ptilonorhynchus violaceus

SATIN BOWERBIRD   AU

The Satin bowerbird lives on the eastern and southeastern coast of Australia in rain forests and adjacent areas. The male's bower consists of two side walls made of twigs and stalks stuck in the ground. The bird is truly keen on the color blue and therefore adornes the structure with blue flowers and feathers, and also with other blue items like beer caps, clothes pegs, etc. In addition, it paints the inner walls using a piece of bark which it steeps in blue-black fruit juice mixed with saliva and charcoal. The bower is used for courtship display and as a place where the male mates with several females. The female builds a nest at a fair distance from the courting platform, 7–50ft/2–15m above the ground, and lays 1–3 eggs in it.

Diphyllodes respublica

Diphyllodes respublica (Cicinnurus respublica)

WILSON'S BIRD-OF-PARADISE   AU

Both sexes have bare and blue tops of their heads. In addition, the male features spiral curved tail feathers. The species frequents wooded hills at altitudes above 984 ft/300 m on just two islands, Waigeo and Batanta, near New Guinea. The male prefers a courting arena on the ground. Its diet is comprised of fruit and various arthropods.

Cyanocorax yncas

GREEN JAY   NA NT

The Green jay lives in South America in the area from Colombia and Venezuela to central Peru and Bolivia. Through Central America, the range stretches into Texas. It is found in forests up to an altitude of 8,200ft/2,500m, and in shrubs and vegetation along rivers. It is noisy and curious and often visits farms, ranches and suburban gardens.

Garrulus glandarius

JAY   PA OR

The jay frequents all kinds of forests, nor does it avoid larger field groves and spacious old parks and gardens. This tendency has been apparent in Western and Central Europe from the 1930s and in Eastern Europe since the 1960s. Besides Europe, it inhabits northwestern Africa and its range spans in a wider zone through Central Asia all the way to Japan. Another strip goes south of the Himalayas to China. It is mostly non-migratory.

Cyanocorax yncas

However, the birds from the northern areas may migrate southwards in an invasion-like manner. The nest is situated close to the forest edge, more often in conifers. The diet consists of invertebrates and small vertebrates, and from the end of the summer, also of berries, beechnuts, hazel nuts and, above all, acorns.

Perisoreus infaustus

SIBERIAN JAY   **PA**

The Siberian jay is a non-migratory inhabitant of taiga, the continuous boreal coniferous forest between latitudes 50–70 degrees North. It prefers unbroken woods in the uninhabited areas. It breeds early in the spring while there is still snow on the ground. The nest is found in trees, often pines, near the trunk. It is comparatively small, but features thick walls and warm insulation of lichens plus a lining of hair. The complete clutch consists of 3–5 eggs.

Perisoreus infaustus

Cissa chinensis

Cyanopica cyana

AZURE-WINGED MAGPIE   **PA**

The Azure-winged magpie can be found in two completely distinctive regions: in southwestern Europe and in eastern Asia. This huge gap is explained either by a division of the original range during the Ice Age, or by the release of birds brought over by Portuguese seafarers in the 16th century. The bird primarily frequents light ilex and pine forests, but also can be found in dunes overgrown with introduced eucalyptus, in olive groves, pastures and orchards. The nest is usually placed in the top of a tree crown.

Pica pica

MAGPIE   **PA OR NA**

The magpie favors park-like country where fields intersperse with meadows and groves, cultivated tree rows and vegetation along watercourses. It avoids unbroken forests. The nest may be placed in both tall trees and low shrubs or in fruit trees. It is made of dry branches and turfs and there is a characteristic roof over it. Both members of the pair build several nests. Afterwards, they pick one for breeding. The clutch of 5–8 eggs is incubated solely by the female. The magpie lives in almost all of Eurasia, in northwestern Africa and in the western part of North America.

Cissa chinensis

GREEN MAGPIE   **PA OR**

The bird can be found in Asia in a region from eastern Pakistan and foothills of the Himalayas to the Greater Sundas. It is a non-migratory species living in mountain forests. It is noisy, but also shy and therefore it can be heard rather than seen in thick vegetation. The nest is a massive, broad and shallow structure situated in low trees in dense jungle. The diet is comprised mainly of insects and other small animals.

Cyanopica cyana

Pica pica

Nucifraga caryocatactes

Pyrrhocorax pyrrhocorax

Nucifraga caryocatactes

NUTCRACKER   **PA OR**

The nutcracker is distributed throughout the boreal coniferous forests of Eurasia and in mountain forests of more southerly regions. From central and eastern Siberia its range reaches to Kazakhstan and the Himalayas. It can also be found in unbroken coniferous forests at lower altitudes and, in some locations, in beech woods. Its relatively small. A high nest with thick walls is built early in the spring when there is still snow in the woods. It is almost invariably interwoven with thick conifer branches. The diet of nutcrackers consists of cone seeds, beechnuts, acorns and in the autumn it is made up of primarily hazel nuts. If there is a shortage of seeds in the northern areas, the birds make invasions southwards.

Pyrrhocorax pyrrhocorax

CHOUGH   **PA AF OR**

The range of the chough is large but scattered, reaching from southern Europe to Central Asia and Africa (Morocco, Ethiopia). The bird is associated with coastal cliffs and inland rocks, and in some locations it also occupies buildings and ruins, especially stone ruins. It ranges up to an altitude of 12,000ft/3,600m. It breeds in colonies in crevices in rocks, on ledges in caves, beneath overhangs, and occasionally on or inside buildings. The clutch of 3–5 eggs is incubated only by the female. After breeding, the birds group in large flocks.

Pyrrhocorax graculus

ALPINE CHOUGH   **PA**

Its distribution range is limited mainly to the alpine areas from southern Europe and Morocco all the way to China. It is non-migratory, apart from descending to lower altitudes and to the vicinity of human settlements in the winter, often in large flocks of 30–500 birds. It frequents rocky cliffs and grassy slopes between the tree line and permanent snow line. It ranges considerably higher than the chough and in the Himalayas, it can be found up to 22,000ft/6,500m. It breeds in colonies of up to 20 pairs or in individual pairs. The nest is placed in holes and cracks in rock faces.

Pyrrhocorax graculus

Corvus monedula

Corvus monedula

JACKDAW   **PA OR**

The jackdaw frequents places with many old trees and inhabits rock formations, ruins, castle and church towers and the attics and chimneys of town buildings. It breeds in colonies. The breeding pairs usually unite for life. The nest is built by both sexes in all kinds of hollows and also freely in building attics. After long use and additional building, the nest may become a huge, 2ft high by 3ft wide structure. Its base is formed by a pile of branches broken from a tree, and by clay, grass, hair, even paper and rags. In autumn, jackdaws join flocks of rooks in a migration from the northeastern areas to the south. The range includes al-most all of Europe as far as the Himalayas, central Siberia to the east and as far as Morocco in the south.

Corvus frugilegus

ROOK   **PA**

The rook is a highly gregarious bird with a broad range: most of Europe, and a considerable part of Asia as far east as Japan, Korea and China. It shows preference for open country with interspersed groves and old vegetation growths along streams. It also nests on the edges of forests and even in parks in town centers. It requires a habitat that is close to fields, meadows and pastures, with a substantial supply of plant and animal (mostly invertebrates) food. It nests in tall trees in colonies, some of which comprise more than 1,000 pairs. It is migratory and winters in numerous flocks in the southern parts of the range.

Corvus corone

CARRION CROW   **PA**

There are two groups of the Carrion crow subspecies that differ in color: the black and gray one. They have all been included within a single species because they crossbreed and their offspring are fertile. The black subspecies live in western Europe and in Asia from the Yenisei River eastwards. Two subspecies from these two groups are found in Europe: the Black Carrion crow *(C. c. corone)* and the Gray Carrion crow *(C. c. cornix)*. Their ranges join in a zone that stretches from Scotland through Denmark and Austria to Italy. The subspecies evolved during the last Ice Age when the genus was split by a glacier in the two isolated populations in the Iberian and Balkan Peninsulas. The bird always nests individually in open country where groves, vegetation

Corvus frugilegus

Corvus corone

Corvus macrorhynchos

Corvus corax

along streams and groups of trees are found along with fields and meadows. It is also found in forests and in the eastern regions as well as in towns. The breeding pairs are bonded for life. Both birds build their nest high in a tree. The Carrion crow is a non-migratory species. The gray subspecies make longer migrations during the winter.

Corvus macrorhynchos

LARGE-BILLED CROW   **PA OR**

The Large-billed crow is found throughout most of tropical Asia. It also lives in eastern Asia and as far north as Manchuria. It frequents woodlands, cultivated areas and can be found also near towns and villages. It lives in pairs, and only gathers in flocks in the vicinity of rich food sources. It feeds mainly on animal food including carrion, and takes advantage of garbage dumps near human settlements.

Corvus coronoides

AUSTRALIAN RAVEN   **AU**

The Australian raven can be found in eastern, southern and southwestern Australia in literally all types of environments, excluding deep forests. While calling, it ruffles the feathers on its throat, thus forming a beard. It is omnivorous and feeds on carrion, insects and small animals as well as on grain and other plant-based food. It does not breed until the age of three years. The nest is built high up in a tree.

Corvus corax

RAVEN   **PA OR NA NT**

The raven's broad distribution range, which encompasses all of Europe, Asia and most parts of North America, is based on its flexibility regarding breeding lo-

cations. It nests in all kinds of forests as well as in fully open country where it builds its nests in tall trees or on steep cliffs. Increasingly, it enters towns. The pairs live in a firm relationship for their entire lives. Ravens are not migratory. Their main diet is carrion and they can fly for more than 6 miles/10km to find a place to feed. Otherwise, they hunt live prey ranging from insects to animals the size of a hare. They also take advantage of garbage near mountain huts and human settlements.

Corvus coronoides

Index